W9-CFC-630

ABOUT THE AUTHOR

James Fulford is a Fellow of The Institute of Chartered Accountants in Ireland. He obtained first place in Ireland in the pre-final examinations and, since qualification, has studied commercial law and, more recently, computing.

Based outside Belfast, James is a contributor to the Institute's professional journal, *Accountancy Ireland*, as well as being a partner in both a computer consultancy firm and an accountancy practice. He started his career in a large local accountancy practice. After qualification he joined an international practice, with responsibility for technical and quality control matters, and later moved to the accounts department of a sole practitioner. James is also a member of The Institute of Chartered Accountants In Ireland's IT Committee.

THE ACCOUNTANT'S GUIDE TO EXCEL

James Fulford

Oak Tree Press

Dublin

Oak Tree Press
Merrion Building
Lower Merrion Street
Dublin 2, Ireland

© 1997 James Fulford
Reprinted 1998
Revised 2nd Edition 2000

A catalogue record of this book is
available from the British Library.

ISBN 1-86076-162-3

All rights reserved. No part of this publication may be reproduced or
transmitted in any form or by any means, including photocopying and recording,
without written permission of the publisher. Such written permission must also be
obtained before any part of this publication is stored in a retrieval system of any
nature. Requests for permission should be directed to
Oak Tree Press, Merrion Building,
Lower Merrion Street, Dublin 2, Ireland.

This book and accompanying CD are sold *as is*, without warranty of any kind, express
or implied, respecting the contents of this book or compact disk,
including but not limited to implied warranties for the book or compact disk's quality,
performance, merchantability, or fitness for any particular purpose. Neither Oak
Tree Press nor its author, dealers or distributors shall be liable to the purchaser or
any other person or entity with respect to any liability, loss or damage caused or
alleged to have been caused directly or indirectly by this book or compact disk.

Printed in Ireland by Colour Books Ltd.

ACKNOWLEDGEMENTS

There is always a long list of people to thank when a book finally reaches the end of a long, long road. There are also always a lot of backroom people whom I do not even know by name.

I would therefore like to thank everyone at Oak Tree Press, the publishers, for their professionalism and hard work, not individually, but as a team. They applied no pressure during the writing of the book, and that pressurised me more than anything else could.

In a broader context, I would also like to thank the people who have helped to shape me into what I am today — from past employers, authors of the countless computer books that I have read along the way, and the wider group of individuals who, from speaking to and interacting with, have shaped the book into what you hold in your hands.

And lastly, I would like to acknowledge the support, criticism and professional input from my wife — the best blend of accountancy qualification and common sense I have met.

This project is the hardest thing I have ever done in my life, soaking up vast reserves of mental energy that I didn't think possible. When I reread the book, it seems effortless. I hope you think the same as you work through it.

James Fulford
July 2000

CONTENTS

INTRODUCTION

This book is about spreadsheets! But it also covers much more — Windows basics, spreadsheet design, object linking and embedding (OLE) — and it includes practical examples of how to build spreadsheets, from first design to completed project. Sales Voucher Tax recording and calculation, Wages pay calculator, Financial Accounts and Projections — all are fully explained and discussed, so that the principles learnt will allow you to build well-designed and well-managed spreadsheets of your own.

WHAT CAN YOU DO WITH SPREADSHEETS?

Spreadsheets are principally used to "slice and dice" data. They are then used to present this information in a meaningful way — tables, charts or suitably formatted summaries.

The power and capabilities that should be tapped in a spreadsheet are:

- Using multiple sheets within a workbook
- Linking cells, sheets and workbooks
- Formatting of both text and numbers
- Formulae
- Drag and drop
- Mouse-driven functionality and control
- Object linking and embedding with other programs — principally word processing packages.

By properly controlling the spreadsheet environment, efficiency, accuracy and speed increase.

WHO IS THIS BOOK FOR?

Spreadsheets are an essential tool for personal productivity. They are used by engineers, statisticians, mathematicians, programmers, accountants and many others — and the needs of each, whilst different, are all catered for in Excel!

However, this means that a lot of functionality is built into Excel which is not needed by any one audience. The purpose of this book is threefold:

- To identify those aspects of Excel particularly relevant to accountants
- To explain good spreadsheet practice
- To demonstrate both of the above, by building three different working models.

Possible improvements to the models are discussed at the end of each chapter — improvements which are not just restricted to Excel, but which may include using databases or Visual Basic programming. The purpose is to provide you with a good knowledge of Excel, as well as broadening your perspective.

It is therefore suited to anyone involved in finance who uses, or wishes to use, spreadsheets. This includes:
- Auditors and accountants in public practice
- Accountants in industry and commerce.
- Accountants in government departments and the public sector
- Trainee accountants
- Non-accountants, suitably experienced in finance
- Business degree students.

WHAT IS COVERED IN THIS BOOK?

This book is written in order to make you proficient in using Excel. In order to do this, you must understand, not only Excel itself, but also Windows, the operating system in which Excel runs, because you have to know how to manage files, control your printers, etc. To provide all of this knowledge in an easily accessible format, the book is divided into the following sections:
- Windows
- Excel Functionality
- Spreadsheet Design
- Building Spreadsheets
- The Business Plan.

There are appendices to explain the use of the Extended Trial Balance in the Projections spreadsheet, and a quick reference guide to the parts of the Excel program explored within the book.

The book therefore covers:
- The essentials of Windows — starting programs, file management, print manager, etc.
- Excel menus, toolbars and screen layout
- Spreadsheet design and development of spreadsheet solutions
- Spreadsheet solutions in Excel
- Presentation skills — charts, OLE and report presentation.

WHAT IS NOT COVERED IN THIS BOOK?

Excel is a vast program, and it is not possible to cover all of its features in one volume. This book takes the reader from beginner to intermediate "Power User". The advanced Power User aspects which are beyond the scope of this book are:

- Visual Basic Applications Edition programming
- Consolidation capabilities
- Database capabilities
- Pivot tables
- Advanced functions and analytical techniques
- Import and export of data between Microsoft Office components or between Excel and other (non-Microsoft Office) programs (except for those aspects relevant to Word, covered in the chapter on report presentation).

However, before these aspects can be learnt, a solid foundation of knowledge must be laid. This is what the book sets out to achieve.

EXCEL 2000 OR EARLIER VERSIONS?

This book explains how to build spreadsheets and because there are many advanced features in Excel 2000 that you do nor necessarily need, you will be able to build the spreadsheets in this book using earlier versions of Excel. Therefore, despite the fact that the screen shots are in Excel 2000, the spreadsheets on the CD have been saved in a multiple format which allows them to be opened in Excel 2000, Excel 97, Excel 95 and Excel 5.0. However, my recommendation is, as you advance into Power User you will appreciate the more up-to-date version of Excel more and more. If you have the opportunity I would recommend you study with this guide using Excel 2000 in order to maximize your familiarity with the program.

WHY WINDOWS? WHY EXCEL 2000?

Two questions arise: Why choose Windows? And why choose Excel rather than another package?

As an operating environment, Windows provides huge power to manipulate information, well beyond that possible in DOS. Using Windows is beyond dispute, but which version?

Windows 3.x is a 16-bit operating system, written to be compatible with DOS versions 6.22 and earlier. Windows 95 and later versions are 32-bit, with a 32-bit version of DOS for using old DOS-based software.

PCs have been 32-bit for many years – from the 386 generation of processor, through the 486 and 586 (Pentium), and into Pentium II and MMX. The Pentium III pushes the technology further. Using a 32-bit operating system harnesses the full power and capabilities of your PC.

Why Excel 2000? Excel is the most popular spreadsheet package presently sold — and deservedly so! With over 80% of market share in the office suite market, it offers an excellent user interface, first rate functionality, superb co-ordination with the other Microsoft Office suite software and, essential for serious users, a common look and feel between this program, Word, Access, and PowerPoint.

HOW TO GET THE MOST FROM THIS BOOK

You will gain more from Excel if you practice, and you will gain more from this book if you follow the exercises on your own PC.

All of the models built in **Sections Four** and **Five** are included on the enclosed compact disk for you to review, and the files at the various stages of development are also included, so that you can check your model at each stage in the building process.

To access the files directly, follow the steps below:
1. From Excel, choose Open from the file menu
2. In the Open File dialogue box, change to the CD drive (usually D:)
3. Search for the appropriate file, and click on it to select. Double-click to open, or choose the Open button.

The CD-ROM is read only. If any amendments are made to the file and you wish to keep the updated file you will have to save it to your hard drive (usually C:).You cannot save it on the CD.

If you prefer, any or all of the files can be copied to your hard drive by using Explorer. To do this:
1. Start Explorer and select the CD drive.
2. Select the file(s) with the mouse, while holding down the Control key. The selected files are highlighted in blue.
3. With the mouse cursor on one of the files, right click and select Copy.
4. Change to the hard drive (usually C:), select the appropriate folder, and right click the mouse. Choose Paste.

See the Windows section of the book for detailed instructions on working with Explorer, Files and Folders.

The more you put into using this book, the more you will get from it. Good luck on your road to Power User status!

Section One

WINDOWS

SECTION INDEX

SECTION OVERVIEW

As we shall see later, Excel includes menus and toolbar buttons to save your work or print it out. However, saving files and printing are actually controlled by Windows, the operating system.

You may find Excel runs too slowly for your liking. Can the operating system speed it up?

Both of these aspects, and many others, demonstrate that a broader perspective is needed before actually approaching Excel itself. Useful background information is given in this section on Windows.

This section provides an understanding of:

- The concepts of files, directories and folders
- Organizing work on the desktop and the hard disk
- Good housekeeping
- Using the Windows program.

The section will be useful to those who do not know the Windows operating system well and require a quick review of how to use it. It will also be useful to those who, although they know how to use the program, do not have enough background knowledge to understand the broader perspective.

Chapter One

HARDWARE CONTROLLED BY THE OPERATING SYSTEM

It's not the hardware in your life that counts — it's the life in your hardware.

In this chapter, we want to look briefly at how to control the hardware we are most likely to interact with on a daily basis.

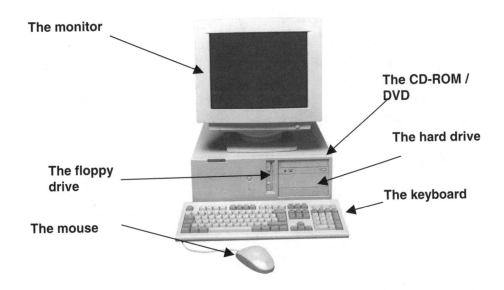

WHICH HARDWARE?

You should already be familiar with most, if not all, of the hardware. For our purposes, we are not interested in the full technical specification of the equipment, only the basics on how they work, and how we use Windows to control or fine-tune the settings. The items of computer hardware we want to look at are:

- Keyboard

- Mouse
- Monitor
- Disk drives (floppy, hard and CD-ROM / DVD)
- Memory and processor.

The printer (not shown), although not directly part of the computer, is controlled by it, and is an important peripheral device — arguably, the most important piece of equipment at your disposal. When thinking about computers, you must think of controlling the printer, because it will produce the final reports upon which your spreadsheet expertise will be judged.

THE BASIC COMPONENTS
Keyboard
The same computer is sold world-wide: in the USA, UK, France, Germany and the computer can, therefore, be re-programmed to respond to keys in different ways. Windows will let you change the symbols and characters produced by the keys.

Mouse
Left-handed, right-handed, three-button, two-button ... other controls as well. The mouse is an input device in the same way that the keyboard is, and it can be fine-tuned and reprogrammed to suit the user. The mouse is used to activate parts of the screen that cannot necessarily be activated from the keyboard. It may also provide a quicker input than can be achieved with a keyboard.

Monitor
Screen-savers, power management, screen resolution, number of colors ... the screen is one of two main output units (the printer is the other). Setting the display correctly for your purpose will minimize strain and maximize accuracy when reading the displayed information.

Disk Drives
There are three types on a standard PC:
- Floppy drives (for floppy disks)
- Hard drives (for fixed disks)
- CD-ROM drives or the higher capacity DVD drives (both are for CD-ROMs).

They are (collectively) the place to load new files or programs onto the computer, to transfer information from the computer and to store a permanent copy of the files being worked on.

Memory

There are different types of memory, and different ways to categorize memory as well. For our purposes, in order to maximize speed and efficiency, and minimize the risk of losing data, we are interested in understanding:

- Random access memory (RAM)
- Permanent and temporary memory
- Virtual memory.

Printers

There are several different printer technologies in use, and the capabilities of the printer will determine what can be achieved with the spreadsheet in terms of the output generated.

INTERACTING WITH THE OPERATING SYSTEM

The operating system is the buffer between you, the hardware and the spreadsheet. If the hardware stops responding, or if the spreadsheet crashes, the operating system may be able to resolve the problem.

Using the Keyboard

As well as the alphabet and number keys, there are other keys on the keyboard. These other keys are very important, because they are used to interact with programs or the operating system as appropriate. They are:

• Escape (Esc)	Used to escape from the current procedure. This could be cell editing, file save, printing etc. If the program appears to have locked up, this is the first key to press to try to release control back to the program.
• Alt	This is used to access drop-down menus. Pressing it once will highlight the menu bar. Arrow keys can then be used to move across the menu items.
• Control (Ctrl). There are two Ctrl keys, one on the bottom left and the other on the bottom right of the alpha key pad.	This is used in association with another key to complete an operation. For example, Ctrl and X pressed simultaneously will cut the highlighted item to the clipboard. The key does not function on its own.

- Shift. There are two Shift keys; each is marked with an up arrow ↑. One of the keys is below the Caps Lock key on the left of the alpha key pad, and the other is below the Return key on the right of the alpha key pad.

  The key may be combined with the F keys, Tab key etc. to perform specific operations. Exact functionality is determined by the program running, rather than Windows.
  The key does not function on its own.

- Control Alt Delete (Ctrl+Alt+Del)

  Pressing all three keys together causes the operating system to break into the running programs. If a program has stopped responding, Windows can be instructed to close it down by pressing these keys.

- Return and Enter. Return has the symbol ↵ and is located in the alpha key pad. Enter has the same function as the Return key and is located in the numeric key pad.

  Pressing this key tells the program that the input is finished and that the program should process the transaction.

The keys are highlighted in the diagrams below. Locate them on your own keyboard for future reference.

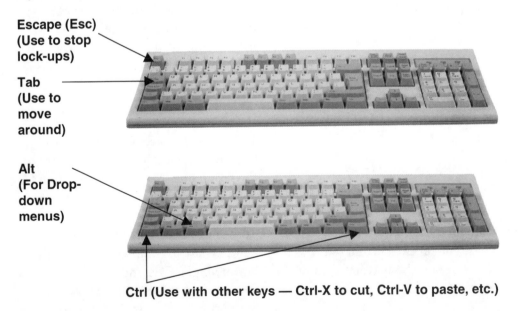

Escape (Esc) (Use to stop lock-ups)

Tab (Use to move around)

Alt (For Drop-down menus)

Ctrl (Use with other keys — Ctrl-X to cut, Ctrl-V to paste, etc.)

**Shift
(Use with
other keys in
programs to
access
specific
functions)**

**Return and Enter
(Confirms input and instructs the program to process the transaction)**

**Ctrl   Alt   Delete
(Press at the same time to unlock a program that is not responding)**

Exercises

We will practice using Control (Ctrl) and Shift (↑) in **Chapter Four**, when we have programs running. For now, we will practice how to use the other keys used to control programs: Escape, Return, Alt, Arrow (direction) Keys, and Ctrl+Alt+Del combined. The exercises below will illustrate how to use each of the keys, or combinations of keys, and the results that should be achieved.

Turn the computer on. The screenshots used in this book are taken from Windows 98 Second Edition. If you are using a different version of Windows your screenshots may not be exactly the same. However, the principles we are exploring will still apply to your computer provided you are using Windows 95 or later. Please note that Windows 2000 is for use on a business computer, and includes enhanced security features. These advanced aspects of Windows are beyond the scope of this book.

My ——▶
Computer

Double-click on **My Computer** to activate it.

The screen changes to:

Press **Alt** once. This activates the drop-down menus. **File** is now raised to show that it is active. The screenshot shows My Computer with View as Web page selected. We will adjust this shortly.

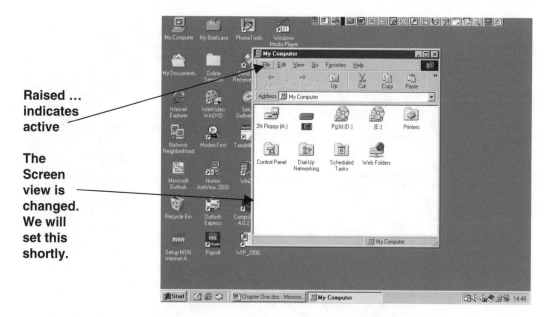

Raised ...
indicates
active

The
Screen
view is
changed.
We will
set this
shortly.

Press **Esc**. The raised menu item becomes flat again, because the command sequence was safely exited by Undo.

Activate File again by pressing **Alt**. Now press **Return** or **Enter**. The File menu item now shows a drop-down list of items.

The arrow keys (left and right) negotiate the menu items from File to Edit, View, Go, Favorites and Help, with their associated drop-down menus shown.

Arrow keys Up and Down move to items within each main menu heading.

**Right
arrow
moves
the
drop-
down
menu
right**

The arrow keys are in a block on the bottom, middle right, of the keyboard or in the number pad area (switch number lock off). See the diagram below.

**Number
lock**

**Number
keys**

**Arrow
keys**

Down arrow moves menu items down

Up arrow moves menu items up

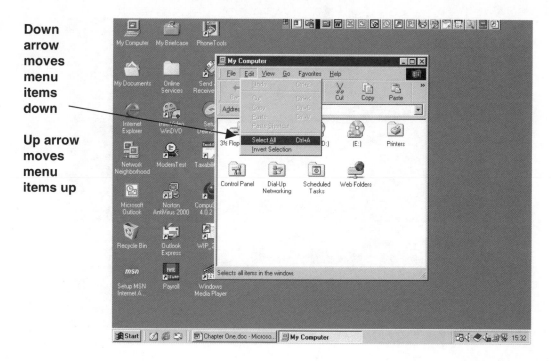

We now know how to handle the keyboard to instruct programs or to cancel commands given to Windows programs. But what if the program fails to respond to the keyboard?

System Crash

If a program will not respond, we can do two things:

- Turn the machine off and on again, which will terminate all of the programs running and lose all of the unsaved data in all of the programs we were working in
- Restrict the data loss to the single program which has crashed by pressing **Ctrl+Alt+Del**. Windows will attempt to trap the fault, and give us an analysis of the running programs. We can then identify the program at fault and terminate only that program.

We will now practice recovering from a system crash.

Press **Crtl+Alt+Del**.

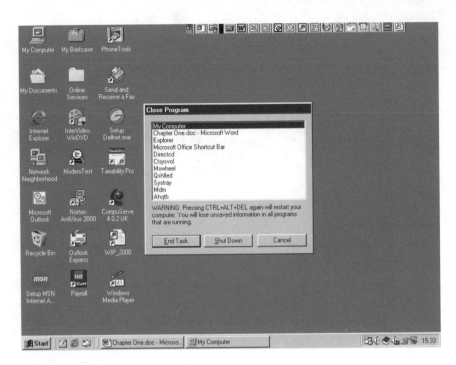

A dialog box appears, which analyses all of the programs running. You have the options of:

- Selecting one of the programs and closing it down (End Task)
- Closing down Windows completely (Shut Down)
- Canceling the request (Cancel). Pressing Esc will also close the dialog box.

If a program has locked up, Windows will give the program name and state (Not Responding) beside it. If this occurs, select that program using the up and down arrows, then select **End Task**.

For the moment, press **Esc** to close the dialog box.

We have now covered everything we wish to practice on keyboard at present. If you wish to exit Windows and return to the exercises later, click on the **Start** button, then click on **Shut Down** and **Yes**. This closes Windows down safely, and the screen will display a message when it is safe to turn off the computer. The computer will not display the message if it automatically powers off itself when Windows shuts down.

Using the Mouse
The mouse can be used as an alternative to the keyboard for selecting items and for input of commands. It can also fulfil special functions in programs and provide access to shortcut menus.

We will try some examples to illustrate how to use the mouse.

Exercises

Start **My Computer** on the main screen by double-clicking it.

Move the mouse pointer to **File** and click on it. The screen will look like this:

Move the mouse up and down the drop-down menu (do not hold down the mouse button). The blue highlighter moves to each item as the mouse passes over it.

Clicking the left mouse button selects the item.

Move the mouse to **View** and click the word. The drop-down menu appears. Move the mouse down to **Arrange Icons**. Another drop-down menu appears. Move the mouse on to this list (without clicking the mouse button).

The screen should look like this:

Move the mouse down until it is resting on **By Type**. Click the left mouse button. The drop-down menu closes and the view shown by My Computer changes to:

When clicked, the left mouse button acts as an alternative to using the Enter (or Return) key on the keyboard.

We now want to change everything back to the original screen layout.

Click on **View**. Without touching the mouse button, move the mouse down to **Arrange Icons**, and then move it on to **By Drive**. This time, press **Return**.

The screen returns to this:

Return (or Enter) produces the same result as clicking the left mouse button

Notice that pressing **Return** (or **Enter**) produced the same result as clicking the left mouse button.

Now we will see how to use the right mouse button.

In this example, the second mouse button (or the one on the extreme right on a three-button mouse) calls up a shortcut menu.

Close My Computer by clicking on **File**, **Close**.

Click on the green background on the Windows screen with the second mouse button. A small menu list appears.

**Mouse
right-click
brings up
menus.
Use the
left button
to select
from the
list**

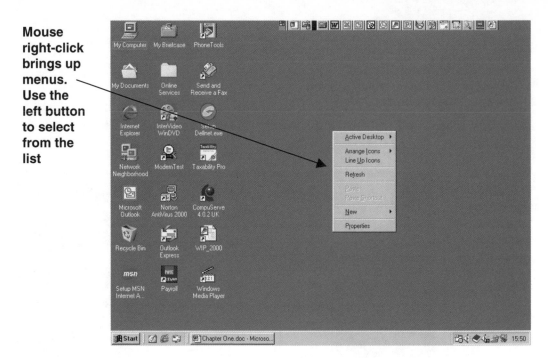

Move the mouse pointer over the list and select **Arrange Icons**, then select **By Name** and left-click. The computer now acts on the mouse input.

Remember: Left mouse button, always enabled; right mouse button, sometimes enabled.

MONITOR

For most purposes, if the monitor details have been set already, they should be left alone. However, there will be occasions when you want to change the type of monitor, the screen resolution, screen-savers etc.

Windows controls the monitor from the control panel. Double-click on **My Computer**, and then double-click on **Control Panel**.

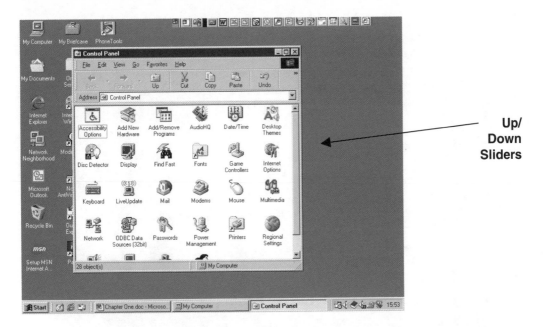

Up/ Down Sliders

Scroll through the screen using the Up/Down slider on the right-hand side of the screen until you see the Display Icon.

Double-click this icon, and the following screen appears:

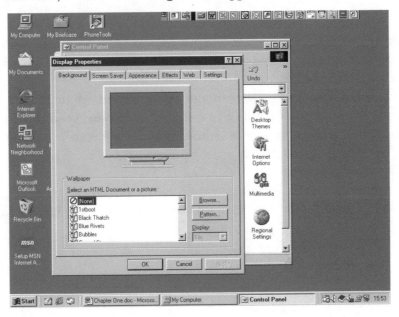

Click on the **Settings** tab, and you will see two settings:

- Colors
- Screen area.

Click on the down arrow on the **Color** box. A drop-down list is shown and, by clicking one of the values, the depth of color can be changed. Note the setting before changing and then experiment. If difficulties are encountered, change back to the original setting.

In order to increase the amount of information displayed on the screen, change the screen resolution by sliding the **Screen Area** bar from left to right. Either click and hold the mouse button while the mouse pointer is on the slider bar, and then drag it to the right and release, or click in the bar area and the slider will jump across.

Experiment with different resolutions and colors, checking the resulting screenshots in Excel. This is where you will achieve the benefit (or detriment) in screenshots because of the changes.

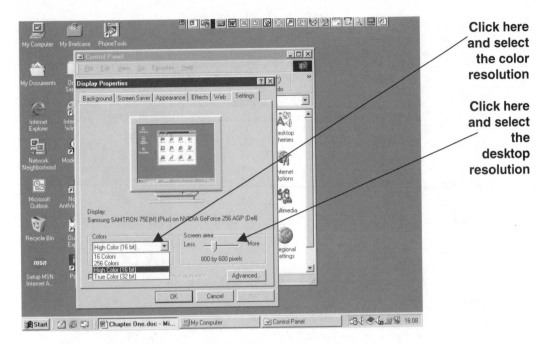

Click here and select the color resolution

Click here and select the desktop resolution

DISK DRIVES

We have to know how to read files from disk, save files to disk, review disk contents and find the files we are interested in.

Opening files, saving files, exploring the disks, etc. is covered in **Chapters Four** and **Five**. But here we want to consider disk organization, naming conventions for the various drives and other background information.

Which drive letter?

Each drive (floppy, hard disk, CD-ROM / DVD and network) is allocated a letter to identify it. How are the letters chosen? What about missing letters?

Computers used to come with two floppy drives installed — there may or may not have been a hard drive installed, particularly in older machines. The first floppy drive, usually the one on the left, was designated as A: drive. The second floppy was designated as B: drive. With two floppy drives fitted, the lowest letter for the hard drive was C: and, by convention, the hard drive is allocated from letter C: — even when no second floppy is fitted.

CD-ROMs are designated the next letter after the letter used by the hard drive, so it is usually allocated as D: drive. If there are two hard drives fitted, or if the hard drive is split into two logical drives, the CD-ROM will be drive E:

Double click on **My Computer** to see the drives on your PC. This PC has the following drives:

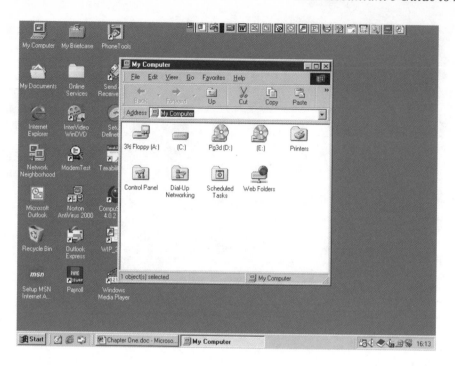

- Drive A: Floppy
- Drive C: Hard Drive
- Drive D: DVD
- Drive E: CD-ROM

There is no drive B: (second floppy) installed.

Floppy Disk Size

The floppy drive capacity of your computer is probably 1.44 MB (megabytes), which means that it will read from floppy disks with a capacity of 1.44 MB or less. It also means that, if the file you are trying to save is greater than this size, it will not save to floppy, unless you use special software to split the file over several disks, or zip the file (condense it) using utility software.

Floppy Disk Speed

The floppy disk rotates at approximately one-tenth of the speed of a hard disk. This is why it is slower to work from floppy disks (opening, saving and closing files) than it is to use files stored on the hard drive.

Storing Information on Floppy and Hard Drives

Floppy disks, hard disks and CD-ROMs all store the information in the same way, using a path from the root directory through sub-directories, to the individual files themselves.

The addressing structure can therefore be represented as a tree branch diagram, like this:

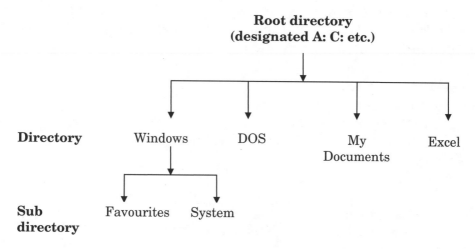

The full address of a file in Favorites is therefore:

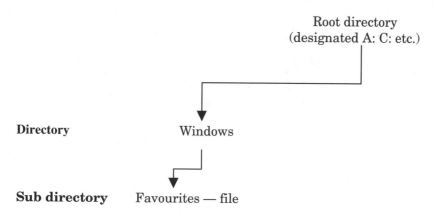

Assuming we are using drive C: to store a file, its full path will be:
C:\Windows\Favourites\Filename.

The backslash (\) is used to identify when a sub-directory is involved. The final backslash precedes the file name.

If the file was on the root directory, it would be C:\Filename, or just C:Filename.

If the same file were stored on the floppy disk, the path would be A:\Windows\Favourites\Filename if the directory structure shown above were duplicated on the floppy.

MEMORY

The next area we should look at is memory, so that the hardware is firmly in context as regards the operating system.

Memory has several different meanings, the meaning usually coming from the context in which it is used. So, let's outline some of the contexts.

An Overview

The computer sends information from disk or CD-ROM to Random Access Memory (RAM). From there, the information passes to the Central Processing Unit, and then back out to RAM, and from there to the hard disk. Diagrammatically:

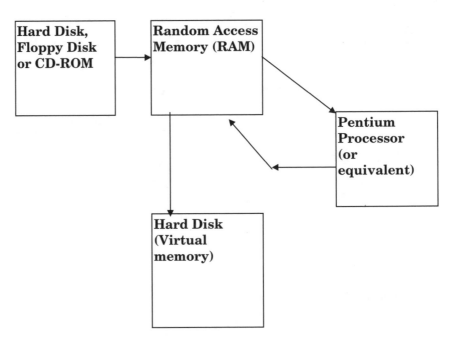

The operating system controls the ins and outs of the information flow. However, from our point of view, we want to analyze the memory into permanent and temporary. If the power fails, or if the system locks up, we lose temporary memory and everything stored in it. If the memory is permanent, we do not lose the information.

Looking at the diagram again, and annotating it, we get:

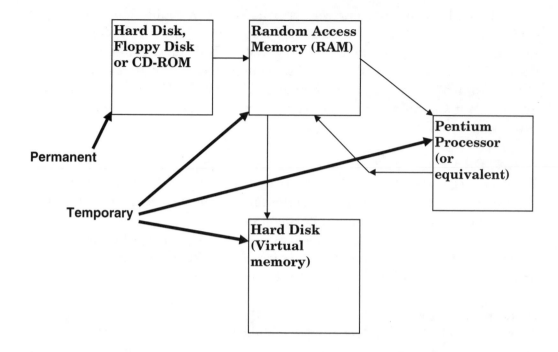

Every time we turn on the computer, the virtual memory on the hard drive is created. When we turn the computer off, it is deleted.

The RAM holds information because electricity is passed through the memory chips. Switching off the power means all circuits are wiped clean of information.

Files and data held on the hard disk using the operating system's Save function are written to the hard disk. Because it is a magnetic medium, it is not affected by switching power on or off UNLESS the operating system is writing to the disk when the power goes down and it has not completed the write operation.

From the above, you will see that there are two things which we can do to assist the operating system in making our life as easy as possible:

- Either regularly save manually to hard disk or instruct the computer to automatically save on a regular basis. This is covered in **Section Two**.
- Minimize the amount of information transferred from RAM to Virtual memory. RAM works faster, and the system speeds up accordingly. However, as with most things in life, there comes a point when extra RAM makes no difference, because there is excess capacity available.

Read Only Memory (ROM)

The above does not cover CD-ROMs. Unless special equipment has been purchased, the CD-ROM unit on your computer is read only, therefore, information cannot be stored on it.

If information is needed (to record your name, log in details, etc.), this will be stored on the hard disk and accessed by the program when you start the CD-ROM. If this data is important, you may wish to back up the information from the hard disk. The CD-ROM cannot be corrupted because it is read only — no write operations are made by the computer to the CD-ROM drive, so no files are updated on it and there can be no write errors if the computer locks up or if the power goes down.

PRINTERS

The operating system loads a printer driver so that, when you want to print out your work, you can select the right printer for the job, and the file output is sent in the correct form for the printer to understand.

There are many different technologies in printers, although for our purpose the differences between them are largely irrelevant. What we are interested in is how to set up a new printer, and how to change from one printer to another.

Printer Exercises

We want to look at the printers already installed, and to check their properties.

Turn the computer on, and close down the Welcome Screen if it appears. Double-click on **My Computer**. The screen should look like this:

The printer icon

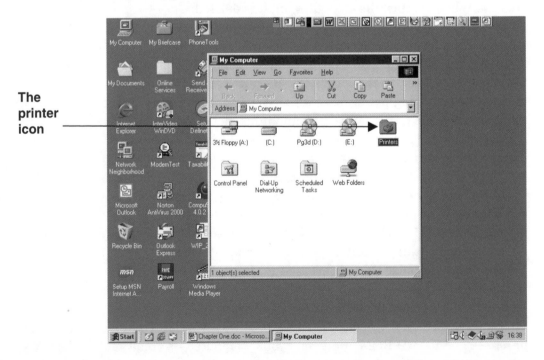

Double-click on the printer icon. The screen changes to:

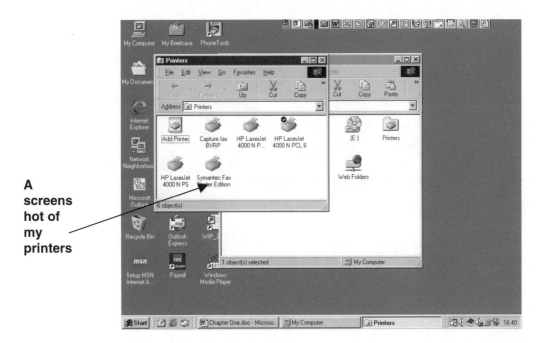

A screens hot of my printers

Double-click on **Add Printer**, and Windows will guide you through the installation procedure. The first step is:

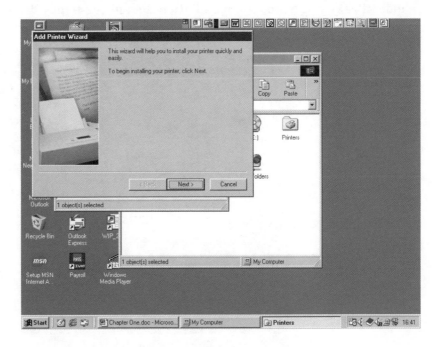

Click **Next**.

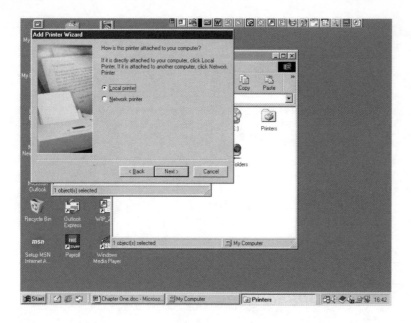

The options are to select a local printer or a network printer. Select the manufacturer in the left window by clicking on the name (scrolling up and down the list, if necessary), and then select the printer model in the right-hand box. Windows asks you to put the installation disk in the floppy drive or CD-ROM as appropriate, then it loads the appropriate driver.

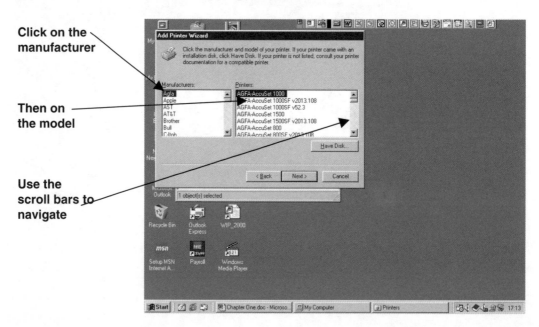

Click on the manufacturer

Then on the model

Use the scroll bars to navigate

Select the port to which the printer is attached. This is usually LPT1.

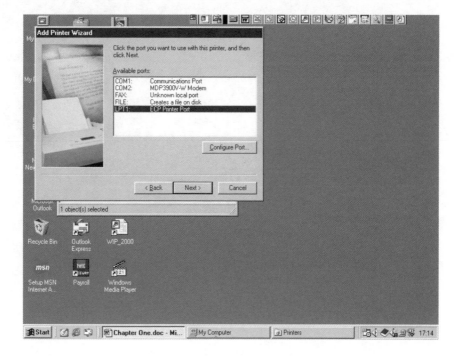

Click **Next**.

Setting the printer as default means that it will be the printer suggested every time you print, whether from Excel or any other program.

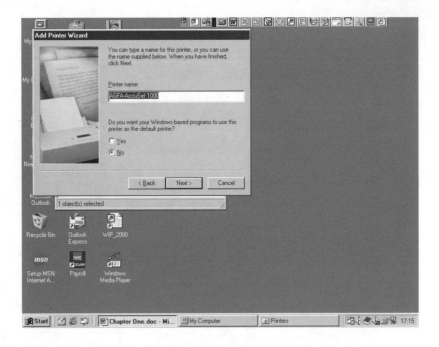

Click **Next**.

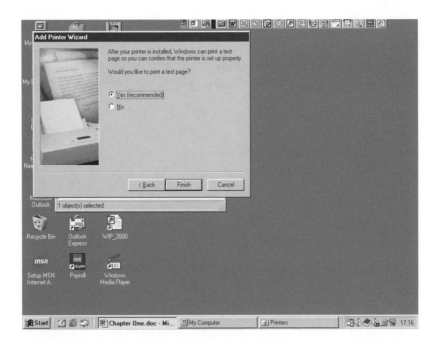

Click **Finish**. The screen changes to this (or refers to A: drive):

Click on Cancel to close the wizard. If you click **Finish** Windows will build a driver database and the printer will be installed. If the drivers are not already on your computer you will be prompted to insert the Windows CD into the CD-ROM drive.

The printer then appears in the list of available printers in the Printer folder.

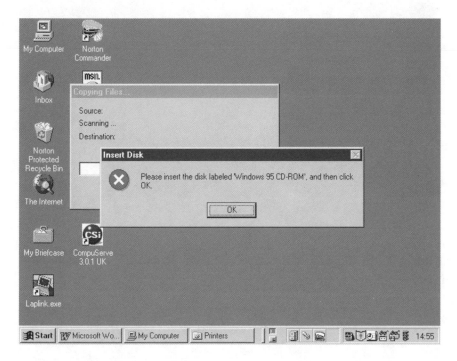

Insert the disk, and there you have it — a new printer installed.

Changing the Default Printer
Once the printers have been set up, you may want to change which printer is set as the default printer, cancel print jobs or interact and control the printer in some other way.

We will look at the control that can be exercised over the printer.

To access printer controls, double-click on **My Computer**, then double-click the **Printers** icon.

Select the printer you wish to deal with by double-clicking on it. The following screen appears:

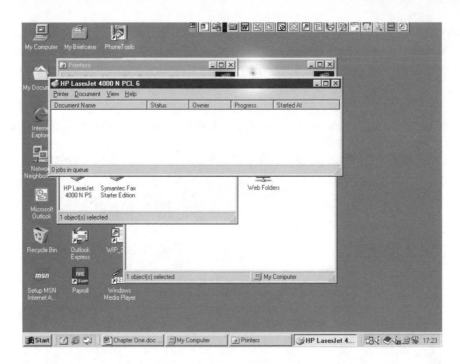

Click on **Printer** in the menu, or press **Alt** then **Return** — the drop-down menu is displayed as shown below:

**Click on
Printer or
press Alt
and Return**

The options are:
- Pause Printing
- Set As Default
- Purge Print Documents
- Properties
- Close.

We wish to toggle the **Set As Default** option on and off, using the keyboard. If the printer you have chosen is already the default printer, choose another.

Notice that the menu item Set As Default has the letter **F** underlined. If a letter is underlined, pressing the letter will select that item.

Look at the menu again. Notice that an underlined letter only appears once. This avoids any confusion as to which item you are selecting.

In general, selecting items using the mouse or Up and Down arrow keys is quicker, but there may be occasions when the mouse proves to be faulty and an alternative is necessary. Smaller keyboards, especially laptops, do not have separate arrow keys and letter-selection is more convenient.

With the panel active, press **Alt+P** to display the drop-down menu, then press **F**. The window closes, and the new printer is set as the default. Double-click on the **Printers** icon and press **Alt+P** to check — there should be a tick mark against Set As Default.

Close the window, select the original printer and make it the default printer once more.

We will look at printing again in **Section Two**.

Understanding Printing Using Windows

It is important to understand how printing works in Windows, in order to be able to control the output properly, and to solve problems.

The file is sent from (say) Excel to the printer along the following route:

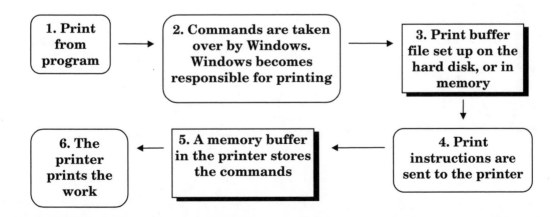

We may want to interrupt the printing process for several reasons — the printer is printing gobbledygook, we sent the wrong information to the printer or we sent the right information to the wrong printer. We will use the diagram above to describe how we can interrupt the printing process:

Step 1: The print command is invoked. Once invoked, the process cannot be interrupted.

Step 2: The print command is invoked. This passes the information to a buffer on the computer and, once invoked the process cannot be interrupted.

Step 3: The information for printing is stored here, ready for passing on to the printer.

Deleting the buffer file will cancel the print job. We have seen how to access the printer command screen earlier, but there is a shortcut when we print. A printer icon appears at the bottom of the screen — double-clicking on this icon provides access to the printer screen, and the job can be cancelled.

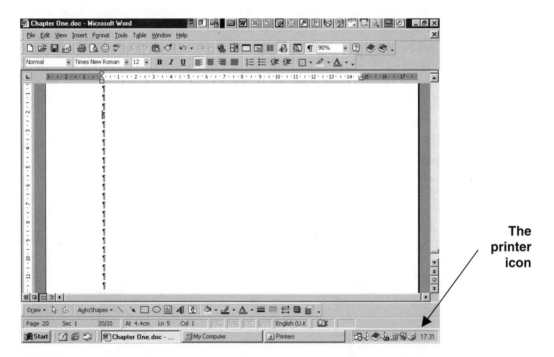

The printer icon

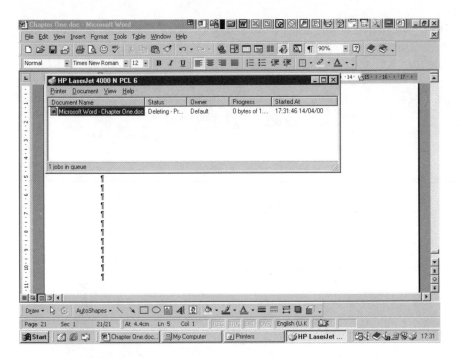

The printer control panel appears. Click on **Printer** in the menu, and then on **Purge Print Documents**. The job is deleted.

If several jobs are listed and you only wish to cancel one of these, highlight the job by clicking on it with the mouse and then press the **Delete** key on the keyboard.

If the print file is small, the file will be passed to the printer before you have chance to interrupt its progress. In this case, we will have to move to Step 4.

Step 4: This passes the information to the printer and, once invoked, the process cannot be interrupted.

Step 5: To clear the memory buffer in the printer, turn it off and then on again. Depending on the size of the file being processed, and the size of the printer memory, it may be necessary to turn the printer on and off several times, allowing the memory to be filled each time, and then flushing it out. Failing this, we move on to Step 6.

Step 6: If the printer starts to print, remove the paper from the paper tray. The printer will stop automatically, allowing you to return to Step 5. In addition, the printer will send a message to Windows that it is off-line, and the following message box appears:

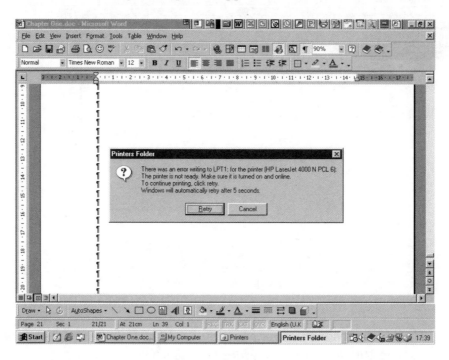

Pressing **Cancel** will cancel the print job.

CHAPTER TWO — DIRECTORIES, FILES AND FOLDERS

Now that we know how to use the hardware, and how to interact with the operating system, we will now learn more about directory structures, etc. in **Chapter Two**. This will show you how to organize your work to suit you best.

Chapter Two

Directories, Files and Folders

Once a directory, always a directory . . .

In **Chapter One**, we saw how files are organized on the disk drives, and we explained the concept of directories and file addressing.

In this chapter, we want to look at the concept from the Windows perspective. The term "directories" is no longer used in Windows, and everything is either a file or a folder. We therefore want to look at the concepts, and to understand what they mean.

By doing this, we will be able to navigate with ease through the computer representation of where our files are stored, and be able to use the file manipulation software with confidence.

DIRECTORIES RECAP

You will recall that in **Chapter One** we represented the file structure as a tree diagram and that the file address was given by describing the path along the tree that has to be taken to reach it.

Windows gives us a pictorial representation of this structure, and we see this in Explorer. To start Explorer, click on the **Start** button — a list of items appears, one of which is Programs.

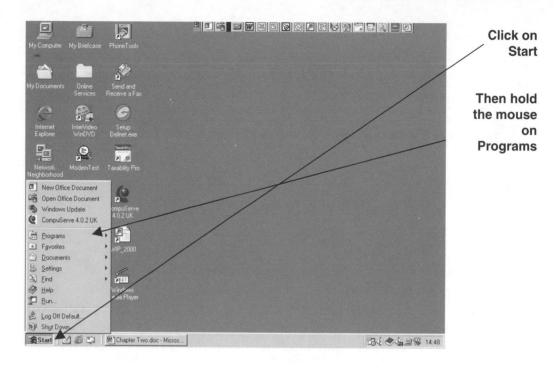

When you move the mouse pointer to **Programs**, a further list pops up; this time the list shows the programs loaded on the computer, as well as shortcut keys to DOS etc. The last item on the list is Explorer.

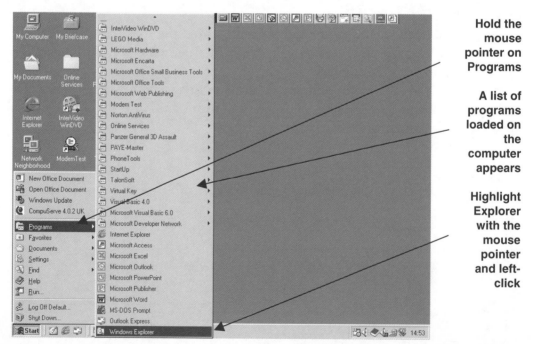

A screenshot similar to that shown below appears. Note that the content of the computer shown is different from your own, so whilst some individual items will be the same the majority will not.

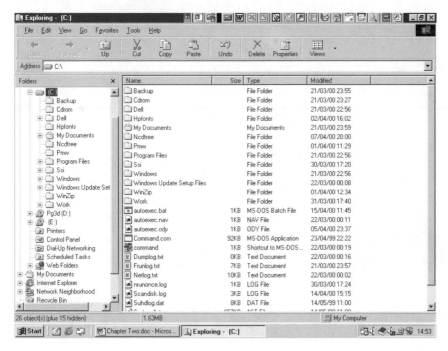

There are two panes: The one on the left identifies the sub-directories in the directory you are reviewing; the pane on the right identifies the sub-directories and files in the directory under review.

The left pane shows the directory structure.

Click with the left mouse on the Windows yellow folder. It is highlighted in blue, and the information in the right pane changes.

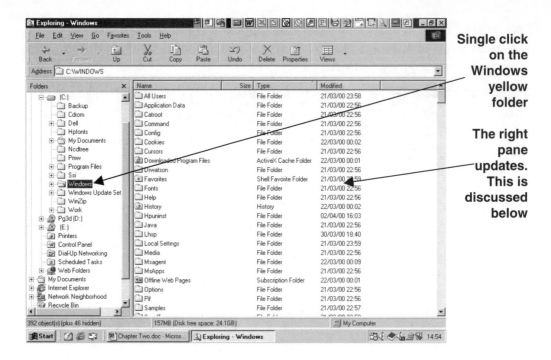

Now double-click the Window yellow folder in the left pane. The yellow folders in the right pane are now shown in the left pane.

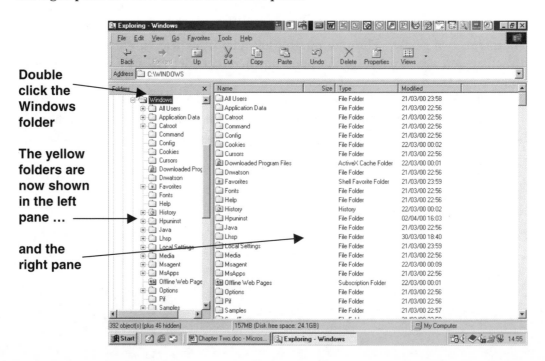

So what's the difference? Scroll down the left pane to the bottom, then scroll down the right pane to the bottom.

The left pane only shows the directory and its sub-directories. The right pane shows what is in each directory — the directory contains the sub-directories and files.

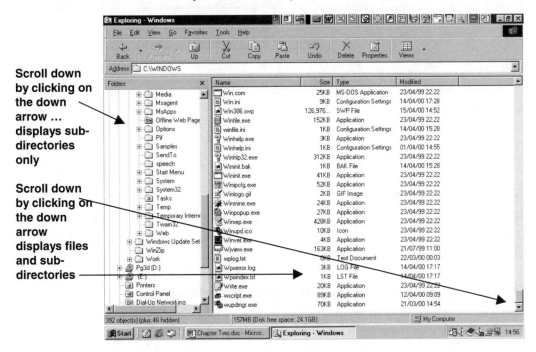

To go back to our original diagram of directory structures, the layout in each pane is therefore:

LEFT PANE

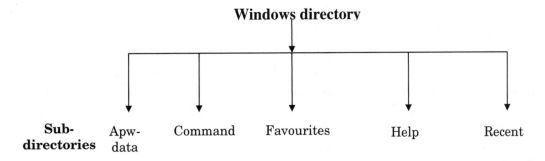

There are a lot more sub-directories than this, but you get the point. You can only move up and down the directory tree. Individual contents of the directory are not shown in this pane.

RIGHT PANE

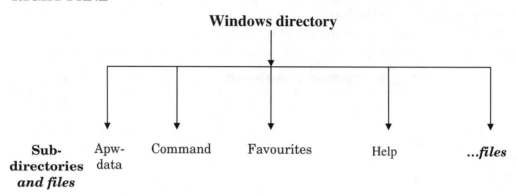

Windows directory

Sub-directories and files | Apw-data | Command | Favourites | Help | *...files*

The files will usually be by far the largest part of the content of the right pane.

So, to Summarize

Negotiate through the directories and sub-directories in the left pane. View the directory contents (files and sub-directories) in the right pane. The sub-directories are repeated in both the left and right pane.

By double-clicking on the directory in the left pane, the View Sub Directories/Hide Sub Directories alternative is invoked.

Folders or Directories? What's in a Name?

Windows '95 introduced the term Folder. Why? It seems just like a DOS directory.

The reason is to make you change the way you (perhaps) think about storing information on your hard (or floppy) disk.

DOS Programs and Directories

Load a DOS program and it creates the working directory, then functions as per the manuals.

Load a Windows program and likewise.

However, they are substantially different when it comes to running the program. The DOS package requires the data files to be in one (specified) location — in the main program directory or in a sub-directory of that main directory. There is no discretion on the part of the operator as to where data files are located.

Windows and Folders

Windows programs do not have this constraint, and working files can be kept anywhere, irrespective of the location of the program. This allows users to save files in a logical place, or in user-defined sets, to suit the way their work is organised.

The Folder concept makes it easier for users to conceptualize the way their work is stored. Just as a folder in a filing cabinet will contain all relevant documents, irrespective of source — spreadsheets, graphics, word processed documents, databases — a folder can be set up in Windows for a project, rather than having the related files spread throughout the hard disk in the directories of the various programs being used.

As a starter, Windows includes two folders for immediate use: My Documents and Favorites.

Exercises

We want to store any work we prepare in this book in three separate folders:
- Practicing Spreadsheet Techniques
- Projections and Accounts on Spreadsheets
- The Business Plan.

You will note that the titles are self-explanatory. This is one of **the** benefits of Windows: Long file names, ones that are actually meaningful compared to the 8-character limit imposed by DOS.

Start **Explorer** (refer to the earlier part of the chapter, if need be).

Click on **File**, then on **New**.

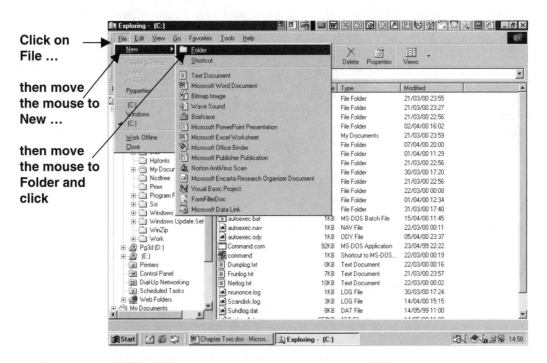

Click on File ...

then move the mouse to New ...

then move the mouse to Folder and click

A new folder (directory) is created within the current folder (directory), with the name **New**. Type in **My Spreadsheet Folder** to replace the default text. Click outside the folder, and the folder titled My Spreadsheet Folder will appear.

The new Folder

Type in the name My Spread- sheet Folder

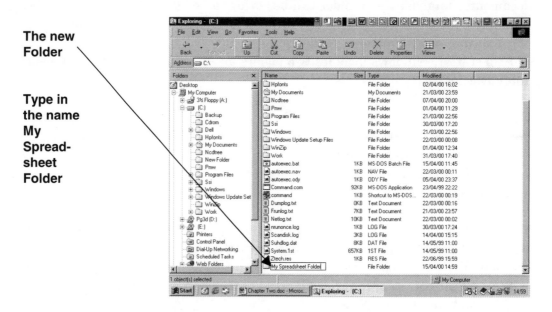

Click on the folder My Spreadsheet Folder, and you will see that it is empty — we have not placed anything in it yet. So . . .

Click on My Spread- sheet Folder

Nothing displays in the right pane — the folder is empty

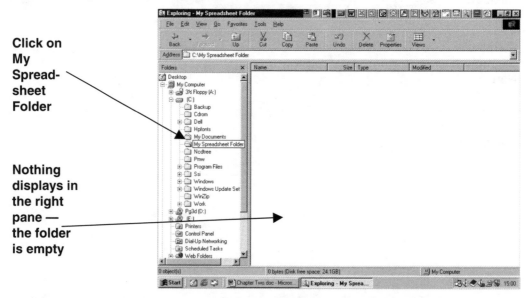

We now want to create the three folders referred to earlier, and place them in this folder. With the folder My Spreadsheet Folder highlighted in the left pane, all of the actions we are about to undertake will affect this folder, rather than any other.

So, highlight **My Spreadsheet Folder** in the left pane. Click on **File**, **New**, **Folder** (as we did to create My Spreadsheet Folder previously).

Type in the name **Practicing Spreadsheet Techniques**.

Click in the right pane, outside the folder name, and the task is completed.

Repeat this for two further folders, named:

- Projections and Accounts on Spreadsheets
- The Business Plan.

The procedure is shown below:

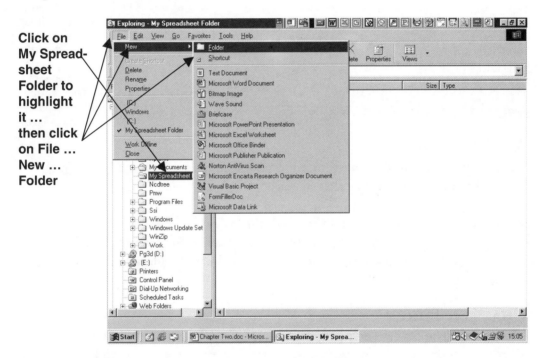

The screen should look like this when completed. If not, click on **View**, then **Details** in the menu.

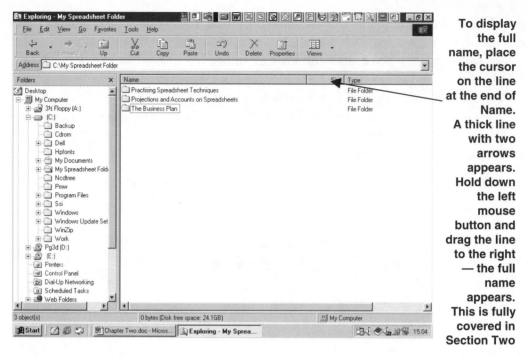

To display the full name, place the cursor on the line at the end of Name. A thick line with two arrows appears. Hold down the left mouse button and drag the line to the right — the full name appears. This is fully covered in Section Two

TO CONCLUDE

That covers everything we need to know about Folders, Files and Directories.
You should now understand:

- That a folder is a directory.
- That a folder can contain another folder, files, or both.
- The full path name for a file, by tracing its location through the tree diagram.
- The importance of organizing work in a logical set of folders to suit the way you work.

CHAPTER THREE

Chapter Three covers the navigation of programs using the Windows interface. Your understanding of directories, files and folders above is a foundation for the next chapter.

Chapter Three

START, TASKBAR AND DESKTOP PROGRAMS

That's not a Desktop! That's a Mess-top . . .

In **Chapter Two**, we saw how Windows stores information, and how to organize the folder structure to suit your own way of working.

In this chapter, we want to take a step further back and get a wider perspective on controlling programs and organizing the screen to suit the way you work.

THE WINDOWS SCREEN REVISITED

Let's take another look at the opening screenshot. This one is tailored — some of the content will be the same as your own; some is specific to my own set-up.

The important items (for this purpose) are highlighted.

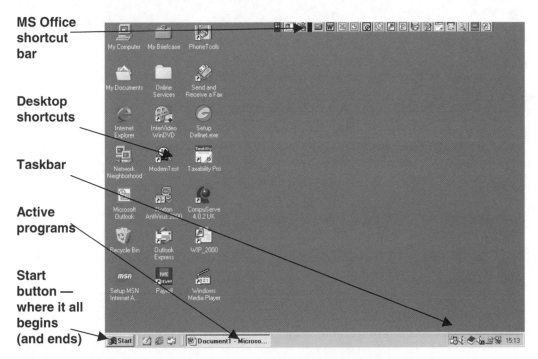

What is the significance of each area, and how do we tailor it to our needs?

START

You can navigate manually to the program file (for example, Excel) that you want to execute, or you can use the shortcuts provided by Windows.

When you click on **Start**, a range of choices is made available, as follows:

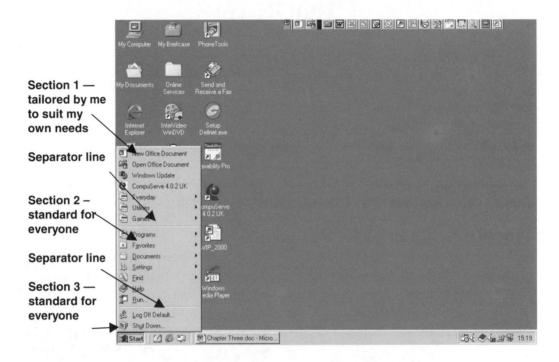

The menu list is split into three sections, separated by lines.

This format for splitting sections within menus is consistently applied throughout Windows packages, as we will see with Excel later.

With Start, we have a direct route to control the loading of programs. It does other things as well, but these are covered later.

STARTING WINDOWS PROGRAMS

We want to start all of the programs we are interested in using. The standard route is through the Programs section. If we highlight **Programs**, a list of available Windows programs appears.

Note that DOS-based programs do not appear in the listed programs — these have to be added separately.

In this case, there are quite a number of programs loaded:

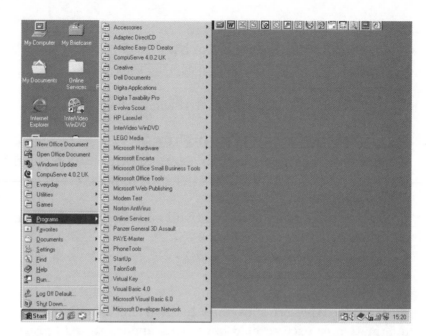

Highlight one (say **Microsoft Office Tools**) and a further list of programs appears.

Place the mouse pointer on MS Office Tools …

Then place the mouse pointer on MS Binder and click – the program starts.

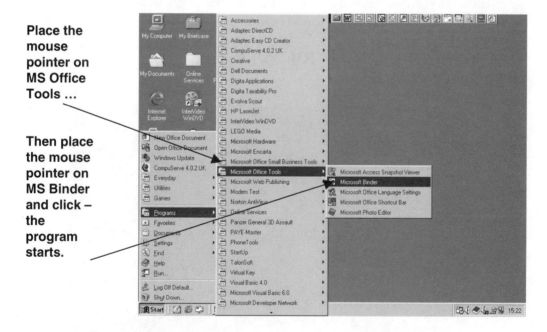

If you want to cancel the command, click on the green area of the screen and Start closes.

If you regularly run a program, this can be a long circuit to navigate. You have three alternatives:

- Change the menu structure
- Add it to the MS Office shortcut bar
- Place an icon on the desktop to run the program.

We will look at each in turn, but first some information on file types.

EXECUTABLE AND OTHER FILES

When we run a program, such as Excel, Set-Up, Install, etc. the program starts. If you try to run a data file, it doesn't start (unless it is associated with the original program). Why?

There are two types of file that will execute (run) when you type the filename (with or without the file extension):

- Executable files (extension EXE)
- Batch files (extension BAT).

All other file types are subsidiary to these and are either used by the program for information or used to hold data. This applies to DOS programs and Windows programs alike.

In the next section, we will identify the executable file in our program and use Windows to write a small batch file to run it.

CHANGING THE MENU STRUCTURE

Look at the screenshot below:

It shows a tailored entry in the Start menu. We will now enter Excel on a new section of the menu — the only reason for choosing Excel is to ensure you have the same program, and can follow the steps and test your result.

Click on **Start**, and then place the pointer on **Settings**.

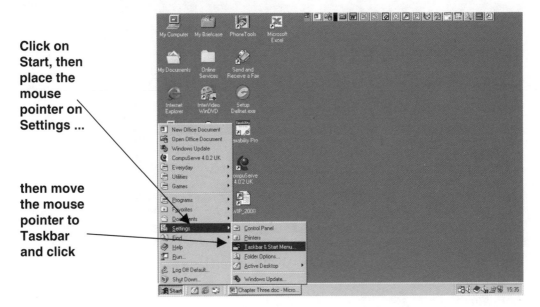

**Click on
Start, then
place the
mouse
pointer on
Settings ...**

**then move
the mouse
pointer to
Taskbar
and click**

There are six choices: Control Panel, Printers, Taskbar & Start Menu, Folder Options, Active Desktop and Windows Update. We looked at Control Panel and Printers in **Chapter One**. You will recall we activated these programs through the My Computer icon on the desktop — the Settings section is another way of reaching it, as shown above.

The following screen appears:

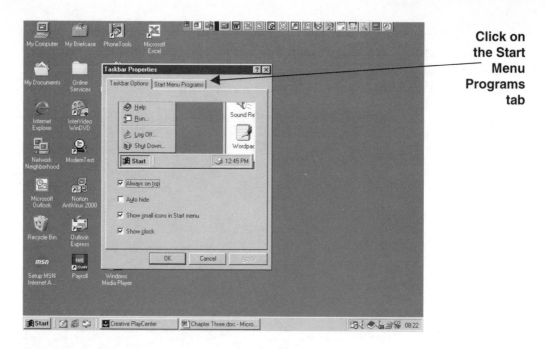

Click on
the Start
Menu
Programs
tab

Click on the **Start Menu Programs** tab. The choices are:
- Add
- Remove
- Advanced.

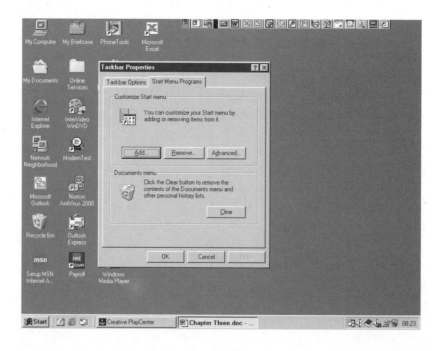

Click on **Advanced**.

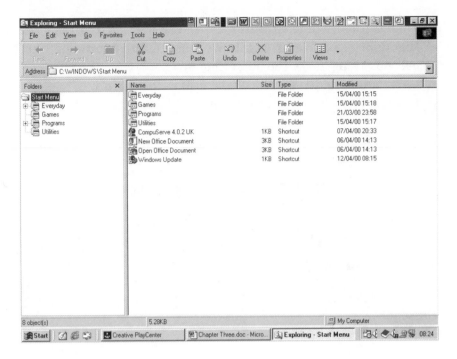

Notice that this has started a special screenshot from Explorer. We used Explorer in **Chapter Two** to navigate around the hard drive, but its display can be adapted to display selective information. If you wish to do this, review the online help facility.

The screen has a similar layout to the Root Directory/Tree Diagram we discussed in **Chapter Two**.

Redrawing the structure shown on the screen above gives:

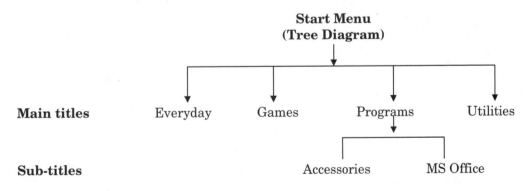

We want to enter a new Main Title, and then put a Sub-title within this called Excel.

From the above (and **Chapter Two**), you will see that the procedure is:

- Highlight **Start Menu**, so that we insert a **Sub-Menu** off Start Menu and not off something below the main item level.
- Insert a new folder — we will call it **My Collection**.
- Insert a shortcut to Excel in the new Folder.

This is shown below:

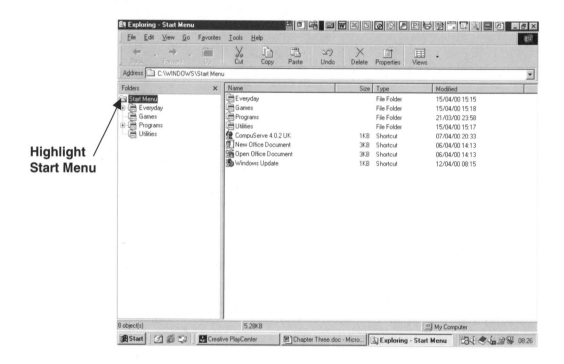

**Click on
File ...**

**Move the
mouse
pointer to
New ...**

**and then to
Folder.
Click on
Folder**

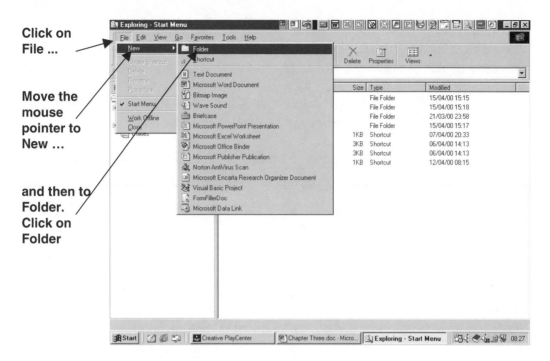

Type in the name **My Collection**.

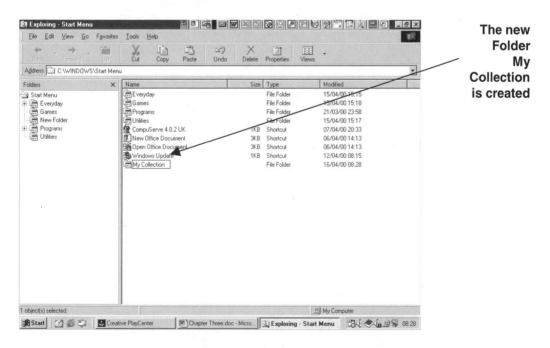

**The new
Folder
My
Collection
is created**

Click in the left pane so that the name is accepted and processed.

Then click in the left pane on **My Collection**. This gives us the content of My Collection (which is nothing), but it also means that anything we now do will go into the My Collection folder.

This time we want a shortcut to Excel, rather than to a folder. Go through the same procedure, but click on **Shortcut**. The following dialog box appears:

With My Collection highlighted, click on File ...

then New ...

then Shortcut

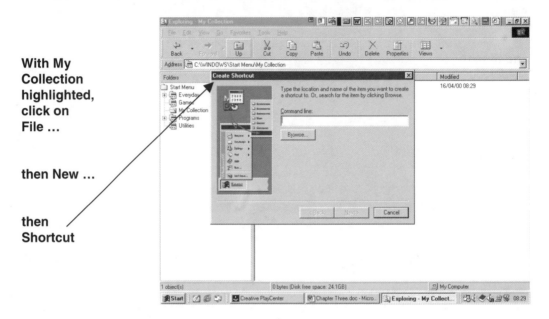

Click on Browse and . . .

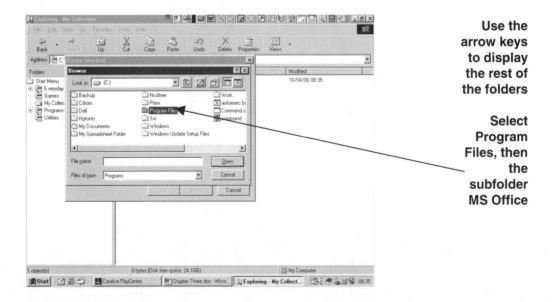

Use the arrow keys to display the rest of the folders

Select Program Files, then the subfolder MS Office

. . . Move to the MS Office folder. Double-click.

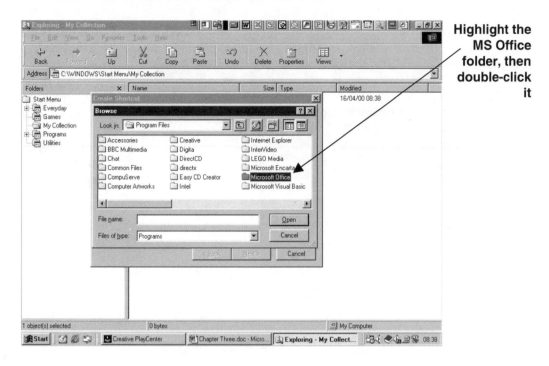

Highlight the MS Office folder, then double-click it

A set of sub-folders displayed. Select Office and double-click.

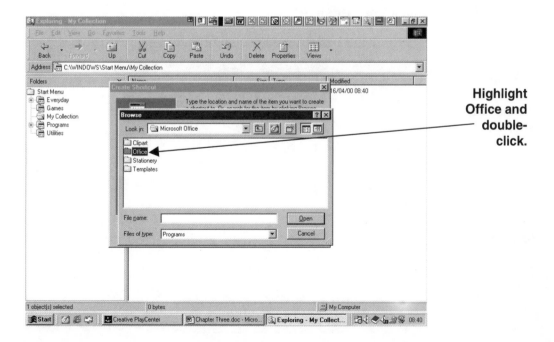

Highlight Office and double-click.

The contents of the MS Office folder are then displayed. Select **Excel** and double click on it.

The **Excel.exe** file is entered in the shortcut batch file prepared by Windows.

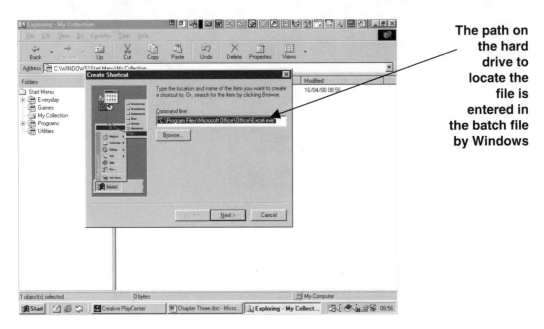

The path on the hard drive to locate the file is entered in the batch file by Windows

All we need to do is enter a name (or accept the default), click **Next**, and then, on the next screen, click **Finish**. An icon is entered in the menu beside the name.

We will use the name **Spreadsheet**.

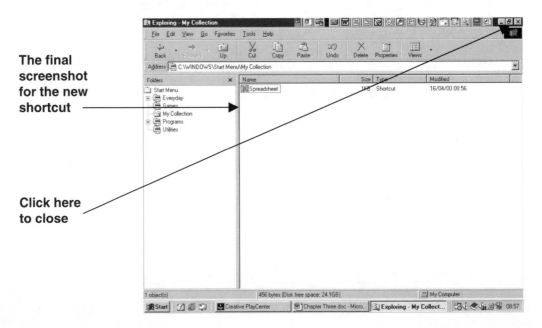

The final screenshot for the new shortcut

Click here to close

Close the Exploring screen (**File, Exit** or click on the X in the top right-hand corner of the screen).

Click on **Start**.

The new section My Collection appears

The shortcut Spreadsheet appears, with the Excel icon

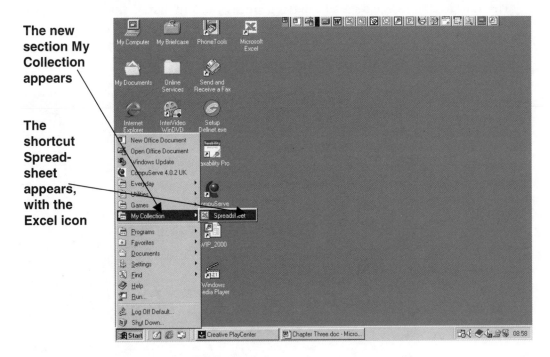

Click on the **Spreadsheet** shortcut to confirm it works correctly.

If you want to move My Collection so that it appears above another menu item, left click the icon on the left of My Collection and drag it up. Release the mouse and the menu item is relocated. If you drag it outside the menu it will appear on the desktop instead.

If you have DOS programs, you will need to put a shortcut for them on your Start menu, because they will not appear on the Program section without special programming.

The only difference in the procedure with DOS programs is that, because there is no default icon for the shortcut, a selection of icons appears, any of which can be chosen.

If You Could Not Find Excel.exe
If you could not locate Excel.exe, use Explorer to search your hard drive — click **Tools, Find, Files** or **Folders**. Type in the name of the file (Excel.exe) and start the search from the C: drive. Do not forget to include sub-folders in the search.

DESKTOP SHORTCUTS

Instead of (or as well as) having the program shortcut available in the Start menu, a shortcut can be placed directly on the screen desktop.

The requirements, in terms of setting up a shortcut batch file and icon, are similar. In order to start the process, **right-click** on the desk-top background.

This produces a small menu of options, one of which is **New**. Place the mouse pointer on it to see the **Folder/Shortcut** options.

Right click in an empty part of the desktop to display the menu

Place the mouse pointer on New

Move the pointer to Shortcut and click

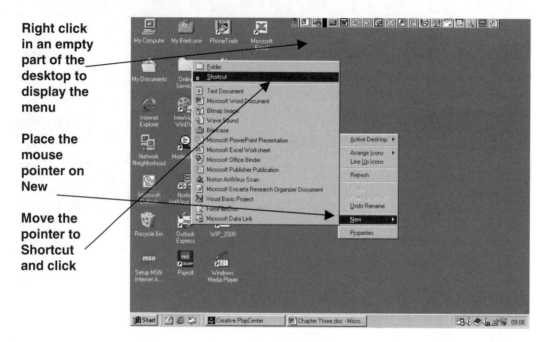

After clicking on Shortcut, the procedure is the same as for the Start menu — the same dialog boxes, etc. appear.

MICROSOFT OFFICE SHORTCUT BAR

The final option, in terms of creating shortcuts to programs, is to add them to the Microsoft Office shortcut bar. The procedure for this is explained below.

Click on the icon at the extreme left of the bar to see a drop-down menu.

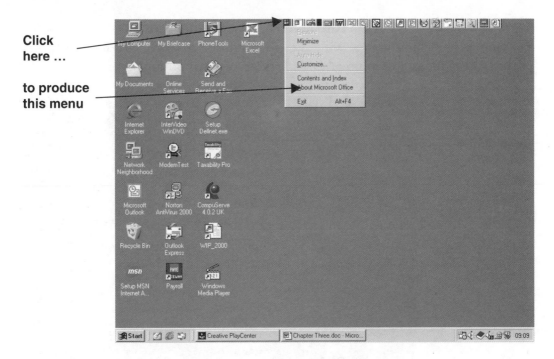

**Click
here ...**

**to produce
this menu**

We want to add program icons and shortcuts to the standard bar, so click
Customize. This produces:

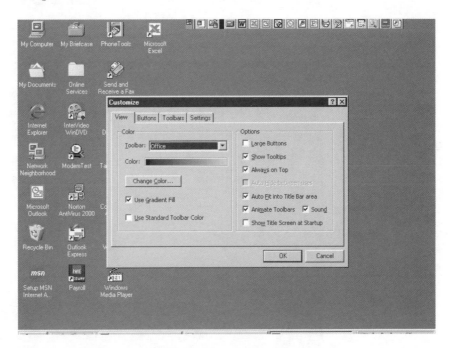

There are two choices: Add to the buttons on the Office toolbar, or change toolbars.

To add buttons, select the **Buttons** tab, then click on **Add File** (to add the executable file). If the file is a Windows program, an appropriate icon will be displayed; if the file is a DOS program, a pre-set icon will be displayed.

**Click on this
tab …**

**then on the
Add File
button**

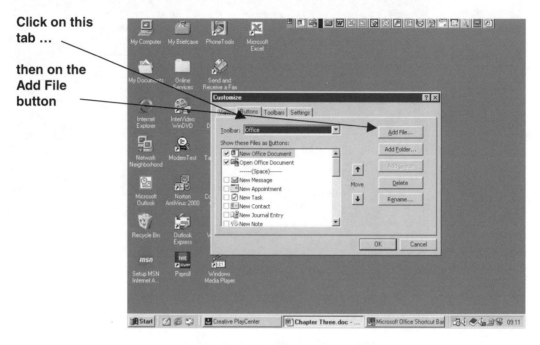

This takes us to the Folder Selection screen we saw earlier:

We can complete the insertion as before.

The other possibility is to select the **Toolbars** tab. Choose the **Desktop Toolbar**. Clicking on the **Office Toolbar** then will change from Office to Desktop and *vice versa*.

**Click on the
Toolbars
tab ...**

**click on the
check box to
include the
Desktop ...**

**then click
OK**

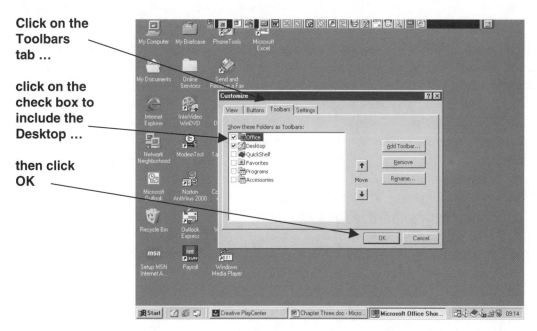

The toolbar changes to this:

**Click here
to change
back to
Office**

**If clicked,
the Office
toolbar is
shown, and
there is an
icon to
switch to
the
Desktop
display**

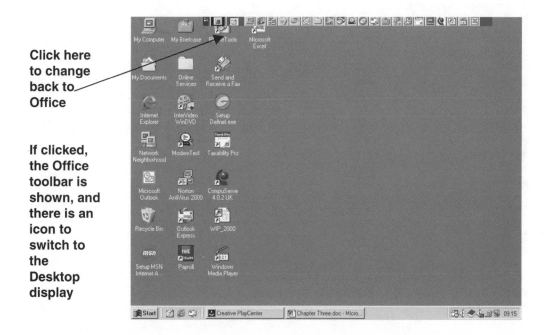

So, as illustrated above, there are many ways to take control of the computer and to personalize it to your own requirements. The last control tool we want to explore in this chapter is the Taskbar.

TASKBAR

The main reason for running Windows is to allow several programs to run at the same time, and to allow the easy transfer of information from one program into another.

Control is exercised by using the Taskbar — the space beside the Start button.

When a program is started, it is displayed in a wide box on the spacebar. As further programs are started, the space along the Taskbar is divided between them.

To make a program the "front screen" active program, simply click on its name on the Taskbar. The screen is updated to take you into that program while the other programs work in the background.

As we shall see in the section on Excel, this means that if we have information in Excel which we wish to paste in to Word a single click transfers the focus from one program to the other, simplifying the task.

The screen below illustrates the Taskbar with Word and Excel running, both minimized so that the Desktop is visible.

To minimize all windows, right-click on an empty space in the Taskbar and select **Minimize All Windows** from the pop-up menu.

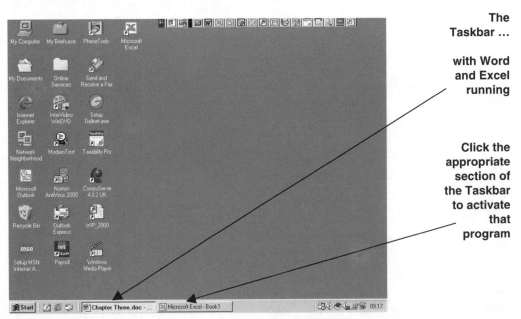

The Taskbar ...

with Word and Excel running

Click the appropriate section of the Taskbar to activate that program

Click on **Word** in the Taskbar. The background of the Word box goes white to show it is active, and the screen changes to:

Click here to activate Word...

Word Box shaded white to show it is active

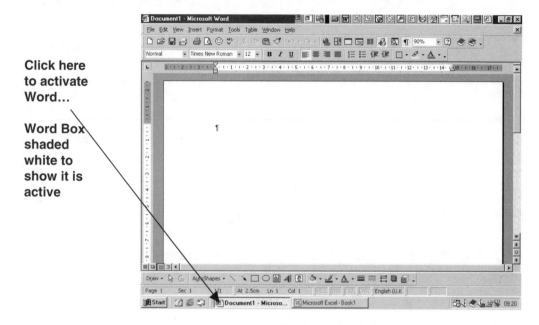

Click on **Excel** . .

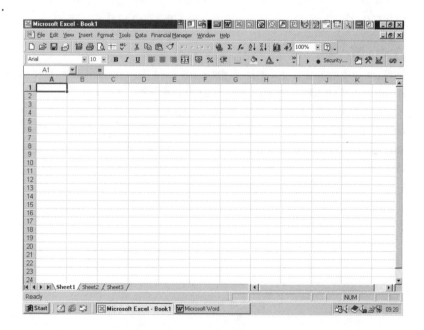

Finally, place the cursor in the Taskbar, and click the right mouse. Then select **Minimize All Windows**.

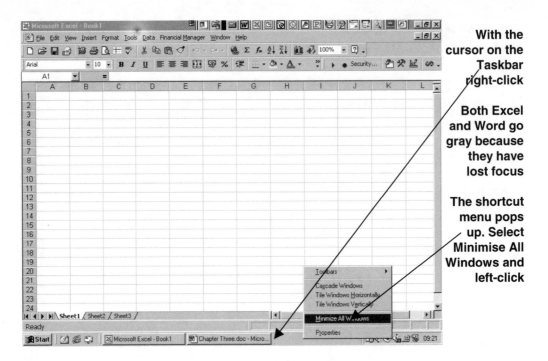

With the cursor on the Taskbar right-click

Both Excel and Word go gray because they have lost focus

The shortcut menu pops up. Select Minimise All Windows and left-click

Neither Excel nor Word is in focus any longer. Both are running in the background. Both become gray, and the Desktop is displayed.

AND NOW . . .

We have gained a good insight into how to control the Desktop, and how to manipulate Windows to suit the way we work.

In **Chapter Four**, we look at the Control Panel, Printer and Clipboard, so that we can take charge of the transfer of information between packages, its output on to paper, and also how we can put Windows in charge, with ourselves at the helm.

Chapter Four

MAINTENANCE, BACKUP AND CLIPBOARD

Maintenance doesn't just apply to marriages . . .

The next task we must understand if we are to gain the full benefits of computerization is how to transfer information between packages and how to ensure that information on the hard disk is not irretrievably lost.

HARDWARE CONTROLLED BY THE OPERATING SYSTEM

In **Chapter One**, we saw how the hardware is controlled by Windows, and how Windows accepts input from the keyboard and mouse in order to control actions.

Amongst other things, we added a new printer, changed the default printer and explained how the printing process works, and we explored the filing system.

Now we want to round this information out on the basis of what we have covered in **Chapters Two** and **Three**, and to blend this with an overview of day-to-day hard disk preventative care.

We will also look at the Clipboard, and consider the transfer (or blending) of information between packages.

MAINTENANCE AND SYSTEM TOOLS

As its name implies, System Tools is the nerve center provided by Windows to safeguard your system from data loss and corruption.

If you are unfortunate enough to experience data errors in specific files, then you will need to restore a backup copy. If you do not have a backup copy, you may need to restart the file from scratch. Therefore, taking backups is a good habit to acquire. Backups are covered later in the chapter so, if you need to back up files now, before starting to maintain the hard drive, move to the next section before continuing here.

Assuming everything is ready, we will start System Tools. To access the tools, click on **Start**, then highlight **Programs. Accessories. System Tools**.

The screen looks like this:

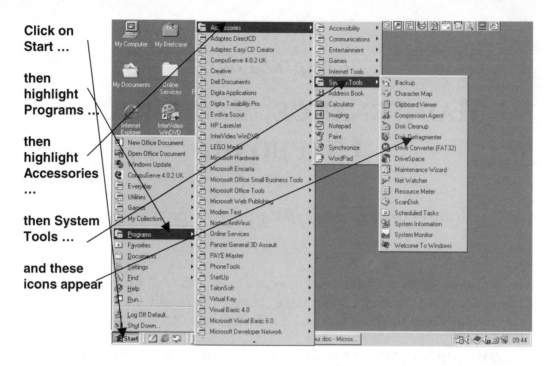

Click on
Start ...

then
highlight
Programs ...

then
highlight
Accessories
...

then System
Tools ...

and these
icons appear

There are a large number of tools available. The ones we are interested in are:

- Disk Defragmenter
- DriveSpace
- ScanDisk.

WHAT DO THE SYSTEM TOOLS DO, AND WHY ARE THEY NEEDED?

We will look at them in the order above.

Disk Defragmenter

We previously discussed the file address, tree structure, directories and folders. This is a logical format rather than a physical format, and Defragmenter is used to bring the two closer together.

Physically, the hard drive is divided into a continuous series of blocks (sectors), and each sector can have data written to it. A section is allocated to record a map of the disk (the File Allocation Table or FAT sector) and, if information is included in two (or more) sectors, the FAT sector records the link of information.

When information is saved to disk, it either overwrites the information that was there (if it is an update) or it is written to the next available block (if it is new). This means that, although two pieces of information are related, they can be physically separated if other disk activity occurred between the times that they were saved.

This does not make any difference to the user, because the computer has the disk references to access this information. However, the slowest part of the hardware is the disk and, if the read head has to move over the disk surface more often than necessary, the computer will slow down.

In order to minimize read head movement and maximize performance, defragmentation physically moves files so that related files are recorded on the same area of disk, and updates the FAT sector (map) accordingly.

As part of this process, and before any files are moved, the computer checks the current FAT map to ensure that all references to files are correct. Any errors are recorded as Lost Clusters, and they can be saved elsewhere for viewing later or deleted immediately using ScanDisk.

Defragmenting is explained in the diagram below.

Files are written to disk as normal work progresses. The order is the same as the order in which the work is completed.

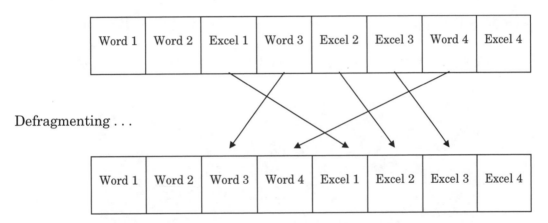

Defragmenting . . .

. . . reorganizes the files to bring them together in related blocks.

Exercises — Defragmenter

We are now going to defragment the hard disk. Take a backup of important files first, if necessary.

Click on **Start**, then highlight **Programs**, **Accessories**, **System Tools** and **Disk Defragmenter**. The screenshot on page 70 shows the path.

You are presented with the following screen.

Normally the drop down box gives a choice of A: or C: drives. If more drives are present these will be shown.

Select Settings to view the options available. The following screen appears.

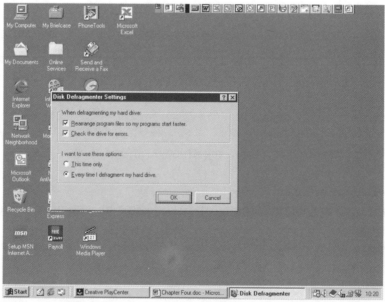

The options are self-explanatory and, unless you are pressed for time, the **Rearrange program files so my programs start faster** and **Check the drive for errors** options should be your preferred choices.

Click OK to close the screen. In the main screen select C: drive, and click OK. Defragmenter starts to run.

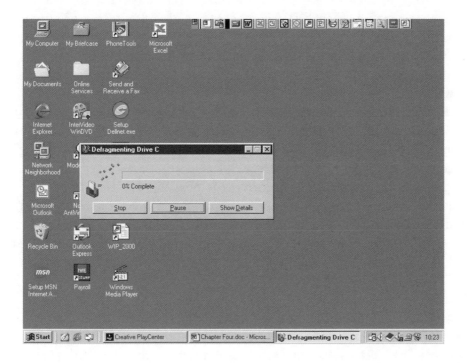

Warning

As explained earlier, the defragmentation process involves moving files and changing pointers to files. It is therefore strongly recommended that no other programs are running when Disk Defragmenter is active. If another program attempts to write to disk during the process, at best it will cause Defrag to quit; at worst, it could cause errors in the files themselves, or their addressing.

DriveSpace

This is a disk compression utility, which creates additional disk space by compressing files and reducing their size. This is compression of live files, compared with zipping older files that you want to have available but are (probably) not going to use.

In broad terms, the capacity of hard drives is now so large that the compression utilities are not required on modern computers. If you do need it, you are strongly advised to install a larger hard drive (or fit a second hard drive) instead.

Separate utility programs to zip files are sold separately. **WinZip** is a very popular utility program, and it would probably be worthwhile obtaining a copy.

ScanDisk

This utility scans the hard drive for any physical defects in the disk and for files that exist but which are not referenced, and updates the FAT sector (map) with the location of any defective sectors. Once a sector is designated as being bad, the computer will no longer attempt to write information to it.

Disk Defragmenter will flash a warning that a disk appears to have errors, and recommend running ScanDisk if there are problems, but it is good housekeeping to run ScanDisk periodically in any event.

To start ScanDisk, click on **Start**, then highlight **Programs**, **Accessories**, **System Tools** and **ScanDisk**. You are presented with the following screen.

**Select the
drive to scan
...**

**the type of
test ...**

**and ensure
Automatically
Fix Errors is
active**

**Then select
Start**

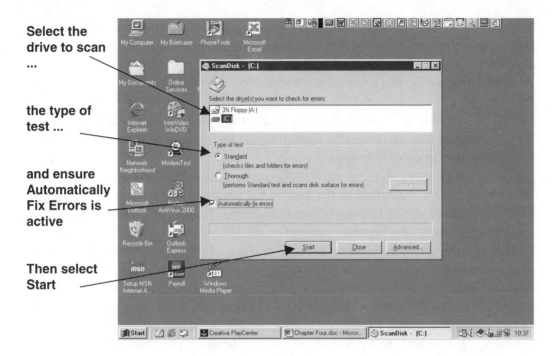

For most purposes, a standard test is enough, although a thorough test should be undertaken occasionally. Ensure Automatically Fix Errors is checked.

THIRD PARTY UTILITY SOFTWARE

Of the Windows tools mentioned above, therefore, you are probably only going to use Disk Defragmenter and ScanDisk. Do you need any others?

If you have any serious problems, a third party utility package is more likely to resolve and (hopefully) cure the problems. One of the most popular of these is **Norton Utilities**. The documentation provided with these third party programs is outside the scope of this book, and reference should be made to the documentation provided with the software.

BACKUP

Backing up data can be achieved in several ways, so first let us define a backup copy of a file:

> A backup copy of a file provides a copy of the information on a file as it existed at the time the backup was completed. It is a snapshot of a moment in time, and will not reflect changes to the file made after the time of the backup.

Why do we need a definition of what a backup is? So that we have a clear understanding of what we are (and are not) achieving by following backup procedures, and of how often to take backup copies of specific files.

Now, let us define the reason for undertaking a backup:

> The purpose of a backup is to allow the restoration of files so that corrupted files are removed from the system, and we always have up-to-date, uncorrupted information on our system.

Why do we need a definition of the reason for undertaking a backup? So that we know where to store the backed up copy of the file. It must be stored in a medium other than the one that becomes corrupted.

Merging these two definitions gives us a clear basis of assessment of whether, in our circumstances, we are achieving the safeguards our backup procedures are in place for. The questions we want to address are:

- Where is the file stored that we wish to backup? In RAM, on a hard drive, on a floppy disk or on a CD-ROM?
- What eventuality are we seeking to protect against? Hardware damage, power loss, system lock up?
- Is the file subject to change? A data file or spreadsheet will change, program files will not.
- How long are we going to keep the backed up file?
- How much work would we lose if a file is corrupted? How frequently should we backup?

Think of the processing of the file you are working on like this:

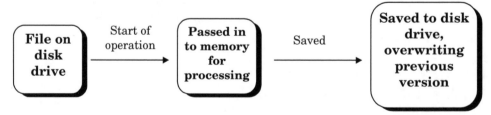

The table below includes the types of hardware, and the failures that can arise:

Stage	Media	Potential Failure
File on disk drive	Hard or floppy disk	Disk fault so that contents cannot be read
↓		
Start of operation		
↓		
Passed into memory for processing	Random Access Memory (RAM)	Power failure — RAM only holds information while power is on
↓		
Saved		
↓		
Saved to disk drive, overwriting previous version	Hard or floppy disk	Power failure, during write operation, corrupting the file

Now, if we merge the table above with the definitions we set out earlier, we can answer the questions we posed.

Question	Media type			
Where is the file stored that we wish to back up?	RAM (working memory)	Floppy disk	Hard drive C:	CD-ROM
What is the potential problem?	Power failure. System lock-up	Disk failure or corruption		None — this is a read-only device, not a write device
Save to . . .	Hard drive	Hard drive or second floppy	Floppy, Tape, (special) CD-ROM	Not applicable
Every . . .	Ten (?) minutes, using AutoSave function of Spreadsheet	Day (?) Week (?) Month (?)		Not applicable

You will note from the table that the threat is different for different media. Note that, to cover against this threat, the backup must be made to a medium different from the one under threat. There is little point saving a second copy of a file on to the same floppy disk, and then dropping or damaging the disk — all your eggs are in one basket.

The important considerations when backing up are:

- To back up all files, including the application programs, takes time. The minimum backup is data files only. However, if the hard disk does crash, you must then reload the application software from the original disks (or CD).
- How many copies? When backing up, computer specialists use the Grandfather, Father, Son approach — they always have three generations of copies available, in case one of them becomes corrupted itself, or in case the restoration process damages the file. Is this necessary for your files? Only you can answer.
- When did the file last change. Backups can be differential or incremental (saving only files changed from the last backup date), or full. Which do you need?
- How long are we going to keep the backed-up file? Can you reuse floppies, tapes etc.?

If you buy a tape backup unit, the instruction booklets provided will fully discuss the mechanics of tape backup.

SECURITY

Ranking equally in importance with backup procedures is security. To copy all of your confidential files on to a backup medium, and then to have the backup stolen, is providing the potential for disaster.

There are simple measures you can take to protect yourself, and you are recommended to buy a good book on Backup and Security Procedures to fully explore this area.

CLIPBOARD

Information transfer between packages is taken over by Windows, and involves providing a buffer zone, called Clipboard, to retain the information. The Clipboard is available to all programs and information transfer is consistent between packages.

There is also a local Clipboard, called Clipbook.

Transfer of information is illustrated below, and is explored in **Section Four**. This illustration is to demonstrate the process only, so you do not need to repeat it yourself at this stage.

Excel and Word are started and some information is typed in Excel. It is then highlighted and copied to Word, via the Clipboard.

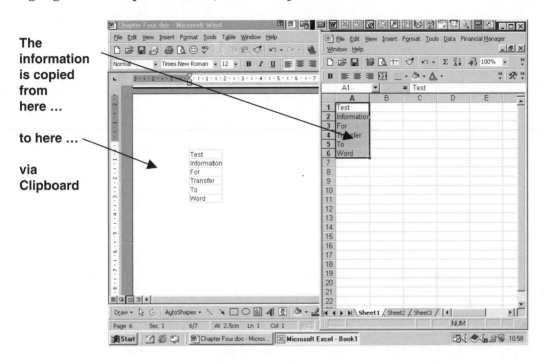

The information is copied from here ...

to here ...

via Clipboard

The Clipboard contents are overwritten each time it is used. To maintain the contents requires a Clipbook to be established.

That concludes the review of the need to maintain the system and backup the files, as well as the introduction of the concept of transfer of information.

... AND FINALLY

Chapter Five deals with the final area of Windows that we want to look at — Common Dialog Boxes. These appear throughout the various application programs, so to cover them here will explain everything once.

Chapter Five

COMMON DIALOG BOXES

That looks familiar!

Windows programs benefit from being able to call on Windows to deal with opening or saving files, printing and other tasks. This means that there is a common look and feel between different Windows packages (a Common User Interface or CUI), enhancing the learning process.

For the exercises below, we will use Excel.

SAVING A FILE

Start **Excel**.

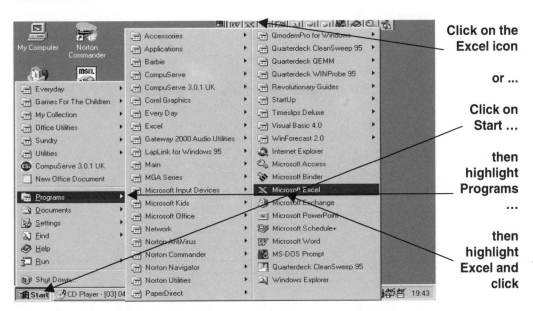

Excel starts, and the file is called **Book 1**.

The menu structure is explained in **Section Two** — here, we are only interested in the aspects that interact with Windows for File Save.

Click on **File** in the drop-down menu, then **Save As**.

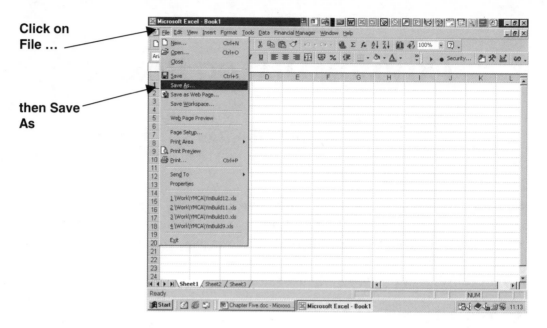

The Windows Dialog box appears.

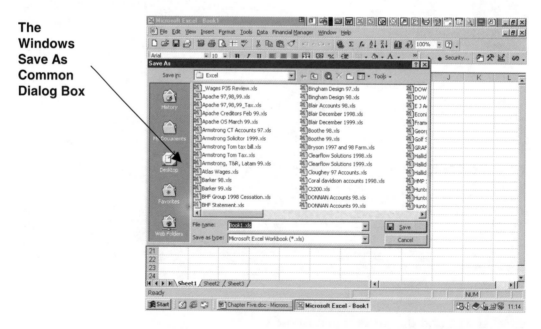

Before we look at how to use the Save utility, let's see the Save As screen from Word (**File, Save As** — the same procedure as for Excel).

The
Windows
save As
Common
Dialog Box
in Word. It
is exactly
the same
as the
Excel
screen,
except for
the default
file format

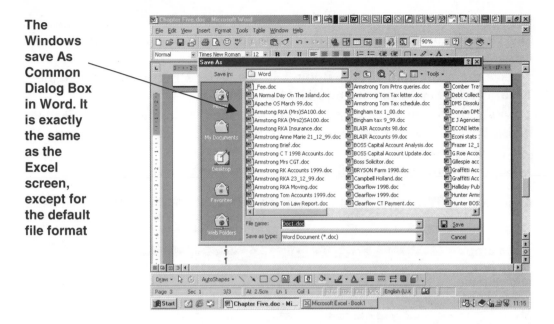

Take another look at the Save As box on your screen. The areas of interest are highlighted below:

Folder
(Directory)
location

Folder
contents
(Sub-folders
and files if
any)

File name to
save as

File
extension to
save as (xls
as default)

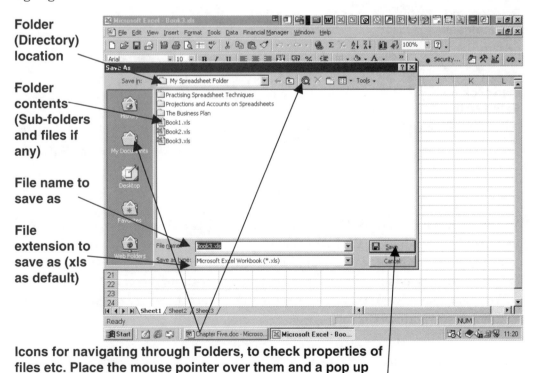

Icons for navigating through Folders, to check properties of
files etc. Place the mouse pointer over them and a pop up
heading appears

Buttons to complete the operation

In **Chapter Two**, we created a folder called My Spreadsheet Folder and, within this, three further folders — Practicing Spreadsheet Techniques, Projections and Accounts on Spreadsheets and The Business Plan.

Save the blank spreadsheet **Book 1** in the folder **Practicing Spreadsheet Techniques**, and rename it **The First Spreadsheet**.

Locate the folder in which we want to save the file. In the Save As Common Dialog Box, click on the box described as **Save In**, and a drop-down list of My Computer appears.

Click on C: drive to see the full contents of the hard drive.

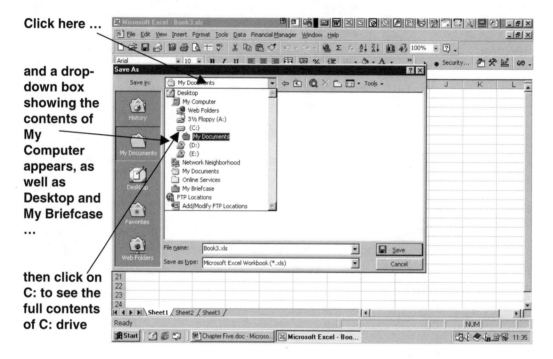

We explored the content of My Computer in **Chapter One**, and looked at directories, folders and files in **Chapter Two**.

The screenshot below looks exactly like the left pane in Explorer, except the folders are displayed left to right instead of top to bottom.

We clicked on C: and, therefore, we are in the root directory of the hard drive. We want to navigate to the folder we are interested in.

**Clicking on
C: places it
in the
Save As
Window ...**

**and
displays
the
contents of
the root
directory**

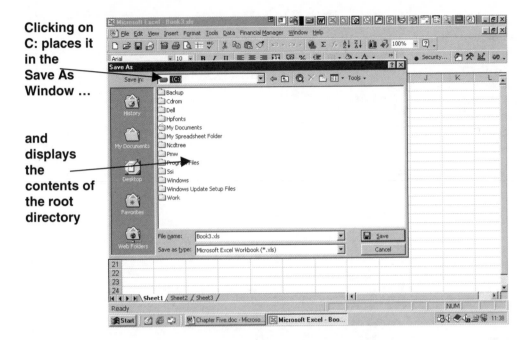

This display is similar to that shown in Explorer's left pane below:

**The root
directory ..**

**and its
contents**

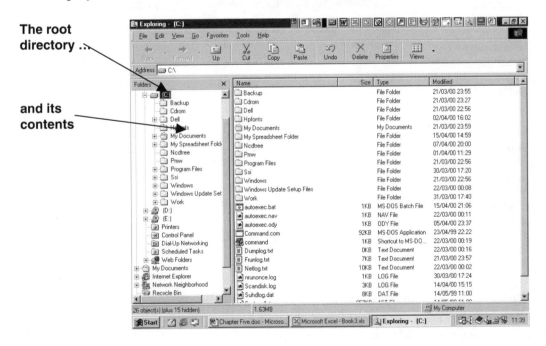

We want to see the contents of My Spreadsheet Folder, so locate it in the pane
and double-click on it. This moves us down the tree diagram we looked at in
Chapter Two, and displays the contents of the folder.

**Click on
the Folder
to highlight
it, and then
double-
click it to
place it in
the Save
As section**

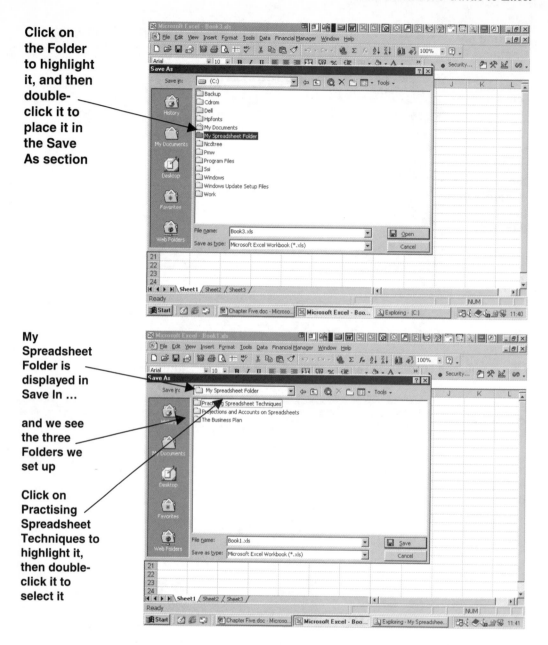

**My
Spreadsheet
Folder is
displayed in
Save In ...**

**and we see
the three
Folders we
set up**

**Click on
Practising
Spreadsheet
Techniques to
highlight it,
then double-
click it to
select it**

We want to save the file in the folder Practicing Spreadsheet Techniques, so click on it, then double-click to change to it and to place it in the Save In section.

We are now ready to save the file, with our chosen name.

**We are now
in the
correct
Folder**

**The default
name is
displayed ...**

**and it will
save as an
Excel
spreadsheet**

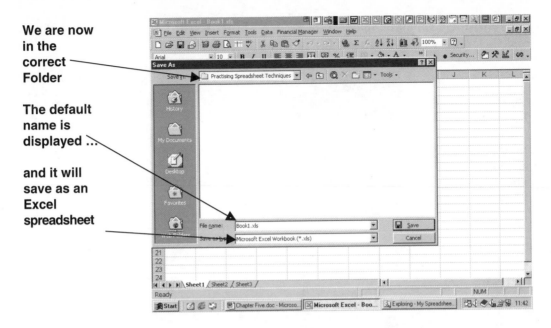

Click in the **File Name Box** and double-click on the name **Book 1.xls**. This selects it. If you start typing, the name is replaced with the new typing. You do not
have to delete it, and you do not have to type the extension ".xls" — this is added
automatically. Click on **Save** to finish the operation.

**Type in the
name ...**

**and click
Save**

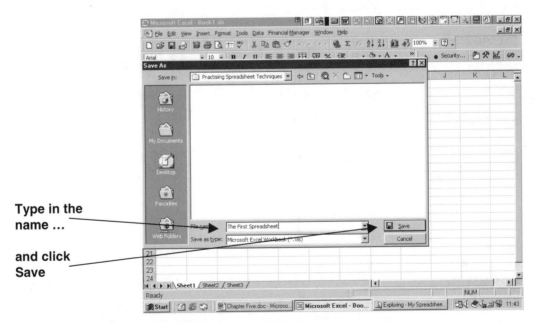

The screen closes, and the file has been saved.

We will use Explorer to check it is there. Start **Explorer** (see **Chapter Two**) and click on **My Spreadsheet Folder** in the left pane.

Start Explorer, then click on My Spread-sheet Folder ...

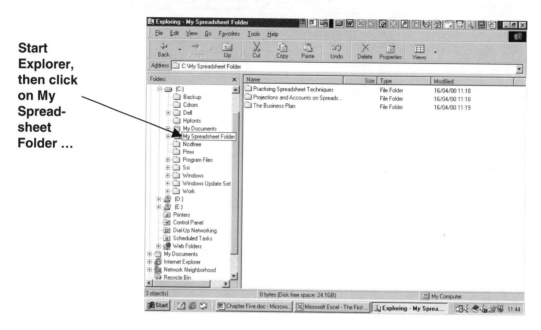

Double-click to display the sub-folders and then click on the one we want. The spreadsheet we saved is displayed.

Double-click to display the sub-folders in the left pane, and highlight Practising Spreadsheet Techniques ...

and the spreadsheet we saved is displayed

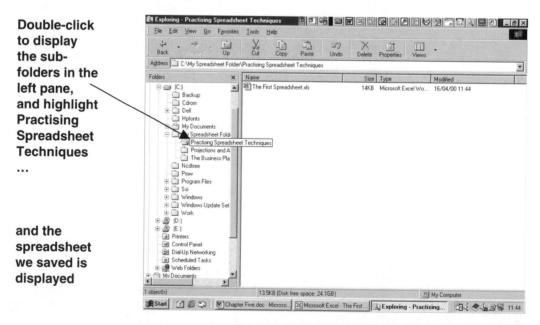

One BIG difference between Explorer and Save As is that Explorer will display all files (Word, Excel, Lotus 123 etc.) but S̲a̲v̲e̲ A̲s̲ will only display the files of the type selected — it filters out all of the "non-relevant" file types.

    This also applies to Open, which we will review now.

    Start **Excel** and click on **File**, then **Open**.

**Click on
File ...**

**then
Open**

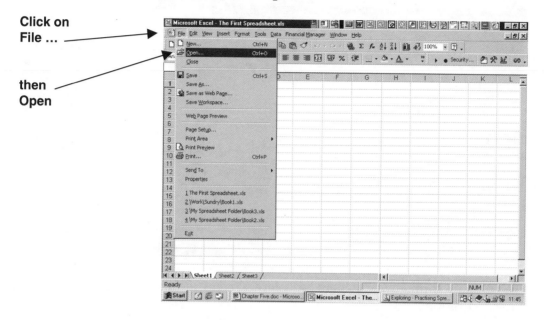

The following dialog box appears:

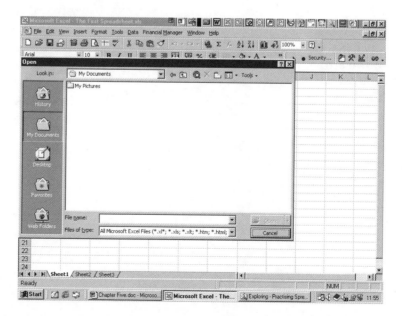

This is virtually the same as the Save As dialog box, but with a few important differences. These are highlighted below:

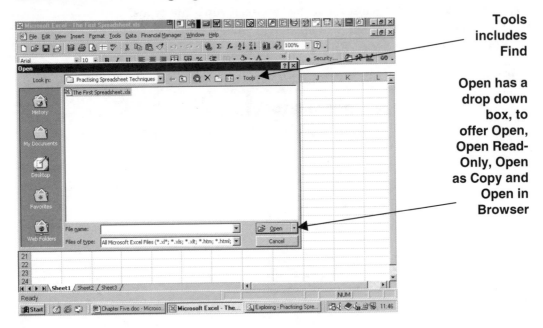

Tools includes Find

Open has a drop down box, to offer Open, Open Read-Only, Open as Copy and Open in Browser

We navigate through the folders as before. Open the file we saved earlier, **The First Spreadsheet**.

Change to the folder **My Spreadsheet Folder**, then to **Practicing Spreadsheet Techniques**. The file will be displayed in the list of files.

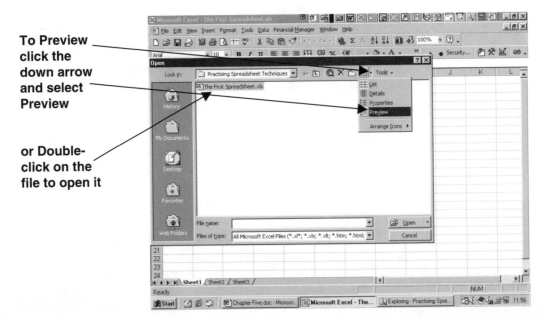

To Preview click the down arrow and select Preview

or Double-click on the file to open it

When you click on **Preview**, it gives a small snapshot of the spreadsheet, so that you can confirm it is the correct one to open.

If the viewers have not been included as part of the Windows installation, you will have to install them before you get a preview of the spreadsheet.

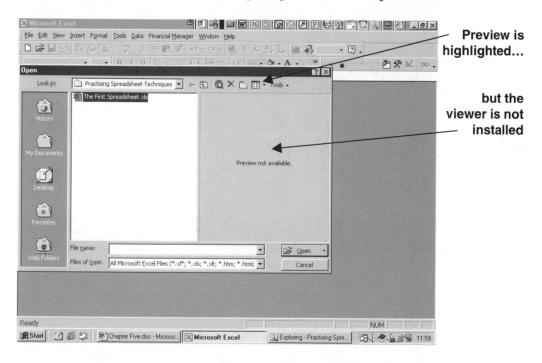

Double-click the spreadsheet name, or click on **Open**, to open the spreadsheet.

We now want to review the final Common Dialog Box we are interested in — Printing.

With the spreadsheet active, click in cell A1 and type "Test", then click on cell A2, so that the entry in cell A1 is processed.

Click in cell A1 again, then click on **File** in the menu, then highlight **Print Area**, then highlight **Set Print Area** and click the mouse.

This tells the program that we want to print the contents of cell A1.

Now click on **File**, highlight **Print** and click. The Windows Common Dialog Box appears, the contents of which are reviewed below. We will return to printing in Excel in **Section Two** but here we are interested in the Printer screen.

Click on File
...

then
highlight
Print Area ...

then
highlight Set
Print Area
and click

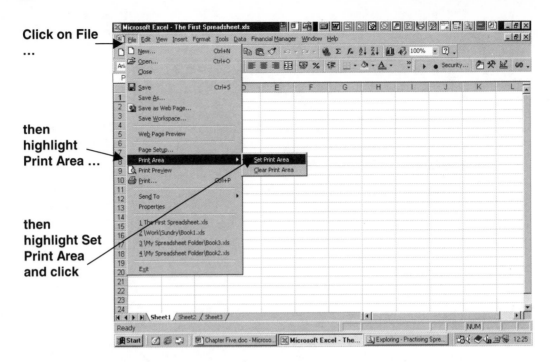

Because only one cell was chosen the following warning message appears. Click
OK

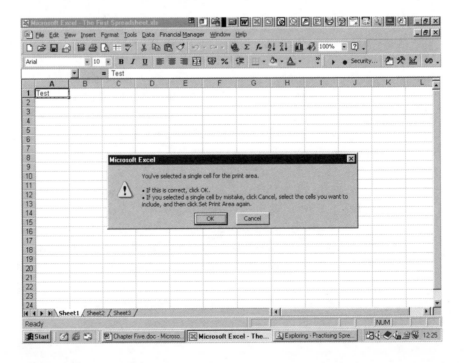

The following Windows Common Dialog Box appears. It is the same style (but slightly modified) in Word, Excel and other programs

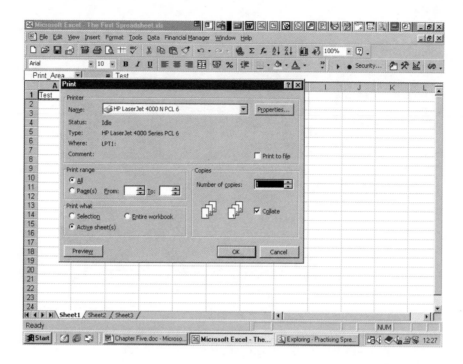

The areas of interest are:

* We can change the printer from this Window, and do not have to go into Printers in My Computer
* We can change the number of copies printed
* We can collate the printouts
* We can change printer properties (portrait, landscape etc.)
* We can preview the printout.

These are highlighted on the screen.

**Change printer
properties
(portrait,
landscape
printing, etc.)**

**Click in the box
to select printer**

**Set the number of
copies, and
collate if desired**

**Specify print
ranges**

**Preview the
printout**

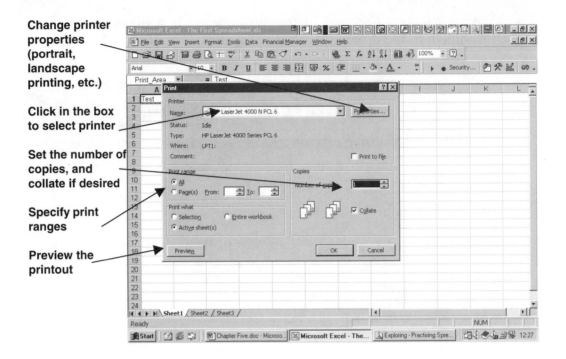

Understanding printing, and choosing between the alternatives available, will be
important when we produce the business plan later in the book.

SECTION SUMMARY

You now have the skills to operate Windows with confidence, and to understand
the storage and retrieval of information from your system.

You are now ready to learn the functionality of Excel, and to put in context
some of the things you have learnt here. Now the hard work begins . . .

Section Two
EXCEL FUNCTIONALITY

SECTION INDEX

SECTION OVERVIEW

In this section, we will examine how to use the menus, toolbars and the working area of the spreadsheet. This covers the mechanics of how to use the program — which buttons to click and how they work.

In this section, we will look at:

- The menu structure
- The toolbar structure
- The screen layout
- Use of the keyboard and mouse to input data.

Sections Three and **Four** build on this information to create a framework for designing spreadsheets to ensure structured, accurate and easily maintained solutions.

Chapter Six

EXCEL OVERVIEW

Good grief! It can do that?

The problem with a program as large as Excel is knowing what it is capable of.

In accounting there is a golden rule: Eighty:Twenty — 80% of inventory value is in 20% of the lines; 80% of the value of accounts receivable is in 20% of the customers, etc. In computer programs, this is more like a Ninety Seven:Three rule — 97% of the time, only 3% of the functionality is used. Identifying the 3% can be difficult, and there are huge productivity differences between using 1%, 2% and 3% of a program's capabilities.

This chapter will provide an overview, from an accountant's perspective, of what Excel can do, and then we will fill in the detail in the rest of the section. Once the technical background has been understood, parameters for spreadsheet design are introduced in **Section Three**.

THE MICROSOFT VISION

The starting point is to consider what Microsoft believed they would achieve by designing their software, and their concept of the way we work. To understand this is to view the software from their perspective and either adapt ourselves to suit their philosophy, or amend their philosophy to suit our own.

Windows is a clear vision of using computer applications and sharing information. The Office suite of programs is built on this vision — and provides users with access to different capabilities in their daily lives: spreadsheets, databases, word processing and e-mail.

In the Microsoft vision, individuals will prepare their own documentation first-hand on the computer, instead of hand-writing it, passing it to secretarial staff, proof-reading it, correcting it, passing it back to the secretary. This means that not only must programs contain a great deal of functionality but also that functionality must be easily accessible.

As we work through the following chapters, we will see to what extent this vision has been achieved.

DEFINE THE CAPABILITIES

The first problem we encounter is defining the boundaries between one package and another, and identifying the best package to use for the task in hand. For example, Excel has spell-checking and text-formatting capabilities, Word has mathematical capability, Access has both.

We will therefore have to prune the scope somewhat, and the best way to do this is to define what we wish to achieve, then map it back through program features. We will do this in **Section Three**, but first we will build our knowledge from the ground up. It will not fully cement until you have also covered **Section Three**, because that section draws all the strands together.

WHO IS EXCEL FOR?

The audience is vast:

* Accountants
* Realtors
* Business managers . . . who form the first tier of users

* Engineers
* Statisticians
* Mathematicians . . . the second, more technical, tier

* Computer programmers . . . the third, and most technically competent, tier.

To cater for an audience this wide requires a huge program with capabilities well beyond our needs as accountant.

EXCEL — THE FIRST OVERVIEW

We will reverse the order of the tiers of users and consider the program's capabilities in relation to each.

Computer Programmers

The Microsoft vision is to provide a computer programming language consistent across the Microsoft programs: Windows, Excel, Access . . . The language is Visual Basic (VB), with Visual Basic Applications edition being used in Excel.

There is no reason why you should not use this programming language yourself to manipulate your data, output and presentation, although to use it properly will require that you study and practice further.

Using VB, computer programmers can program Excel and change its appearance to suit their needs. They can also call upon the program's capabilities in code from another program, and thereby gain access to the powerful functions within Excel without needing to rewrite a spreadsheet program, and without requiring the user to start Excel and provide input.

The Second Tier — Engineers, Statisticians, Mathematicians, etc.

This group of users needs to use the mathematical capabilities of the spreadsheet to calculate complex results. There are a substantial number of pre-defined functions within Excel to cater for their needs.

They would tend to use the program directly (compared to the more indirect use, via VB, that computer programmers make of the functionality), but still at a very technical level.

The First Tier — including Accountants

Although there are functions provided specifically for accountants in Excel, it is more likely that accountants will use the package in conjunction with Word or other packages than as a stand-alone program. Accountants use computer programs primarily for report writing for clients, managers, directors, etc. Spreadsheets are used as one constituent part of a much greater whole.

Whilst there is a large technical content in the spreadsheet from an accounting point of view, there isn't from a program functionality point of view.

CHAPTER SEVEN

With this in mind, we will now look at the Excel program and see how to use its capabilities.

Chapter Seven

THE EXCEL SCREEN

Looking good . . .

We want to look at the Excel screen, identify its components, and become familiar
with the feel of the program.

Start the program. The screen will be similar to, but not the same as, this:

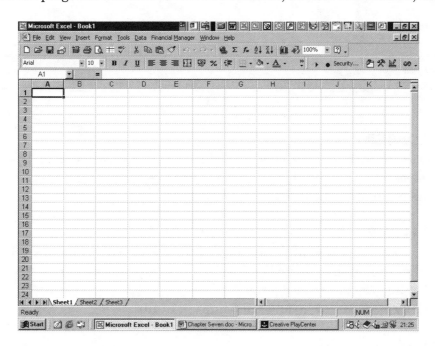

The screen is divided into several distinct regions:

- Spreadsheet name
- Menu items
- Toolbar
- Cell contents viewer
- Spreadsheet working area
- Sheet details
- Status indicator bar.

These are labeled on the screen below:

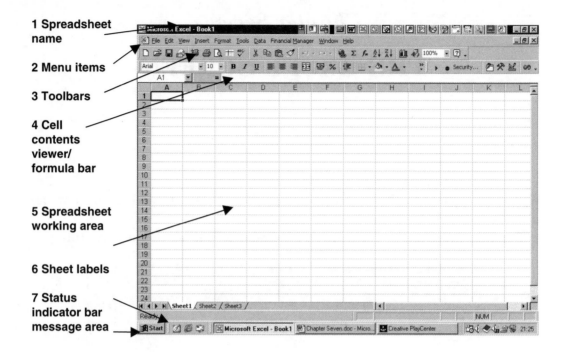

1 Spreadsheet name

2 Menu items

3 Toolbars

4 Cell contents viewer/ formula bar

5 Spreadsheet working area

6 Sheet labels

7 Status indicator bar message area

SPREADSHEET NAME

This can be 256 characters long, including spaces. A meaningful heading is therefore possible, to facilitate easy location when you come to re-open it.

The default name is Book 1.

MENU ITEMS

This is the place to access all operations within Excel. The menu is activated by clicking the left mouse button when the cursor is on the menu bar, or by pressing the Alt key and the underlined letter.

The menu is discussed in detail in **Chapter Eight**.

TOOLBAR

This is equivalent to a macro-shortcut area, with the macros being activated by clicking on them. They provide the same functionality as the menu items, although one icon will fulfil an operation that may require several keystroke or mouse inputs through the menu.

The toolbar can only be accessed by using the mouse.

Toolbars are discussed in detail in **Chapter Nine**.

CELL CONTENTS VIEWER/FORMULA BAR

This displays the contents of the cell as input, as distinct from the cell view, which will display the result.

The cell contents viewer shows the formula, cell references, names etc. used to calculate that cell's result.

SPREADSHEET WORKING AREA

This is, at the end of the day, what it is all about. All of the input is displayed in this area; all of the output, with appropriate formatting, is displayed here; and this is the part of the screen that needs our attention. Everything else is convenient, efficient, helpful or informative. This area is critical.

We will cover the spreadsheet working area throughout the rest of the book, because all other areas impact on it.

SHEET LABELS

There used to be an upper limit of 255 sheets per book, but now the only limitation to the number of sheets that can exist per workbook is the capability of the PC you are using. Sheets are labeled Sheet 1 forward, and each sheet contains approximately 17 million cells. Such a large capacity means that the user has to be very structured in their approach to designing spreadsheets – see **Section Three**.

STATUS INDICATOR BAR/MESSAGE AREA

This provides information to the user on the state of the spreadsheet at any one time, helpful messages are flashed here, and the keyboard or cell settings (number lock on, extension on etc.) are indicated.

These are covered as an integral part of the chapters in this section.

AND NOW THE DETAIL . . .

That draws together the overview of the screen layout. In the next chapter, we look at the menus in detail.

Chapter Eight

THE EXCEL MENUS

I know it's in there somewhere . . .

We now have a general idea of how the screen is organized, and the important areas of the screen.

We want to look at how the menus are organized, to understand the capabilities of the program and how we can control the final product — reports generated for other users.

Start Excel. The screen will look similar to this:

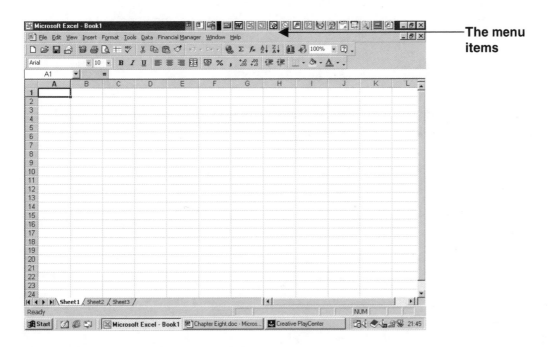

You will see from the screen that the menu choices are: Excel Logo; <u>F</u>ile; <u>E</u>dit; <u>V</u>iew; <u>I</u>nsert; F<u>o</u>rmat; <u>T</u>ools; <u>D</u>ata; <u>W</u>indow; <u>H</u>elp.

In each name, one letter is underlined. Pressing the **Alt** key followed by the underlined letter displays the appropriate drop-down menu.

We will look at each menu item in turn, but first we will take an overview of the menus.

The menus are listed below, with a brief explanation of each:

- Large Excel Icon   Control of the program, and how it displays on screen.
- Small Excel Icon   Control of the individual book within the Excel program, and how it displays on screen.
- File   Interaction between files and the Operating System, by using Common Dialog Boxes as appropriate.
- Edit   Word-processing type facilities for using the Windows or Office Clipboards.
- View   Options in presenting the final product on screen and on paper.
- Insert   Insertion of items into the spreadsheet, ranging from date and time to page breaks and objects.
- Format   Apply formatting to cells, columns, tables etc.
- Tools   This is a catchall heading for anything that does not fit neatly elsewhere.
- Data   This is for database functions and capabilities.
- Window   This is for control of screen presentation of each Window view.
- Help   Access on-line Help files.

Now that we have taken an overview of the menu items, we will start Excel and look at the individual menu options in detail.

EXCEL LOGO — PROGRAM CONTROL

Click on the Excel logo at the top of the screen ...

and a drop-down menu appears

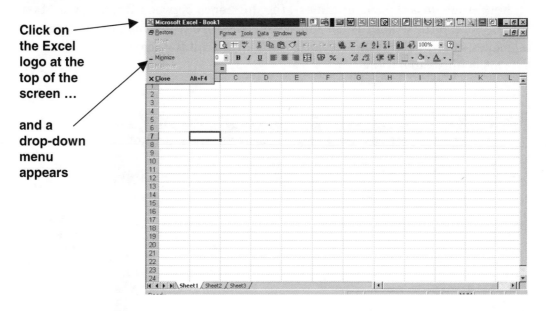

What are the options?

Restore, Move, Size, Minimize, Maximize, Close.

All of these relate to how the full Excel program appears on your screen. Notice that some of the items are grayed, to show that the menu option is not available at the present time.

Click on **Minimize**. We are back to the familiar Desktop screen reviewed in **Section One**.

Clicking on the **Excel** item in the Taskbar restores the screen.

Maximize does the same thing — the difference between Restore and Maximize is that, if the default is not full screen, **Restore** will reinstate the screen at a smaller screen size, while **Maximize** will always fill the screen.

This is illustrated below:

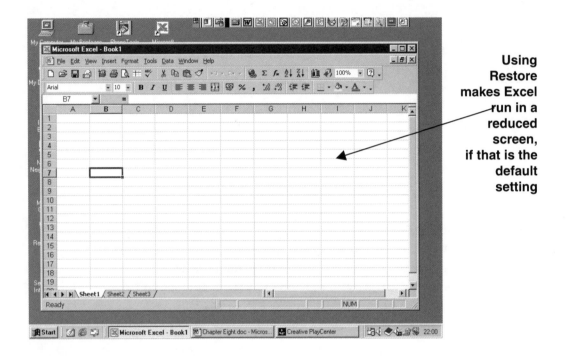

Using **Restore** makes Excel run in a reduced screen, if that is the default setting

Move is for changing the position of the screen (if it does not fill the screen), and **Size** is for changing the default size of the screen when it is **Restored**.

You will rarely run Excel at less than full screen. Too little information is displayed on screen, and mistakes can result.

Click on the **Excel** logo to activate it again, and click on **Maximize** to return it to full screen.

EXCEL LOGO — WINDOW CONTROL

There is a second **Excel** logo, below the one we have just reviewed.

Click on the logo and review the drop-down menu. It is exactly the same except for the last item: **Close (Ctrl+W)**, instead of **Close (Alt+F4)**. This is because the second **Excel** logo refers to Window control within Excel, as opposed to program control.

Let us illustrate the difference.

Click on the **Excel** logo, then highlight **Minimize**.

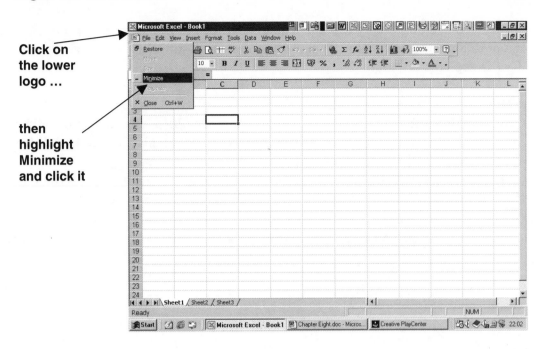

Click on the lower logo ...

then highlight Minimize and click it

The screen changes to:

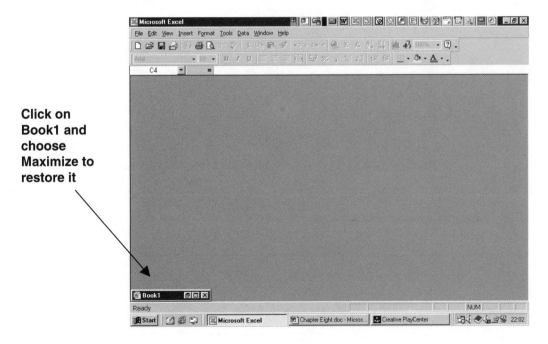

Click on Book1 and choose Maximize to restore it

This is important. To benefit fully from Excel, you must control the Window screen-shots of your spreadsheet, and you must understand the distinction between controlling a spreadsheet window within the program, and controlling the program window within the operating system. Controlling spreadsheet windows is explored later on.

FILE

Click on **File** to display its contents. The system may be preset to display only a reduced list of menu items. If so, either hold the mouse in place until the full list appears, or double-click the File menu heading.

To change the default behavior select **Tools, Customize**, then select the **Options tab** and uncheck **Menus show recently used commands first**.

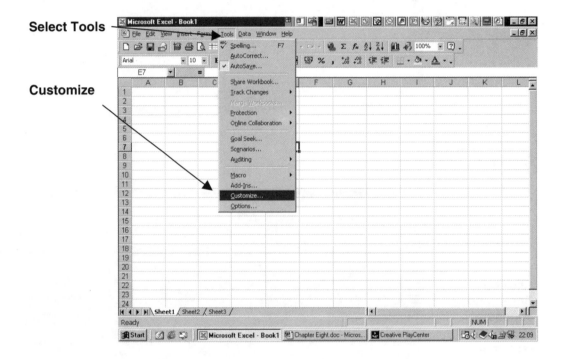

The Customize Dialog Box appears

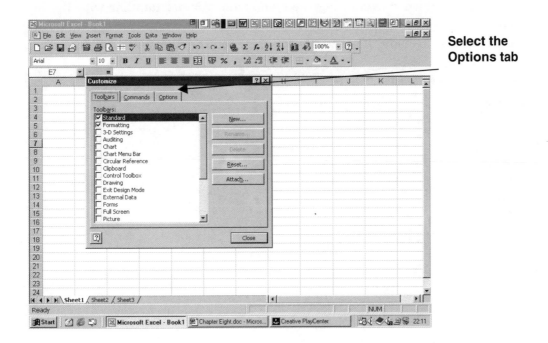

Select the
Options tab

Select the Options tab, and uncheck the **Menus show recently used commands first** item.

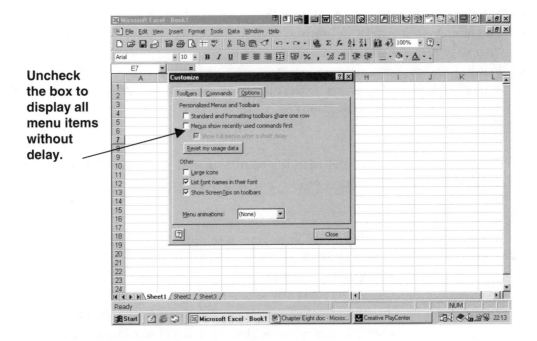

Uncheck
the box to
display all
menu items
without
delay.

When we have finished explaining the menus and you are familiar with the full options you may wish to recheck the box.

Back to the File menu. Its contents are shown in the screenshot below.

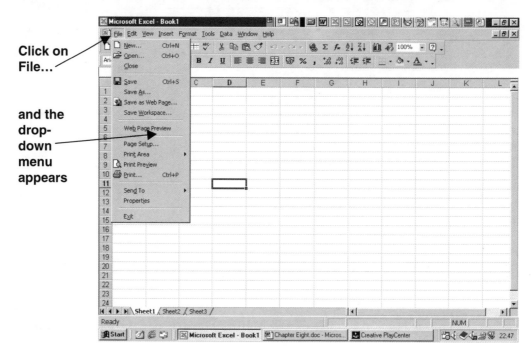

Each major area is separated by a line, the categorizations being:
- File management (first and second sections) — Open, Close, Save etc.
- Web page preview (third section)
- Printing (fourth section)
- Transferring and Properties (fifth section) — Send To and Properties
- Recently Used list (sixth section)
- Exit (seventh section).

All of these relate to interacting with the operating system. Review **Section One** for an explanation of File addresses, Common dialog boxes etc.

The options are:

- New   Creates a new book from a template.
- Open   Opens an existing file. See **Section One** to learn how to navigate the hard drive.
- Close   Closes the currently active book. If it has been saved before, it will overwrite the previous version. If not, a **Save As** Common dialog box will appear. Excel continues to run.

- Save   Saves the file, overwriting the original. If it has not
                  previously been saved, it will enter the **Save As** routine.
                  Once complete, Excel continues to run.
- Save As   Saves the active book by another name. This can either
                  create two copies of a file on the hard drive, save a
                  template as a working file, or save the file in another
                  format (for example, Lotus 1-2-3).
- Save As Web   For Internet publishing.
  Page
- Save   Saves changed documents and creates a workspace file. A
  Workspace   workspace file saves settings, screen arrangements etc.
                  and a group of workbooks can be opened in one step.
- Web Page   Preview the Web page settings established in the above
  Preview   menu item.
- Page Set Up   Changes printing characteristics: Landscape, portrait,
                  reduce etc.
- Print Area   Must be set before printing. Restricts the printing to the
                  part of the spreadsheet we are interested in.
- Print   Shows on screen how the spreadsheet will look when
  Preview   printed.
- Print   Starts the printing process. Calls up the **Windows
                  Common Dialog Box**.
- Send To   Send the spreadsheet to another user on the network. Not
                  relevant to our current needs.
- Properties   Records details about the spreadsheet. You can then
                  locate it by reviewing properties without needing to open
                  the book and review it.
- Spreadsheets   List of last four spreadsheets used. Clicking on one of
                  these achieves the same result as **Open**, but without
                  moving around the hard disk.
- Exit   Closes the program. Achieves the same as the **Excel** logo
                  menu **Close** option.

EDIT
Click on **Edit** and look at the drop-down menu.

**Click on
Edit ...**

**and the
drop-down
menu
appears**

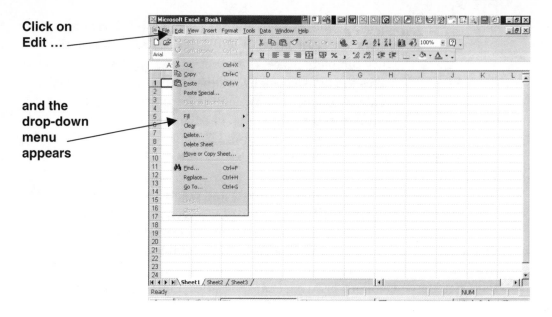

The major categorizations in the menu are:
- Repeating or undoing the last action
- Clipboard controls
- Spreadsheet editing
- Word-processing edits
- Links and inserts editing.

In order to edit something, it must already be present. These controls therefore deal with an already existing condition.

You will notice in the screen-shot shown above that **Links** and **Object** are both inactive (grayed). No links have been established, and no objects have been inserted in the spreadsheet — therefore, they are not applicable and the menu items are disabled. The menu items will be activated when Links are established, or Objects are inserted.

The menu options are:
- Undo   Undoes the last action.
- Repeat   Repeats the last action.
- Cut   Moves the cell contents to the Windows Clipboard, leaving the cell blank. (See **Section One** for Clipboard details.)
- Copy   Copies the cell contents to the Windows Clipboard, leaving the original still in the cell
- Paste   Copies the Clipboard contents to the cell.
- Paste Special   Copies the Clipboard contents to the cell, but with additional options, including Paste Link, Transpose, Values (instead of formulas) etc.

- Paste as   Hyperlink cells.
  Hyperlink
- Fill   Completes entries in a set of cells.
- Clear   Clears cell contents or formatting.
- Delete   Deletes cells or rows/columns.
- Delete   To remove a sheet from the workbook.
  Sheet
- Move or   Either moves a sheet from one book to another (deleting the
  Copy Sheet   original), or copies a sheet to another (or the same) book,
                  leaving the original intact.
- Find   Locates the first entry corresponding to the **Find** search
                  criteria.
- Replace   Replaces cell contents specified with new contents specified.
- Go To   Moves the cell pointer to the appropriate place.
- Links   Allows editing of links established.
- Object   Allows editing of an object previously inserted.

As a general comment, in order to edit a cell, that cell must be highlighted. If this were not the case, uncertain results could be achieved.

VIEW
Click on **View** and look at the drop-down menu.

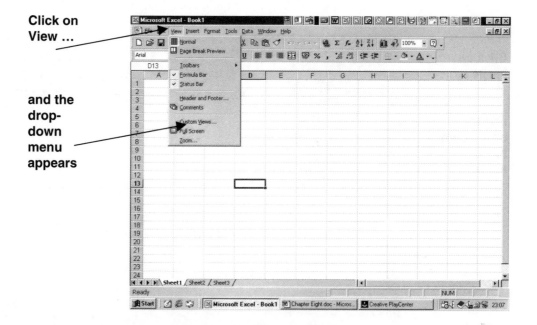

**Click on
View ...**

**and the
drop-
down
menu
appears**

The major categories in the menu are:
- Screenshot type — normal or page break preview
- Toggle screen display of toolbars etc. on/off
- Header and footer and comments
- Magnification and custom views.

The menu options are:

• Normal	The usual display setting.
• Page Break Preview	To show how page breaks affect the printing.
• Toolbars	Sets the toolbars to display. We will customize our toolbar in the next chapter.
• Header and Footer	For printing.
• Comments	Inserting a comment in a cell.
• Custom Views	Set up custom views
• Report Manager	Set up pre-defined reports
• Full Screen	Maximize screenshot
• Zoom	Change magnification settings

INSERT

Click on **Insert** and look at the drop-down menu.

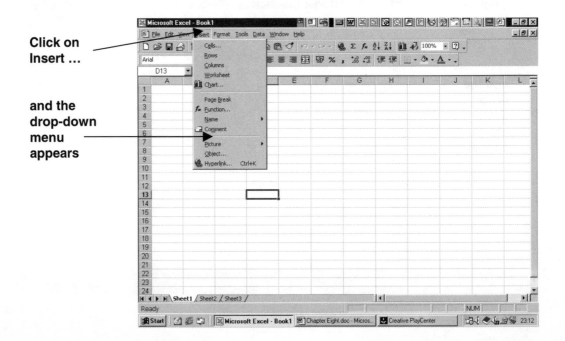

Click on
Insert ...

and the
drop-down
menu
appears

The major categories in the menu are:
- Insert cells, rows and columns in the current sheet
- Insert new sheets and charts
- Insert cell function or annotations
- Insert pictures etc.

The menu options are:
- Cells   Inserts cells, and moves the highlighted cells up, down, left or right as directed.
- Rows   Inserts an entire row. Proceed with caution.
- Columns   Inserts an entire column. Proceed with caution.
- Worksheet   Inserts new sheet into the active book.
- Chart   Inserts chart in the current sheet, or a sheet of its own.
- Page break   Inserts forced page break for printing.
- Function   Starts Function Wizard to build function
- Name   Define, paste apply or create a name (for example, Sales).
- Comment   Cell note, to annotate the spreadsheet.
- Picture   Inserts a picture from a file on the hard disk.
- Object   Inserts an embedded object (it becomes part of the spreadsheet, rather than linked to the spreadsheet).
- Hyperlink   Inserts hyperlink from spreadsheet to another location.

FORMAT
Click on **Format** and look at the drop-down menu.

Click on Format ...

and the drop-down menu appears

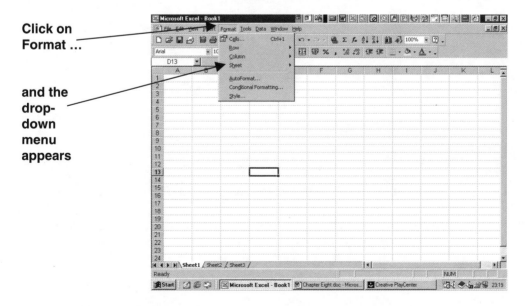

The major categories are:
- Cell, row, column and sheet formatting
- Pre-defined formatting.

The menu options are:

• Cells	Number, Alignment, Font, Border, Patterns and Protection.
• Row	Height, Hide/Unhide. The latter is display rather than format, but it is included in this menu.
• Column	Width, Hide/Unhide.
• Sheet	Hide/Unhide, Rename and Background.
• Autoformat	Pre-defined formats for tables of information.
• Conditional Formatting	Sets format depending on meeting a condition – for example, all items over 10,000 coloured blue.
• Style	Defines the style (Font, etc.) of the sheet.

TOOLS

Click on **Tools** and look at the drop-down menu.

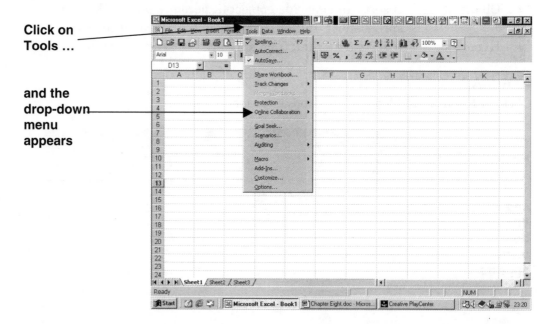

Click on Tools ...

and the drop-down menu appears

This is the catch-all toolbar. The items are grouped, but they are not really related. The important items are:

• Spelling	Word-processor spell-checker.
• AutoCorrect	Automatic type change for common typing errors.
• AutoSave	An Add In — see below.

- Share Workbook   Share Workbook with other users.
- Track Changes   Mark changes made for easy review.
- Merge   To merge changes from one copy of a workbook into
  Workbooks   another.
- Protection   Sheet or book level.
- Online   For Internet access.
  Collaboration
- Goal Seek   Calculation of required value of a variable to give a
                    specific result.
- Scenarios   For reviewing "What If?" scenarios.
- Auditing   Visual on-screen to/from arrows to trace from cell to cell.
- Macro   To run, edit, delete and step an existing macro.
- Add-ins   Optional items that can be included in the menus, if
                    desired.
- Customize   Customize toolbars etc.
- Options   . . . more choices. These will be reviewed when we tailor
                    Excel to suit ourselves in **Section Three**.

DATA

Click on **Data** and look at the drop-down menu.

The term data conjures up visions of databases. Excel has limited database capabilities — limited, because it is a two-dimensional, flat-bed database. That is why Access is supplied in the Office suite, for users who need a serious multi-layered database capability.

**Click on
Data ...**

**and the
drop-down
menu
appears**

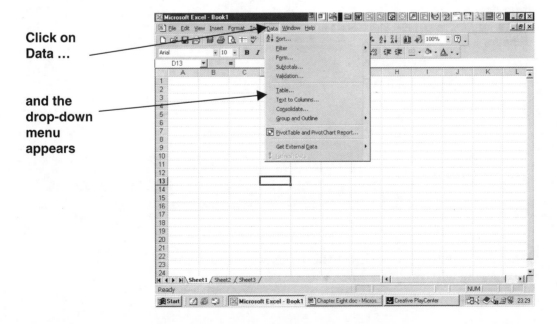

The intention with Excel is two-fold: To provide a basic database facility, and to allow importing of database output so that the results can be "sliced and diced" in Excel.

The major categories are:
- Excel database — data handling, sorting, filtering, input etc.
- Excel database — data grouping capabilities
- Excel slice and dice — pivot tables and data import
- Excel and external database compatibility.

Although the menu list is not vast, the area of databases and uses and abuses of flat-bed vs. relational databases is a book in itself.

If you wish to learn about databases and, for an accountant, it is almost as unavoidable as spreadsheets, acquire a good book devoted solely to the topic. A little knowledge is a dangerous thing, so I will not even whet the appetite here. Nor will I review the menu items.

WINDOW
Click on **Window** and look at the drop-down menu.

Click on Window ...

and the drop-down menu appears

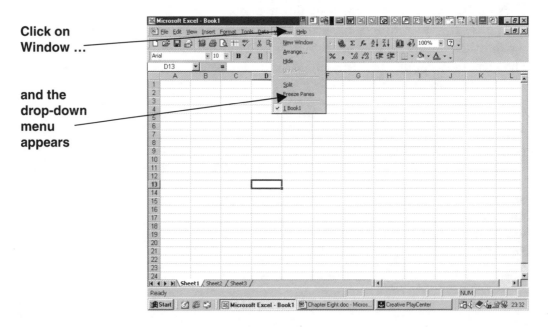

There are only two categories in the Windows menu item:
- Working with multiple windows
- Working with one window.

The menu options are explained below:

- New Window   A second, third, fourth . . . window can be started. Each window then provides a different screen view of the spreadsheet.
- Arrange   Arrange several windows on the screen to see them at the same time.
- Hide   Hide a specific window.
- Unhide   Unhide a previously hidden window.
- Split   Splits the selected window at the active cell.
- Freeze Panes   Freezes the panes for scrolling in the selected window.

Of all of the menu items, Windows is the briefest and the most important. We will see how to use this facility in **Section Three**.

EXERCISES

We will use the menus noted above when we practice the practical exercises in **Section Three**. In the meantime, familiarize yourself with the menu contents and capabilities.

NEXT

In **Chapter Nine**, we look at the **Toolbars**. These are indistinguishable from the menu items, so familiarity with **Chapter Eight** will be a good building block for what follows.

Chapter Nine

THE EXCEL TOOLBARS

That was quick!

We have seen what the menus contain. We now want to explore the efficiencies of the Toolbars. They are there to save you time rather than to do something that you cannot achieve via the menus.

Understanding the menus is, therefore, the precursor to using the toolbars effectively. The menus were discussed in **Chapter Eight**.

The toolbars are at the top of the screen, below the menu.

Toolbars are below the menu

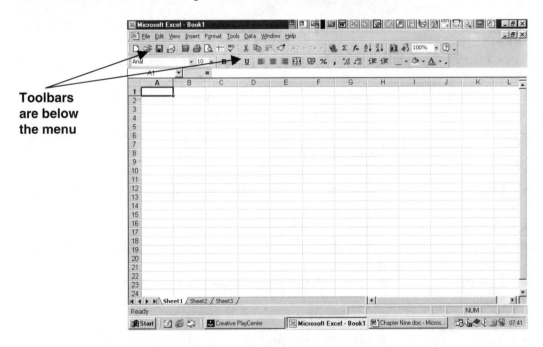

In order to change the default toolbar, access the controls via:

- **View, Toolbars,** or
- **Tools, Customize,** or
- Placing the mouse on the toolbar and right-clicking — a pop-up menu appears.

We will use the last option.

**With the
pointer on
the toolbar,
right-click
...**

**the toolbar
menu
appears.**

**Choose
Customize**

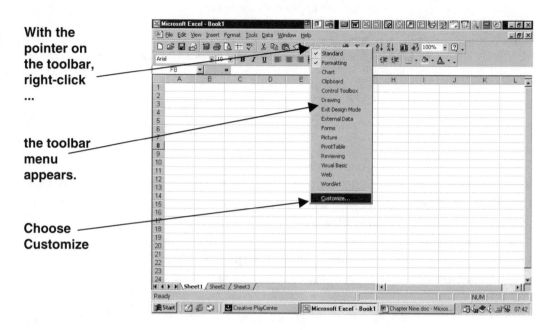

The choices from the pop-up menu are:

- Standard   A basic set of buttons. It is a starting point, but needs to
                   be added to.
- Formatting   Center, Left justify, etc. Some of the buttons are essential;
                   others are not necessary for our purposes.
- Chart   When you chart, turn it on. Otherwise, leave it off.
- Clipboard   Shows the content of the local clipboard (known as Office
                   Clipboard).
- Control Toolbox Relates to VBA programming. Learn VB first.
- Drawing   Lines, shapes etc. Turn on if you want to use it. Generally,
                   leave it off.
- Exit Design   Relates to VBA programming. Learn VB first.
  Mode
- External Data   Interacting with, for example, Access.
- Forms   Relates to VBA programming. Learn VB first.
- Picture   Importing and working with pictures. Leave it off.
- Pivot Table   Data analysis with pivot tables, group, ungroup etc. Turn
                   on if you want to use it. Generally, leave it off.
- Reviewing   Adding comments etc. Turn on if you want to use it.
                   Generally, leave it off.

- VB   To run and edit VB code. Learn VB first.
- Web   Internet tools. Generally, leave it off.
- Word Art   Manipulating fancy text. Leave it off.
- Customize   See below.

Our first task, therefore, is to identify which buttons are going to be useful to us, and to place them on the toolbar.

Start Excel, place the mouse cursor on the toolbar and choose **Customize.** The following screen appears.

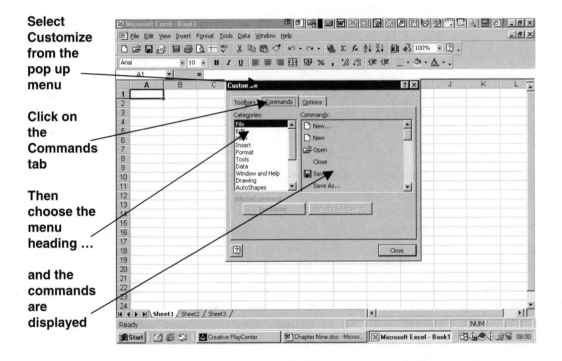

Having activated the dialog box, click on the menu item, and drag the icon that you want to the toolbar. Release the mouse button and the toolbar is updated to include the button.

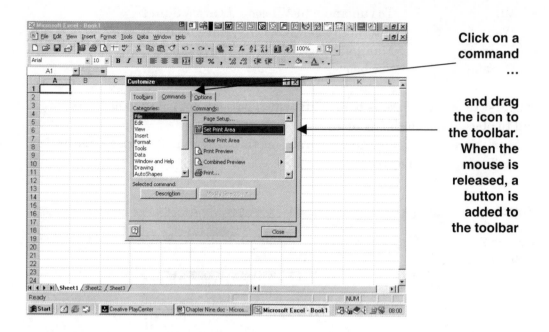

Click on a
command
...

and drag
the icon to
the toolbar.
When the
mouse is
released, a
button is
added to
the toolbar

Note that the buttons are not organized into the toolbar headings.

Which buttons do we need?

The Standard Toolbar contains a lot of essential shortcuts. The Formatting Toolbar is needed if we are going to present attractive and appropriate spreadsheets. However, both contain some buttons that we do not need, and there are buttons scattered throughout the other toolbars that would be useful.

Space is, as always, the limiting factor. We do not want to reduce the working area of the screen too much because we have a lot of buttons that are infrequently, if ever, used. So, as a first step, consider what we are trying to achieve with the spreadsheet, and what we need to do to achieve it.

Click on each button in the dialog box and click on Description to see what it does — if it is needed and we have it already, fine. If we do not have it, click on the button and drag it up to the toolbar. Release the mouse and the button is embedded in the toolbar. If it is on the toolbar and we do not want it, click on the button on the toolbar and drag it down to the dialog box. Release the mouse and it is removed from the toolbar.

I suggest you include the following buttons, if they are not displayed already:

- File   New, Open, Save, Set Print area, Print, Print Preview.
- Edit   Undo, Redo, Cut, Copy, Paste.
- View   Zoom in, Zoom out.
- Insert   Paste Function, AutoSum.

- Format   Font, Font Size, Bold, Italic, Underline, Format Painter, Font
                Color, Align Left, Center, Right, Merge and Center, Increase
                decimal, Reduce decimal, Bottom border, Bottom double border,
                Borders drop-down box, Fill color.
- Tools   Spelling.
- Data   Sort Ascending, Sort Descending.
- Window and   Freeze panes.
  help
- Drawing   The icon to show/hide the full toolbar.
- AutoShapes   None.
- Charting   Chart Wizard.
- Web   None.
- Forms   None.
- Control Tool- None.
  box
- Macros   None.
- Built in   None.
  menus
- New menu   None.

Note that any items not selected (such as Auditing) can be activated at the appropriate time. The fact that particular buttons or functions are not included in the table above does not mean that these facilities are not used.

The amended toolbar looks like this:

TOOLBAR VS. MENU

We want to illustrate how the toolbar buttons are interchangeable with the menu items, and also highlight their limitations. For this purpose, we will enter some information on the spreadsheet and print it out.

Start Excel, and type in the following:

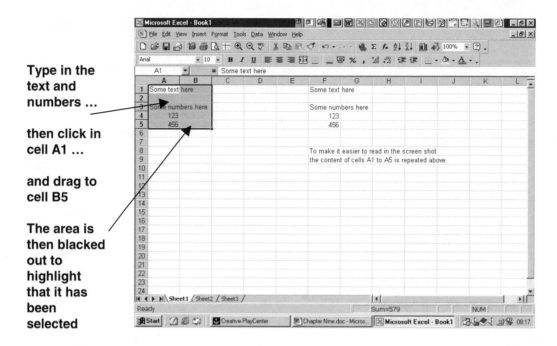

Type in the text and numbers ...

then click in cell A1 ...

and drag to cell B5

The area is then blacked out to highlight that it has been selected

Click on cell A1, and drag to cell B5. This highlights the region in purple.

Now click on **File**, then highlight **Print Area**, then **Set Print Area** and click. This sets the selected area as the part of the spreadsheet that we want to print.

Now click on **File**, then highlight **Print** and click on it. This calls the Print Dialog box. Click **OK**. The page prints.

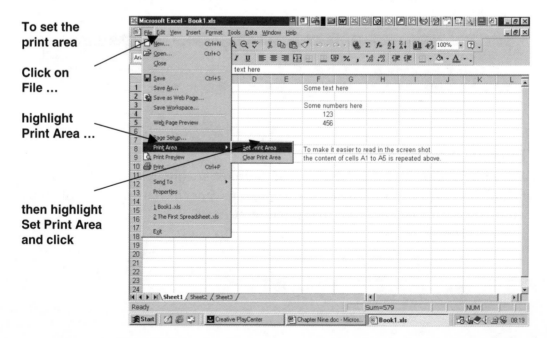

To set the print area

Click on File ...

highlight Print Area ...

then highlight Set Print Area and click

Then ...

click on File ...

click on Print ...

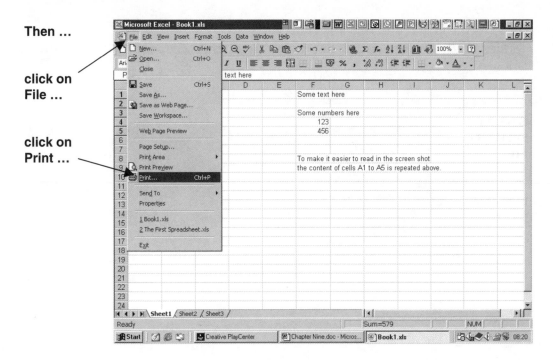

and the Print Dialog box appears

Click on OK, and the page prints

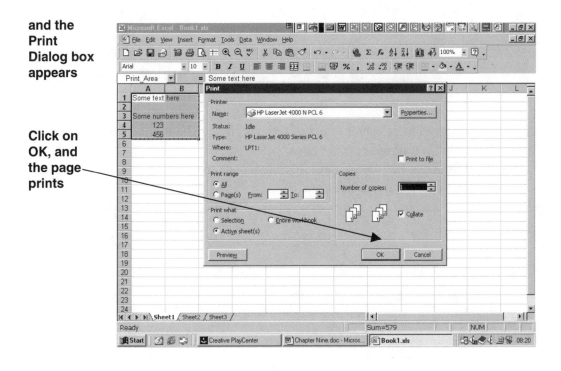

That was the long route. Now the short cut.

Click on the toolbar button **Set Print Area**, then click on the **Print** button. Easy!

Click on Set Print Area ...

then click on Print

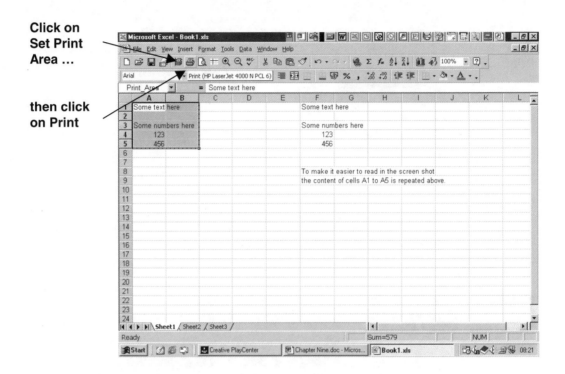

If you are unsure of the correct button to click, leave the mouse over it for a moment. The title then appears in a yellow box.

So, what benefits can menus possibly have over toolbars?

Look at the Print dialog box again.

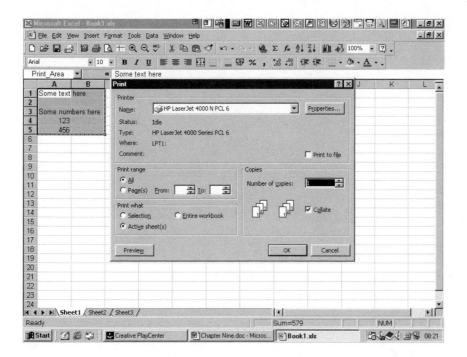

There are plenty of options:

- Change printer.
- Change number of copies.
- Collate.
- Portrait or landscape (via properties).

When you use a toolbar, you accept all of the current settings as your default. If you want to change them, or if you are not sure what they are, the long route via the menus is the only option.

CHAPTER TEN

That concludes the discussion of the toolbars.

In the next chapter, we look at using the keyboard and mouse to input to the spreadsheet. In **Section Three**, we will draw all of our skills together by using worked examples.

Chapter Ten

AUTOMATIC BACK-UP AND
CELL FORMATTING

I'd recognize it anywhere. It looks like this . . .

The screen below shows the areas of the Excel screen — the only area we have not explored yet is the Spreadsheet Working Area, where the cells are.

We have looked at how we access all the other areas by using the keyboard or mouse for issuing the commands, and we are almost ready to look at using the keyboard and mouse for inputting information to the cells, formatting them etc.

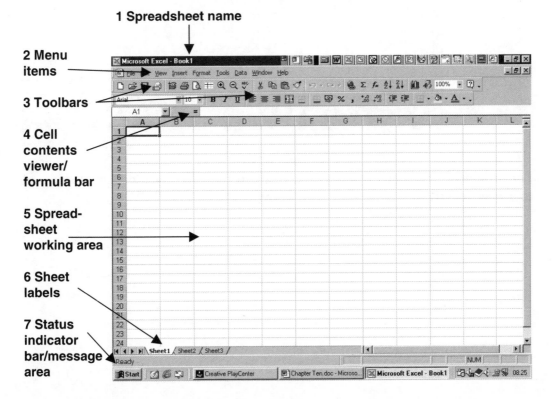

1 Spreadsheet name

2 Menu items

3 Toolbars

4 Cell contents viewer/ formula bar

5 Spreadsheet working area

6 Sheet labels

7 Status indicator bar/message area

But first, we need to protect our work from loss. We can instruct Excel to save our work automatically, saving us the need to break off from what we are doing, and saving us from the consequence of not remembering.

We will initiate **AutoSave**.

AUTOSAVE

Turn on Excel, and check whether **AutoSave** is loaded. If it is not on the Tools section of the menu, click on **Tools, Add In**.

Click on Tools ...

highlight Add Ins ...

and click

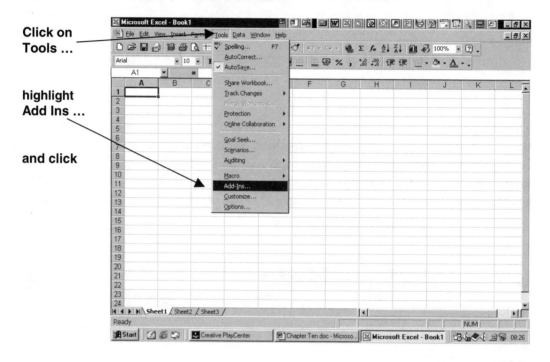

This brings up the Add Ins input box. Click on the check box for **AutoSave** and then click on **OK**.

The Add Ins box appears

Click on the check box

then OK

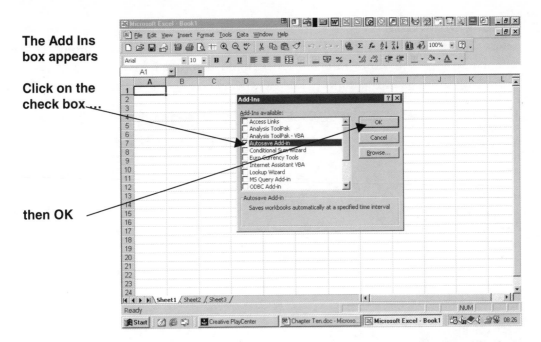

If you now click on Tools, **AutoSave** appears on the menu. Click on **AutoSave** and the following screen appears:

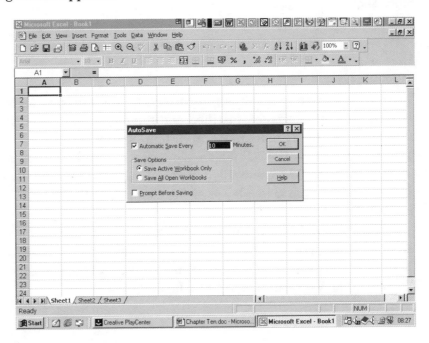

Select your options — mine are on the screen above — and close the screen. Now your work will save automatically.

CELL FORMATTING

Before we start typing in the cells, we must be clear about how to manipulate the cell displays — the same information can be displayed in different ways by formatting the cells in the appropriate manner. Look at the spreadsheet below.

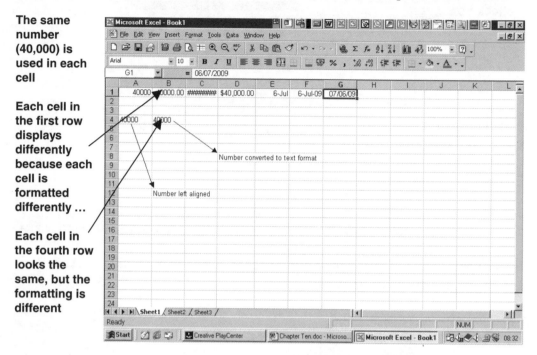

The same number (40,000) is used in each cell

Each cell in the first row displays differently because each cell is formatted differently ...

Each cell in the fourth row looks the same, but the formatting is different

Anything we enter in a cell is interpreted by the program as either number or text. By default, text is left-justified and numbers are right-justified but, as can be seen above, there are many permutations within this.

The issue of how the cell displays on screen and the contents of the cells are entirely separate. We know this for formulae, where the result is shown in the cell, and the formula is displayed in the Cell Contents Viewer, but it also applies to items like dates.

A date is stored as a number, which means that mathematics can be applied (addition, subtraction etc.) to calculate dates based on the first date.

To see what types of cell formatting can be applied, start Excel, and click on the menu item **Format**, highlight **Cells** and click.

Click on Format ...

then on Cells

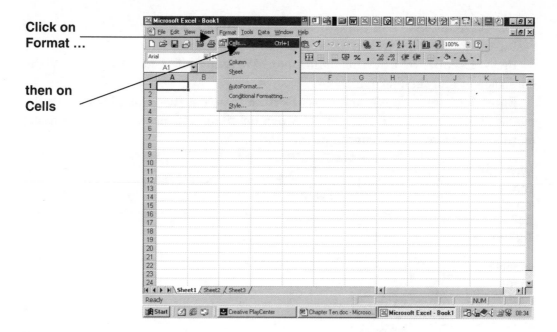

The following format choices appear:

- Number
- Alignment (center, left, right etc.)
- Font (typeface style and size)
- Border (around the edge of the cell)
- Patterns (background, not typeface)
- Protection (on or off).

The format choices are shown on the tabs ...

They are:
Number
Alignment
Font
Border
Patterns
Protection

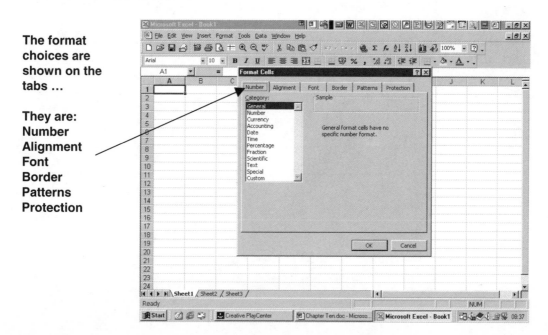

Here, we are interested in the Number format options, rather than Font, etc. The rest of the format options are covered later in this chapter.

Press **Escape** to exit the dialog box. We will put some numbers in the spreadsheet and then format them.

Enter 1000 into cell A1, and press **Return** to accept the input. Then, with the mouse pointer at cell A1, right-click. A pop-up menu appears — one of the items on this is **Format Cells**. Highlight this and left-click.

With the mouse pointer in cell A1, right-click ...

a pop-up menu appears ...

highlight Format Cells, and left-click

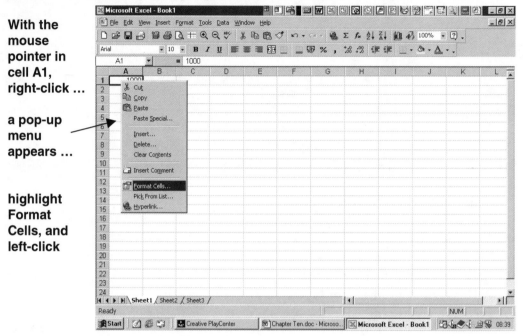

The same dialog box appears as before. Notice that the present format is General. (Click on the Number tab, if necessary.)

**The Format Cells
dialog box
appears**

**The present
format is
highlighted ...**

**and an example
of the style
appears in the
Sample box**

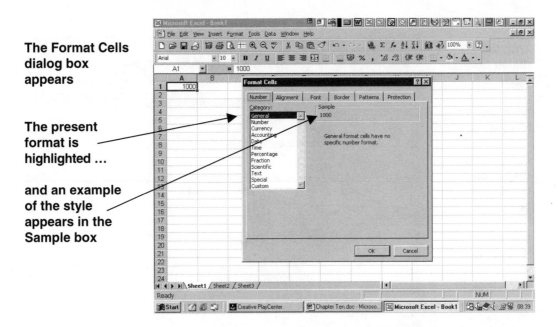

We will change it so that two decimal places are displayed. Highlight **Number**.
A box of choices of format appears (in terms of displaying negatives in red), and
there is a box for choosing the number of decimal places. Two is the default.

You will notice that the display in the Sample box has now changed. Click
OK. The dialog box closes, and the spreadsheet now displays in the same style as
that shown in the Sample box earlier.

Investigate the other options. The most important from our point of view are:

- General
- Number
- Currency
- Accounting (this is Number, restricted to two decimal places. Display of
  currency label is optional.)
- Date
- Time
- Percentage
- Fraction
- Scientific
- Text
- Special
- Custom.

That covers most of the choices available, however, there is a lot of overlap. We
will be using **Format** when we prepare our spreadsheets, so for now we will
leave the topic, except for a special mention of Dates.

**With the
dialog box
open ...**

**click on
Number ...**

**options are
displayed in
the display
box ...**

**and the
Sample box
shows how
it will look in
the cell**

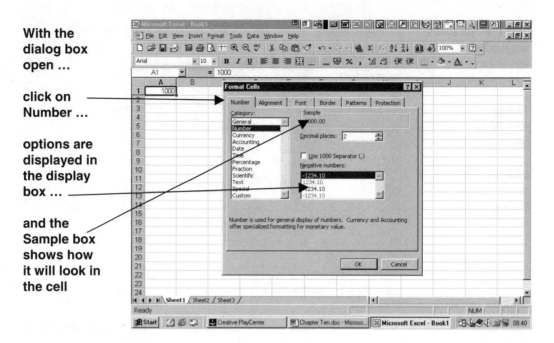

DATES

Dates are entered as numbers, and then the cells are formatted specifically to
display them as dates. This means that you can lose dates (or acquire them), if
the incorrect area of a spreadsheet is formatted. We will manipulate dates in US
and UK formats. You only use US format? Why care? As we said earlier, you can
make any date text instead of digits – and UK format will default to text
automatically, which for our purposes is convenient. As well as that we want to
investigate date manipulation in all of its permutations. The more you know, the
easier it becomes.

Before we start to enter dates, decide how you want them to display. The
choices can be seen by clicking on **Date** in the **Format**, **Cells** menu items (or
right-clicking to access the pop-up menu).

Press **Escape** to close the dialog box and display the blank spreadsheet.

We want to display the date February 28 2001 in various formats:

- In cell A1, type 2/28/01 (US format). It displays as 2/28/01.
- In cell B1, type 2/2001. It displays as Feb-01. Highlight the cell. The cell
  contents viewer shows a date of 1 February 2001.
- In cell C1, type Feb 2001. It displays as Feb-01.
- In cell D1, type 28/2/2001 (UK format). It displays as 28/2/2001 and is left-
  aligned. This indicates it is text, not a number. All of the other entries are
  right-aligned.

Note that either the US format will not work, or the UK format will not work. The Date format can be set for one or the other but not both simultaneously.

Enter dates
...
2/28/01 ...
2/2001 ...
Feb 2001 ...
28/2/2001 ...

The UK
format
28/2/2001
appears as
text,
because the
US keyboard
option was
selected at
set up

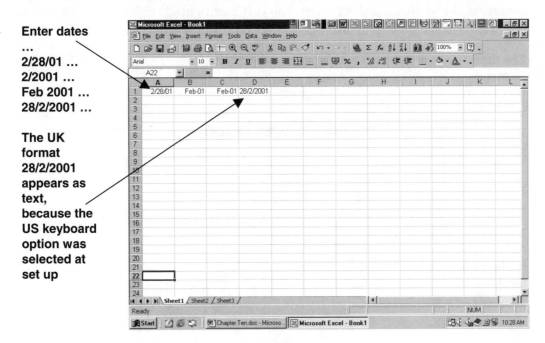

Make the UK format cell active, right-click and choose **Format**. The present cell format is shown.

The UK date
format has
been
allocated as
General, and
is displayed
as text

The sample
looks
correct, but
we cannot
manipulate
the date
unless it is a
number

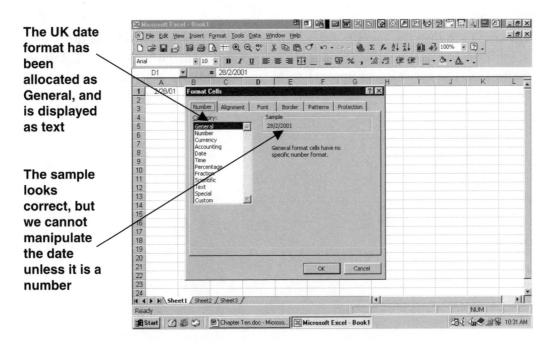

We will change the cell format so that it displays correctly.

Delete the cell contents, type in 2/28/01, and press **Enter**. The date is formatted the same as cell A1. With the cell highlighted, right-click and choose **Format** from the pop-up menu. The format required is **Custom**.

The date format is Custom for UK display

The actual format type is shown in the Type box

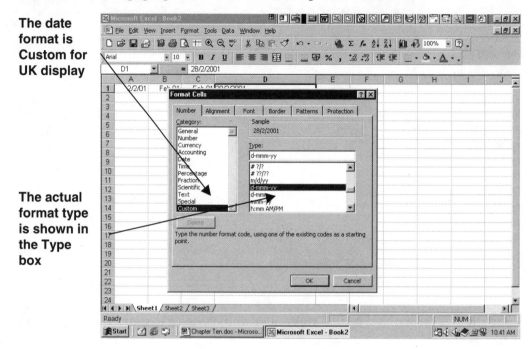

We want to change the way the entry displays. Select Custom and choose d-mmm-yy in the Type box on the right. The display has not changed, but click OK and close the dialog box. The spreadsheet appears to be unchanged. The cells in column D have been widened in the screen below to confirm the entry is still text.

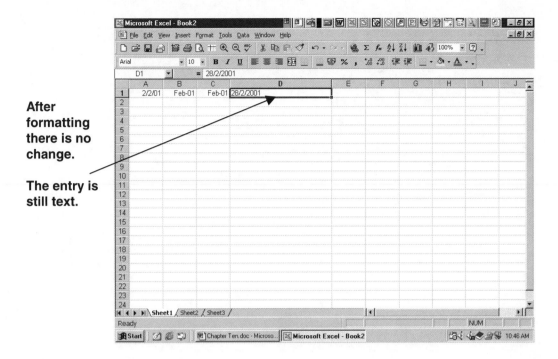

After formatting there is no change.

The entry is still text.

However, now type in the date in US format, 2/28/2001. The display changes to 28-Feb-01. The Formula Bar shows the date as 2/28/01.

In the screen below the format of the cells D3, D5 and D7 have been changed to demonstrate some of the possible options.

Cell	Format
D3	d-mm-yy
D5	d-mmm-yyyy
D7	d/mm/yy

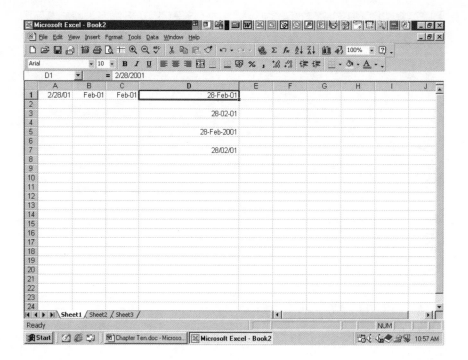

All of the dates are now right aligned, entered in the same way as other dates, but display differently. We will see the importance of dates being recognized as numbers in the next chapter, when we look at **AutoFill**.

The final thing we want to do to the dates is to show the underlying numbers, to prove that they are numbers and not text. For this purpose, in cell F1 type in the UK date 28/2/2001 (the text error date we had previously) and, in cell F3 type **Word**. Select the entire spreadsheet by clicking the box in the top left corner of the spreadsheet – the entire spreadsheet goes purple. Right-click anywhere in the purple area to get the pop-up menu.

Click here to select all cells in the spread-sheet ...

then, with the mouse pointer in the highlighted area, right-click to call the pop-up menu

DO NOT left-click in the purple area or the cells are unselected

Highlight Format cells and left-click

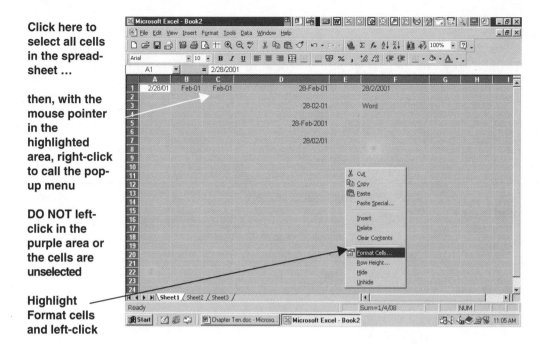

Select General and click **OK**. The cells now display as:

Dates are now in number format

Text is unaffected

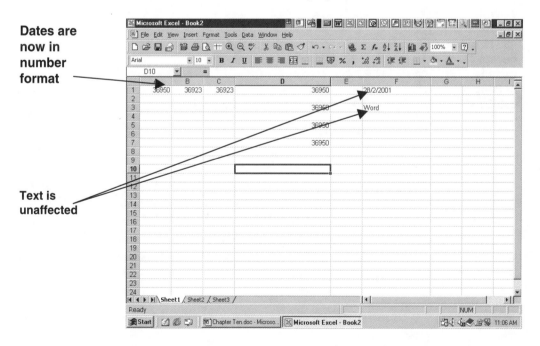

That concludes number formatting for now. We will cover it again when we build spreadsheets, but what about the other formatting options? They are reviewed below.

ALIGNMENT

Clear the contents of the spreadsheet by highlighting each cell and pressing the **Delete** key, or by selecting all cells as shown above and, with all cells highlighted in purple, pressing the **Delete** key.

Type in the following:

- Cell A1   Word
- Cell B1   12345
- Cell C1   A very long sentence

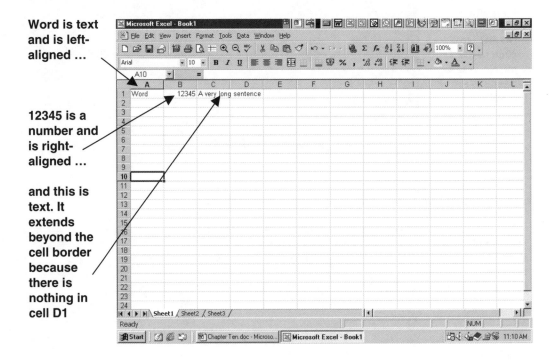

Word is text and is left-aligned ...

12345 is a number and is right-aligned ...

and this is text. It extends beyond the cell border because there is nothing in cell D1

Some cell formatting functions are accessible from the toolbar. When we tailored the toolbar in **Chapter Nine**, we included the formatting toolbar in our choices.

First, we want to right-align cell A1, left-align cell B1 and center cell C1. Click on a cell to activate it, then click on the **Left Justify**, **Center** and **Right Justify** buttons as appropriate. This formatting does not affect the classification of the cell contents as text or number.

**Click on each
cell and
align ...**

**here we have
highlighted
the long
sentence ...**

**and clicked
on Centre**

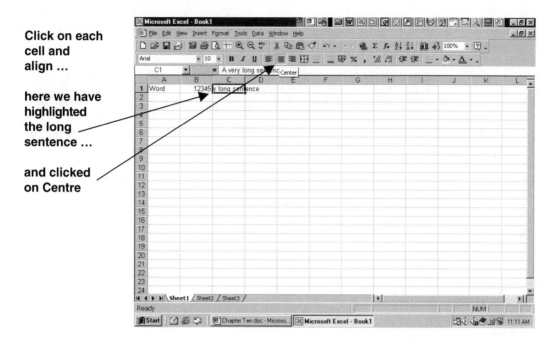

Note that, when a cell is active, the format choices are highlighted in the toolbar. In the case above, the **Center** button is shown as depressed.

Right-click to bring up the pop-up menu, highlight **Format Cells**, and click. Select the **Alignment** tab. The full range of format options appears.

**Call up the
Format
Cells
dialog box
...**

**and click
on the
Alignment
tab ...**

**the full
range of
options
appears**

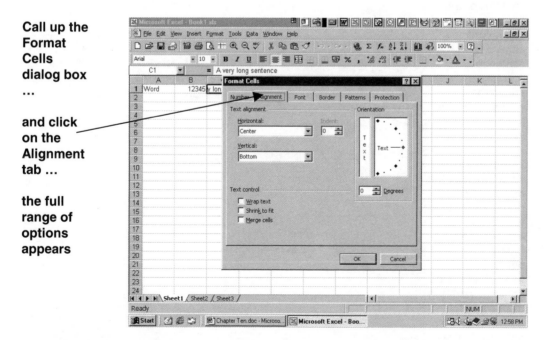

Left-align cell C1 to make the full sentence appear again. Enter A in cell D1, and the contents of cell C1 are cut short to fit in the width of the cell.

With cell C1 highlighted, click Left Align ...

highlight cell D1 and enter A ...

the contents of cell C1 do not fully display

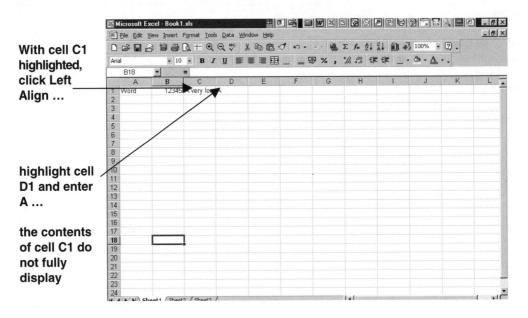

There are two ways around the problem: Widen the cell, or wrap the text, keeping the cell width unchanged.

Text Wrap cell A1.
The height adjusts to fit the sentence

Widen the column to show the full sentence in a single cell

To widen the column, place the mouse on the right-hand side of the column heading. The mouse pointer becomes a black vertical line, with an arrow pointing each way. Hold down the left mouse and drag left or right

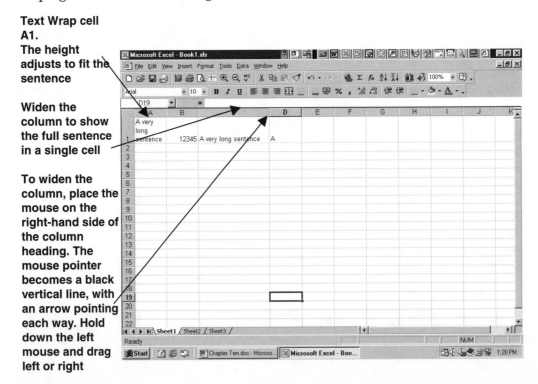

**For text
wrap, click
the check
box so that it
is ticked**

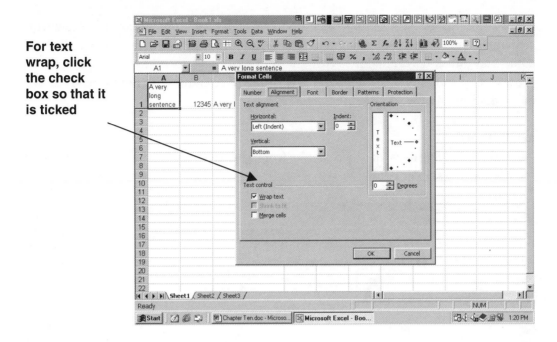

FONT

The font is the style in which characters and numbers appear. The point size describes the height and width of the characters.

There are two ways to access these characteristics: via the menu, as before, or from the toolbar. For most purposes, the toolbar will suffice.

**The Font
type ...**

Size ...

**and special
effects:
Bold
Italics
Underline**

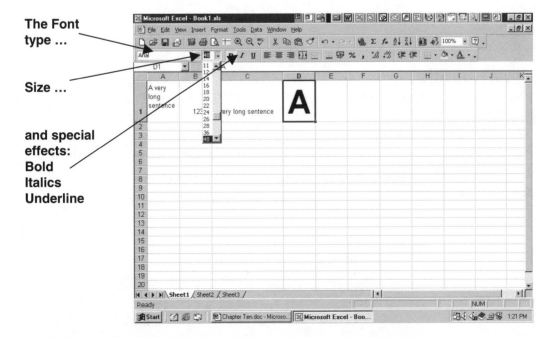

Fonts are extremely important for spreadsheet presentation. However, remember that, when selecting font type, size and highlighting features such as bold, they must be consistent with the font type and format used in the word-processed document — otherwise, the final document will not appear as an integrated piece of work.

BORDERS

As with fonts, borders are accessible from the toolbar or the dialog box. The toolbar item is shown below:

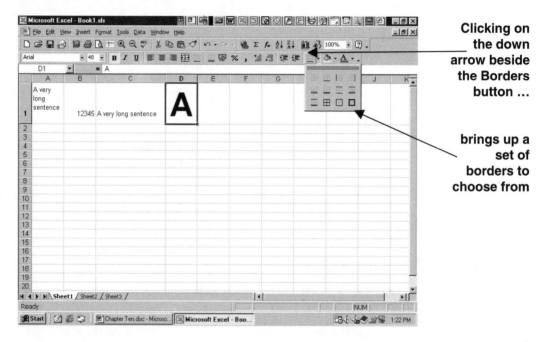

Clicking on the down arrow beside the Borders button ...

brings up a set of borders to choose from

CELL SHADING

This is accessed from either the toolbar or the dialog box. The toolbar item is shown below.

In practice, you will not use shading to any significant degree unless you are using a color printer and all reports are issued in color. Grey shading from a black-and-white printer usually detracts from the physical impact of a presentation.

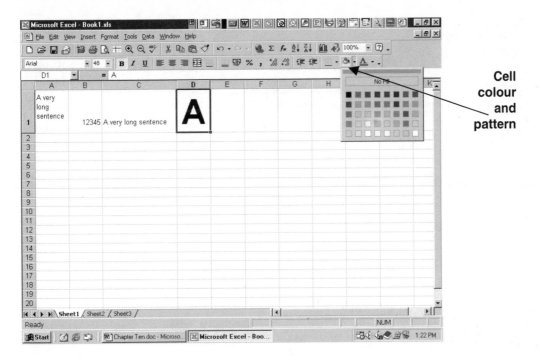

PROTECTION

This can be added to the toolbar, but it is not accessed frequently, and the toolbar space is best left for more day-to-day shortcuts.

It is therefore accessed from the menu — right-click for the pop-up menu, highlight **Format Cells** and click. Then choose the **Protection** tab. To activate protection select **Tools**, **Protection**, **Protect Sheet**. All cells formatted for protection are then protected. By default, protection is active (the check box is ticked in the cells format dialog box), and it must be unprotected before the Tools, Protection, Protect Sheet command is invoked if you want to be able to continue to edit the cell.

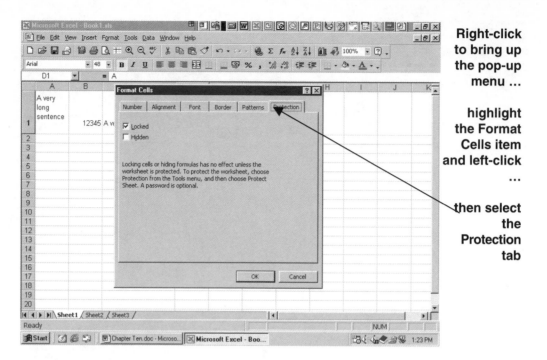

Right-click
to bring up
the pop-up
menu ...

highlight
the Format
Cells item
and left-click
...

then select
the
Protection
tab

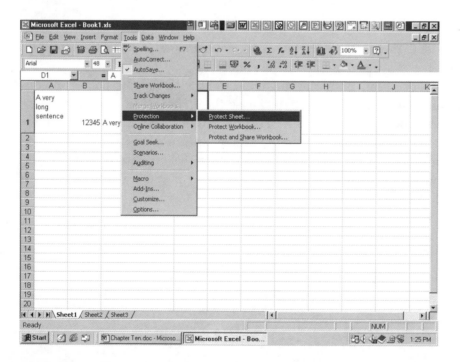

If you do not have some of the buttons shown above, review **Chapter Nine** on customizing the toolbar.

. . . To Summarize

Before we can use spreadsheets in a meaningful way, we have to ensure that what we produce is not lost by a system lock-up while we are working, by using the **AutoSave** facility provided. Backups to other media are covered in **Section One**.

We also have to be able to ensure that what we are going to produce (both numbers and text) will display properly, and that we are able to manipulate cell formatting to ensure the spreadsheet looks exactly as we want it to.

Formatting is a major cornerstone in producing a successful, well-received report, and this area should be practiced until you become proficient.

Next

In this chapter, we have dealt with a single cell each time. In the next chapter, we will see how to use the mouse and keyboard to work with several cells at the same time, speeding up entry and improving efficiency many-fold.

Chapter Eleven

INPUT WITH THE KEYBOARD AND MOUSE

A Mouse? I think I need an Octopus . . .

The screen below shows the areas of the Excel screen, all of which have been reviewed in the previous chapters in this section. We now want to review how to input information to the cells at maximum speed and accuracy, with minimum effort.

We have seen how, by using special keys on the keyboard (Alt, Crtl, Tab and Shift) and by using the mouse, we can access the menus and toolbars. We will now look at using the keyboard and mouse for inputting information to cells.

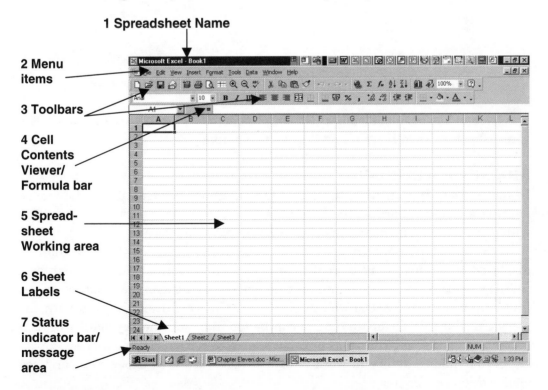

The best way of explaining how to use the keyboard and mouse for inputting into the cells is to use examples. The rest of this chapter therefore comprises exercises, suitably annotated and explained. The best way for you to learn is by following the examples on your screen and practicing until you are proficient.
Start Excel.

EXERCISES

We have a blank screen, like the one shown below:

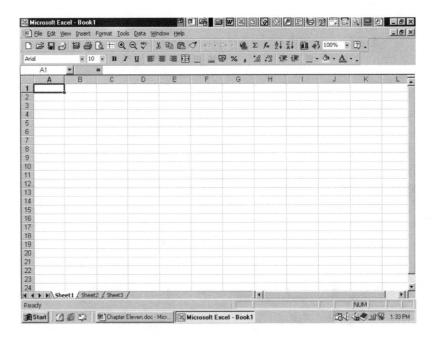

The toolbar has been customized to our satisfaction. The cell area is clear. The spreadsheet is called Book 1, and it is set to AutoSave.

MOUSE OR KEYBOARD?

In this section in particular, there is a big difference between using the mouse and the keyboard. Earlier, the hardware to use was clear — we were dealing with menus and toolbars and these were available in one location only.

With the cell area, we are more likely to be working outside the immediately-displayed area. This can be a problem as regards fine control on the cell pointer.

The keyboard provides definite control, one cell at a time. The mouse provides finger-tip control and speed well in excess of that which can achieved with the keyboard. But this finger-tip control can be too fine, and the keyboard will be a better and, in the long run, quicker input source in certain circumstances.

An individual's ability to work with a mouse varies, so experiment and see what works best for you.

SELECTING CELLS

The first step in working with a spreadsheet is the ability to work with several cells at once. The purpose of this exercise, therefore, is to practice selecting and deselecting a range of cells.

We want to select cells from A1 to E10. Place the mouse in cell A1, hold down the left mouse button and drag to cell E10. Release the mouse.

As the area is selected, it displays purple, except for the first selected cell, to show the region that is affected. This area increases and shrinks as the mouse moves around the screen.

Click on cell A1 — the screen becomes white again.

We will now use the keyboard. Press **F8**. Notice that the letters **EXT** appear at the bottom right-hand of the screen, indicating that Extension has been selected. Navigate to cell E10 using the arrow keys. The procedure is a lot slower.

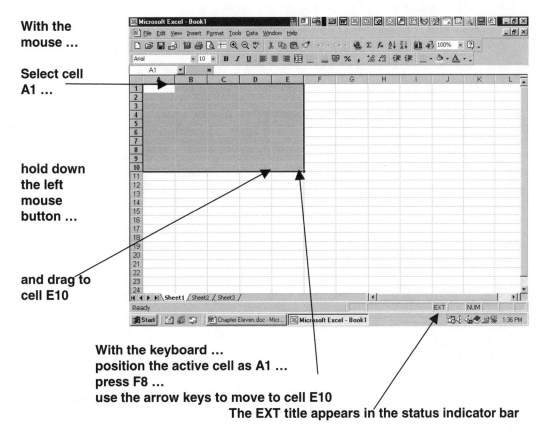

With the mouse ...

Select cell A1 ...

hold down the left mouse button ...

and drag to cell E10

With the keyboard ...
position the active cell as A1 ...
press F8 ...
use the arrow keys to move to cell E10
The EXT title appears in the status indicator bar

The mouse is obviously better.

Press the **Esc** key or **F8** to turn **EXT** off. Click in cell A1 to make it active, and to make the screen white again.

MOVING AROUND

The screen area displayed is small in comparison to the size of one sheet within a workbook — around 150 cells compared to 17 million, so it is unlikely you will stay in the confines of the immediate area. We will look at the methods available to navigate the cell area.

Mouse

If a range of cells is selected and the left mouse button held down, moving the mouse outside the cell area will scroll the screen in that direction. The further towards the edge of the screen the mouse pointer is moved, the greater the scroll speed.

If we are not going to make a range of cells active, but just want to scroll to a new area, click on the scroll bar provided on the right and bottom of the screen. Click and hold down the mouse button on the box within the scroll bar and it can be dragged to speed up the movement. As the area used increases, the size of this box reduces and a wider area can be accessed.

Try moving to cell BA1 by moving the mouse to the extreme right of the screen. It is difficult to stop at the correct place.

Try using the scroll bar. It is very slow.

Select cell A1, hold down the left mouse button and move the mouse pointer to the extreme right of the screen

The scroll speed is too fast to control

Move it part way out of the cell area. The scroll speed is slower

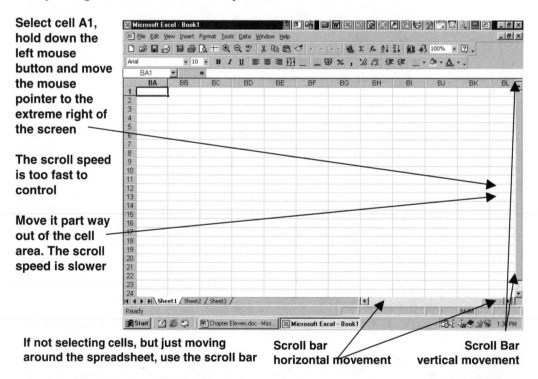

If not selecting cells, but just moving around the spreadsheet, use the scroll bar

Scroll bar horizontal movement

Scroll Bar vertical movement

In order to avoid cluttering the last picture, the slider bars are highlighted below:

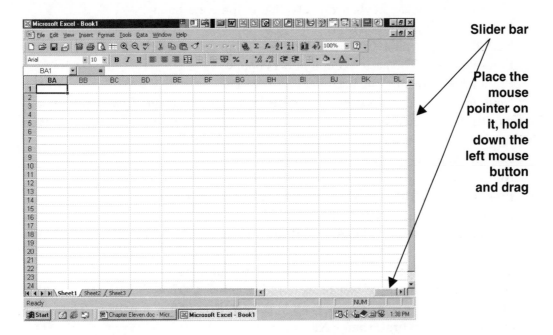

The scroll bars are not ideal. The keyboard gives better control.

The keystrokes to navigate larger areas than the immediate screen are:

- One Screen up   Page Up key
- One Screen left   Alt + Page Up key
- One Screen down   Page Down key
- One Screen right   Alt + Page Down key
- First or last active cell up   Ctrl + ↑ key
- First or last active cell left   Ctrl + ← key
- First or last active cell down   Ctrl + ↓ key
- First or last active cell right   Ctrl + → key
- Move to column A, same row   Home
- Move to cell A1   Ctrl + Home

A word of explanation on the second section of commands. A cell is active if it has anything in it — text or numbers. If cells contain information in a continuous row, pressing **Ctrl** and, whilst holding it down, pressing the **right arrow** key will move to the last entry in that line — be it one cell away, or 100 away.

If you are on the last cell of a block, pressing **Ctrl** and, whilst holding it down, pressing the **right arrow** key will move to the next cell in that row with an entry, or to the end of the spreadsheet if there is no entry.

We will practice the keyboard-controlled maneuvers below.

Start a blank spreadsheet.

With the active cell at A1, press **Ctrl + →**. The active cell is now IV1.

Press **Ctrl + ↓**. The active cell is now IV65536.

Press **Ctrl + Home**. The active cell is now A1.

Hold down **Alt**, and keep holding it down. Press the **Page Down** key repeatedly until you are near cell BA1. Release the keys and move to the final position using the arrow keys only. Enter the text "Stop" in cell BA1.

Now press **Ctrl + →** to move to cell IV1.

Now press **Ctrl + ←**. Cell BA1 is highlighted.

Press **Ctrl + ↓**. The cell pointer moves to cell BA65536.

Press **Ctrl + ↑** to move to cell BA1.

Press **Page Down** until near cell BA900, then use the arrow keys to highlight the required cell.

Enter 1 in cell BA900, 2 in BA901 etc. for 10 numbers.

When the last number has been entered, press **Ctrl + ↑**. The active cell is BA900. Press **Ctrl + ↓**. The active cell is BA909. Press **Ctrl + ↑** twice. The active cell becomes BA900 first, then BA1.

Spreadsheets are now so vast that being able to negotiate your way around is an important skill. Practice this until you are proficient.

Now that we know how to navigate our way around the spreadsheet cell area, the next step is to learn how to manipulate data in the cells, using the mouse or keyboard as appropriate.

Within this, the main speed of entry comes from using the mouse, and to this end it is important to learn what the various styles of mouse pointer mean, and to use this information to maximum effect.

The different styles of mouse pointer are reviewed in the exercises below.

AUTOFILL

We will start by using the mouse to fill in a series of numbers and text. Type the entries into the cells as shown below.

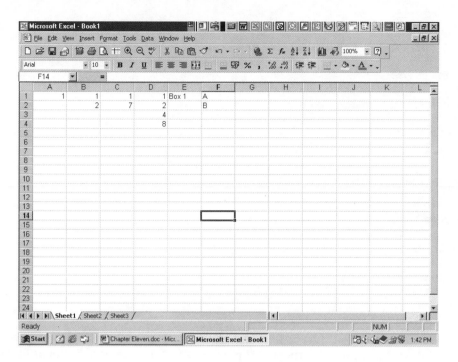

To use AutoFill, we must advise the computer of the extent of the series we are going to expand from, and the cell range over which we want the filled series to spread.

Place the mouse cursor over cell A1 and click. This ensures cell A1 is active.

Move the mouse cursor to the bottom right of the cell — you should see it change to a black cross. When this happens, hold down the left mouse button and drag the pointer down to cell A10. Release the mouse, and the cells are filled with 1s.

Repeat the process on the other cells. If there are two (or more) cells, click in the first cell — this time, ensure the mouse is a large white cross. Click the left mouse button and drag it down to cover the lowest cell with information in it. The first cell is clear, the others are purple.

Now, with several cells highlighted, move the mouse to the lower right of the group. It again becomes a black cross. Hold down the left mouse button and drag down as we did with cell A1. The series is filled.

Click in cell A1 ...

place the mouse-pointer in the bottom right corner. It becomes a black cross ...

hold down the left mouse button and drag down to cell A10. The number 1 is shown in a box. This is the last number the series will fill in

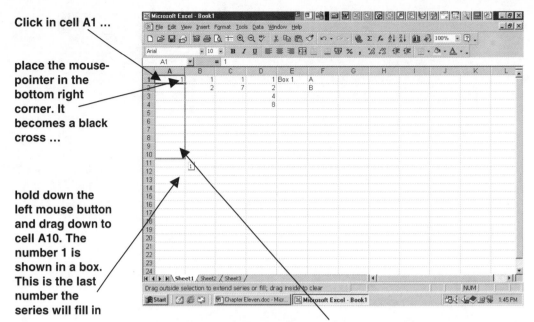

A dotted line appears. This indicates the area selected ... release the mouse button. The series fills automatically

For a fill series of two or more cells ...

place the mouse pointer in the centre of the first cell. The pointer is like a white cross ...

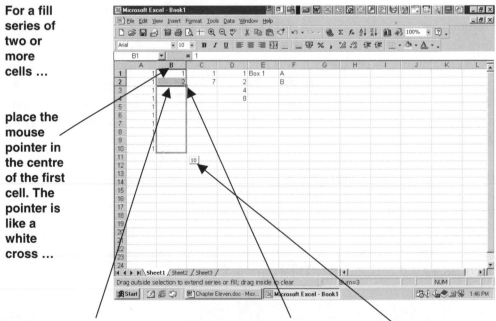

hold down the left mouse button and drag down to the last cell in the series (B2 in this case) ...
all cells are colored purple except the first

Extend the series as before, from the bottom right corner ...

As before, the area you drag down to is highlighted with a dotted border. The number 10 is highlighted

The final screen, with all cells filled, looks like this:

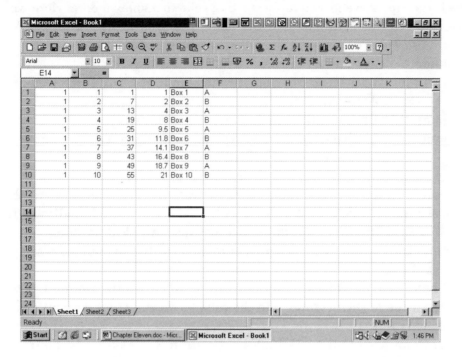

There are six series, and six different results:

- Cell A1   Starting number 1. No indication of uplift required — default of 0 used. The series is therefore unchanged. It is the equivalent of using the **Copy** command.
- Cell B1   The series is stepped by one, and extending the series continues this sequence. This is useful for check listings etc.
- Cell C1   The series is stepped by six, and extending the series continues this sequence. This is useful for dates, as we will see below.
- Cell D1   The series was to double each time. Be careful, and use a formula instead if necessary.
- Cell E1   Text and numbers mixed. And it works . . .
- Cell F1   Text only. It works like copy, repeating what is there.

AUTOFILL WITH DATES

In the last chapter, we looked at formatting cells to display a date. Here we want to see how we can manipulate dates using the mouse and AutoFill. We will therefore use AutoFill to record the following dates in 2001:

*   Column A   Each date from January 15 to January 31.
*   Column B   Each week from January to March, starting at week ending 5 January.
*   Column C   Each month from January to December.
*   Column D   Twelve transactions occurred on January 17. We want to copy the same date 11 times.

If we want a range of dates, then we know from the previous AutoFill that we must place the next date in the series in the cell below — this indicates the interval to Excel. However, the difference between AutoFilling dates and Auto-Filling numbers is that dates are pre-set to increase by one; numbers are pre-set to increase by zero.

Highlight all of the cells as described earlier and press the **Delete** key to clear them. Enter the following dates into the cells — we will try it without specifying a series interval first:

Column A	Cell A1 15/1/2001	**Column B**	Cell B1 1/5/2001
Column C	Cell C1 1/2001	**Column D**	Cell D1 17/1/2001

The results are:

The results of the AutoFill ...

Column A and C correct

Column B and D incorrect

Column E has been AutoFilled to show the difference between numbers and dates

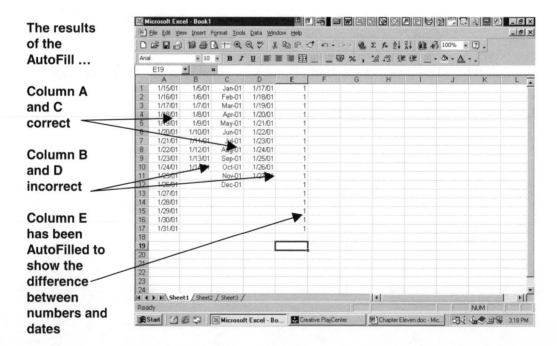

To display columns B and D correctly, enter the next date in the series in the second cell, then highlight both and **AutoFill**.

To AutoFill columns B and D correctly, enter the next date in the series ...

then highlight both cells ...

and drag as before

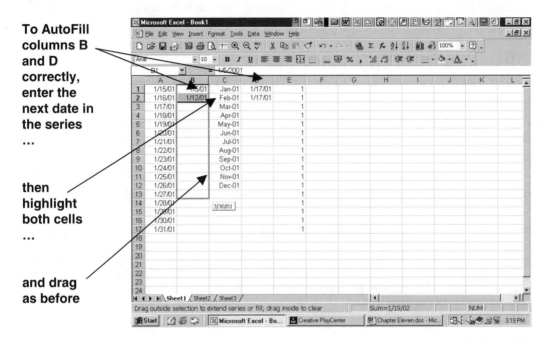

The revised AutoFill works correctly. The other columns have been deleted for clarity.

The AutoFill dates are now correct

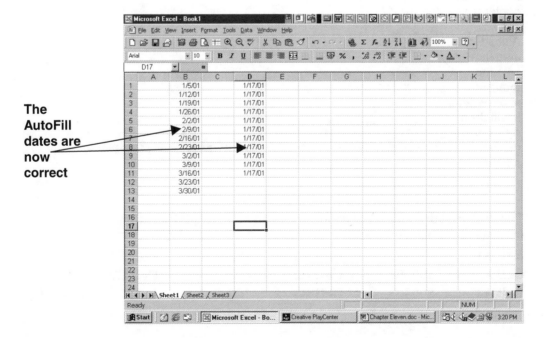

The AutoFill feature is particularly useful when recording check numbers, transaction dates, months in projections etc.

AutoFill can be accessed from the menus, but this is very cumbersome and should be avoided.

DRAG AND DROP / CUT AND PASTE

The mouse can be used to drag cell contents from one location and drop them at another. An example will demonstrate.

Start Excel, and type "Word" in cell A1. Place the mouse on one of the sides of the cell — the cross changes from a white cross to a white arrow-head, similar to the way it appears when it is on the toolbar.

Click and hold the left button, move the mouse to cell D1, and release the button. The cell contents now appear in D1. Now drag it to back to A1.

Place the mouse on one of the sides of the cell. The mouse pointer changes to an arrow ...

drag the cell contents to cell D1. A shaded area moves with the mouse to show where it will drop. A box gives the cell address

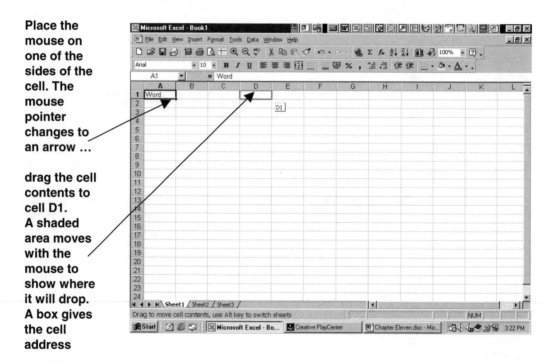

The drag and drop feature can also be used on several cells at once.

Type in the following:

Cell A1	Sales	Cell B1	Purchases	Cell C1	Profit
Cell A2	10000	Cell B2	6000	Cell C2	4000
Cell A3	20000	Cell B3	12000	Cell C3	8000

The resulting spreadsheet looks like this:

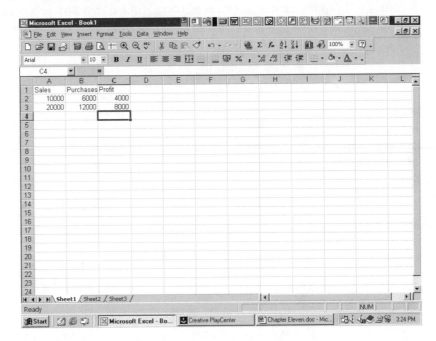

It looks awful — no heading, columns not lined up, no underlines. The first thing we want to do is to create space for the heading. Make cell A1 active and, with the pointer as a white cross in the cell, drag to cell C3. The cells are highlighted to show they have been selected.

Make cell A1 active ...

With the pointer as a white cross in A1, drag the pointer to C3 ...

The cells are all selected, as shown by the area being colored purple

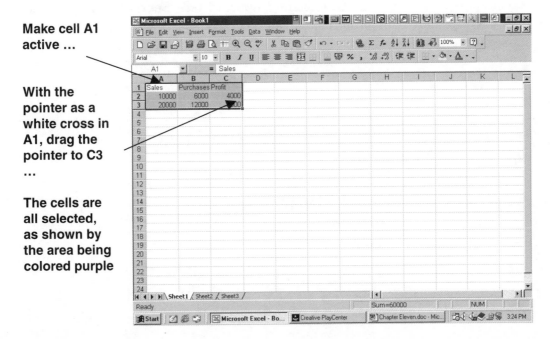

To drag and drop the section, place the mouse on one of the sides of the outer set of cells — the pointer becomes an arrow. Hold down the left mouse button and drag as before. Move the selection so that the top left cell is at B2.

Place the mouse on one of the edges of the block of cells ...

and drag to the new position

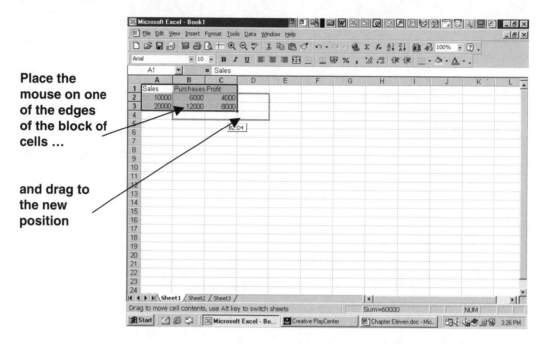

The entire block is relocated. But what about Cut and Paste? This is where we use the keyboard to achieve the same result. Select the cells again — they will become purple. We want to **Cut** to the Clipboard (see **Section One**) — press **Ctrl + X** together. The border of the cell block changes — to indicate we have started to work with that block.

The cells are selected

Press Ctrl + X to cut to the Clipboard

A dotted line appears, highlighting that we are acting of this block

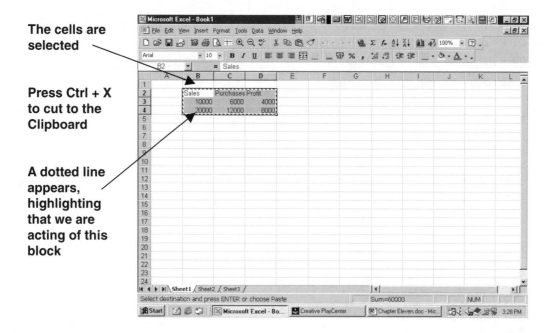

We want to move the block, so that cell B9 is in the top left corner. Click on cell B9. Two things happen: The block changes to white, but the dotted moving line is still there to indicate the block is still selected; cell B9 is activated, but no box appears, and there is no indication of where the pasted block will extend.

Using the mouse, we click in cell B9 to activate it ...

the black area is removed, but the moving dotted line is still there

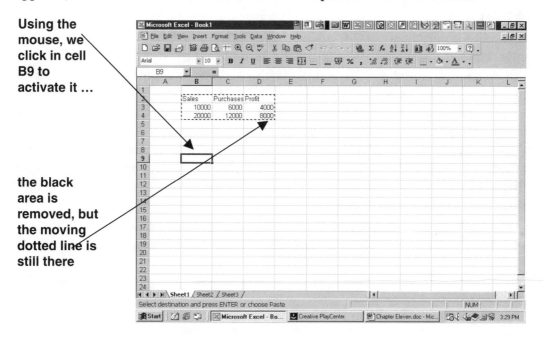

To paste the selection, press either **Return** or **Crtl + V**. The selection appears in a block, starting at B9. Note that the cut and paste facility is available from the Edit menu and from the toolbar — the Ctrl + X and Crtl + V keys are used because they are quicker to access.

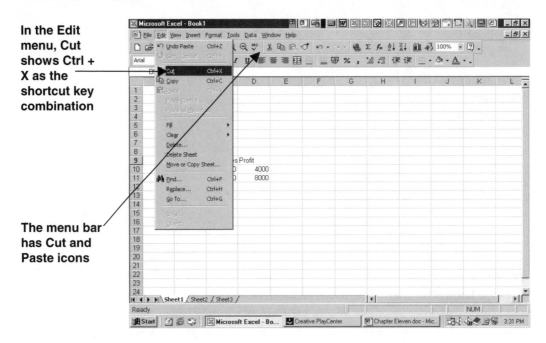

In the Edit menu, Cut shows Ctrl + X as the shortcut key combination

The menu bar has Cut and Paste icons

AUTOSUM

If a series of numbers is to be added together, the function =SUM is used. However, instead of manually typing in the formula and the cell range, the mouse can be used to select the formula from the toolbar, and then the range can be highlighted with the mouse.

This increases the speed of input as well as improving the accuracy of selecting the range. The example below will illustrate.

We want to total the sales, purchases and profit from our previous spreadsheet. We want to leave a space below the present figures to distinguish and highlight the total line, so select cell B13. Drag the mouse to cell D13 so that all three cells are selected (colored purple).

Click on the **AutoSum** icon in the toolbar — the Sigma button Σ. The total figure appears in the three cells and, if you check each, the appropriate formula is present.

Highlight the cells B13 to D13

Click on AutoSum ...

and the totals are inserted, with the appropriate formula

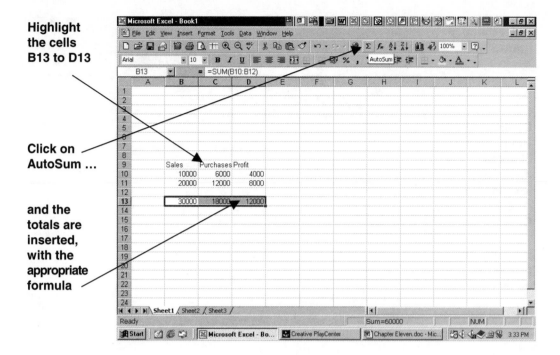

Of course, the table is correct for the present figures but it is incorrect if any of the Sales etc. figures are changed. We will cover this in **Section Three**.

There are limitations in using AutoSum, and you must be aware of them. Always be wary of shortcuts that involve the computer making decisions for you, unless you are fully conversant with how the computer arrives at its suggested solution.

The main problem with AutoSum arises because of the default range it selects. Look at this example.

Select the cell range with the mouse and press the **Delete** key. The cells are cleared. Type in the following entries:

Enter these figures

Use the Centre and Right Justify icons to make the text line up — See Chapter Ten

Heading, Nil and '–' are all text

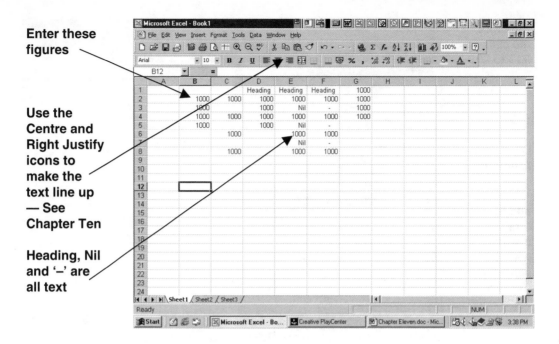

You will notice the Heading has been centered, Nil has been right aligned and – (dash) has been centered in the cell, then moved to the right to center it on the number. All of these adjustments are cosmetic. The totals are all £4,000.

The differences between these columns are:

- Column B   Numbers in a continuous stream.
- Column C   Numbers separated by blank cells.
- Column D   Numbers in a continuous stream, the first cell being text.
- Column E   Numbers separated by cells with text.
- Column F   Numbers separated by cells containing the minus sign.
- Column G   The same as column B, except starting one cell higher.

We want to use AutoSum in several different ways, in order to explore how it is working.

Select cells B10 to G10 and click on **AutoSum**. Everything is correct, except for the last series.

**Highlight
the range
and click
AutoSum**

**Everything
is correct,
EXCEPT
column G**

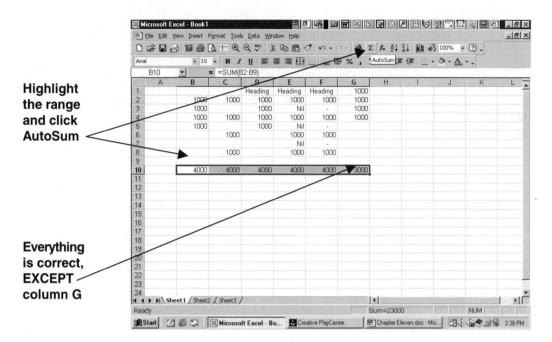

The function has used the first series of numbers (column B), and applied this to
the rest of the highlighted cells. Unless they are all within the same range, the
results will be incorrect.

Now we will **AutoSum** each column individually. Delete the cells from B10 to
G10. Make cell B10 active, and click **AutoSum**.

**Make B10
active, then
click
AutoSum ...**

**a dotted line
appears
around the
cells which
will be
included in
the formula
...**

**and the
formula is
shown in the
cell**

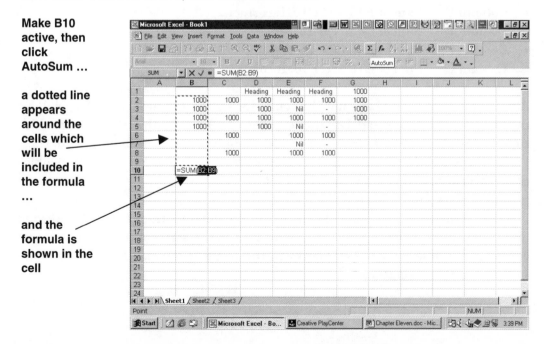

Once all the columns have been finished, the spreadsheet looks like this:

The results of double-clicking AutoSum ...

...so be careful!

	A	B	C	D	E	F	G	H	I	J	K	L
1				Heading	Heading	Heading	1000					
2		1000	1000	1000	1000	1000	1000					
3		1000		1000	Nil		1000					
4		1000	1000	1000	1000	1000	1000					
5		1000		1000	Nil	-						
6			1000		1000	1000						
7					Nil	-						
8			1000		1000	1000						
9												
10		4000	1000	5000	1000	1000	2000					

The results are peculiar:

- Column B   Sum of B2 to B9. Correct.
- Column C   Sum of C8 to C9. Incorrect.
- Column D   Sum of B10 and C10. Incorrect.
- Column E   Sum of E8 to E9. Incorrect.
- Column F   Sum of F8 to F9. Incorrect.
- Column G   Sum of E10 and F10. Incorrect.

AutoSum goes to the source that the computer thinks you are using. This will be the closest number. If you delete the total from C10 and, with D10 active, double-click on **AutoSum**, the figure now becomes £4,000, and the formula is D2 to D9.

The same applies to the cell G10. **Delete F10**, activate cell G10 and double-click **AutoSum**, and it correctly selects G1 to G9.

This is shown in the screen shot below.

The conclusion is, therefore, do not accept the defaults from AutoSum. Always insert your own range. This is especially true if the series of numbers extends beyond the visible screen. Any blanks in the series will cause Excel to stop the AutoSum range prematurely.

Delete C10 ...

then select D10 and double-click AutoSum. The calculation is now correct

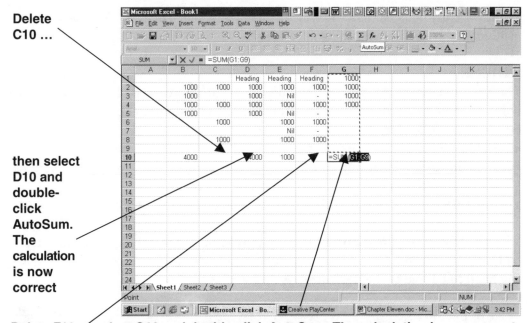

Delete F10 ... select G10 and double-click AutoSum. The calculation is now correct

We will now look at how to use AutoSum to begin the formula, and the mouse or keyboard to select the range of cells.

Select the entries in the spreadsheet and delete them. Enter the following, and click on **AutoSum**.

Enter the numbers in the cells ...

then activate cell B11 and click AutoSum ...

a moving dotted line shows the cell range selected

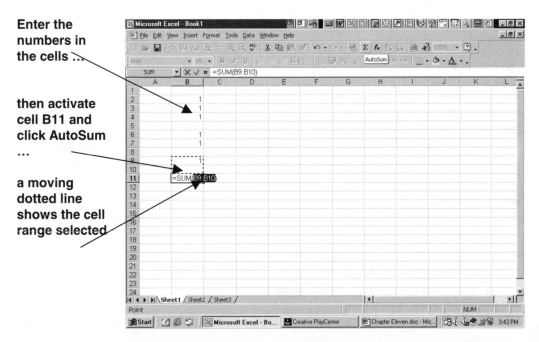

What we must do is change the range of cells selected. To do this we need two co-ordinates: the anchor, and the end reference.

MOUSE

Place the mouse on the first cell in the range (in this case B11, because we are going to work upwards). The pre-selected range is automatically replaced. Then do one of the following:

- Hold down the left mouse button and drag to the new reference
- Hold down the **Shift** key and, without holding down the mouse button, move the pointer to the end cell and click (B2 in this case)
- Press **F8** (this locks the first cell), then click on the last cell in the range (B2).

With all of the above, press **Enter** to inform the computer that the input is complete.

Using **F8** is probably the best, because it provides pinpoint control but allows the hand to be free of the keyboard.

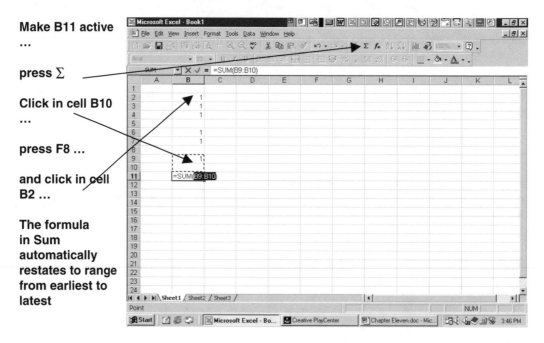

Make B11 active ...

press Σ

Click in cell B10 ...

press F8 ...

and click in cell B2 ...

The formula in Sum automatically restates to range from earliest to latest

KEYBOARD

The keyboard options are similar to the mouse, except for click and drag:

- Hold down shift, and extend the range with the arrow keys
- Press **F8** to anchor, and extend the range with the arrow keys.

The advantages and disadvantages of either input device are the same as discussed earlier — speed of scrolling and control.

Practice, and decide which suits you best in any given circumstances.

ABSOLUTE AND RELATIVE CELL ADDRESSING

When a cell is referenced in Excel, it shows the address in the style =A1, which in English reads as "the cell at the intersection of column A and row 1".

If cell B2 is referenced, there are two ways in which it can be described with reference to cell A1:

- It can be the cross section of column B and row 2 (the absolute reference)
- It can be one column to the right and one row down from the current cell (the relative address).

The method by which we find cell B2 is irrelevant if we only refer to these two cells, and we do not use the formula elsewhere — they both point to the same place. If we move the cells, Excel will change the addresses accordingly, irrespective of whether they are absolute or relative.

The only time the type of addressing becomes important is when we are copying the formula. We must decide then whether we want always to refer to:

- Cell B2
- The cell one column to the right and one row down
- Column B but change the row each time
- Row 2, but change the column each time.

The examples below will illustrate the differences.

Type "Fixed" in cell B3 and "Variable 1" in cell B4. Drag B4 to AutoFill down to cell B8. In cell D3, enter =B3, and copy the formula down to D8. The spreadsheet looks like this:

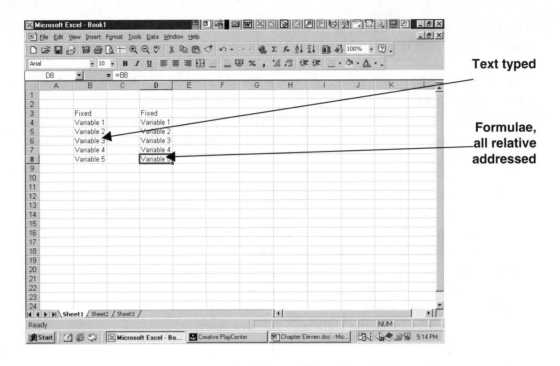

Copy the formula in D3 to D8 to E3 to E8. The results look like this.

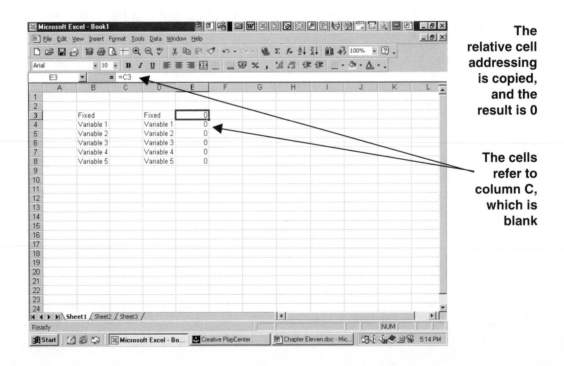

In English, the referencing is "=the cell two columns to the left". Now, delete columns D and E, and enter the formula =B3 in cell D3. Press the F4 key. The formula becomes =$B$3. Copy the formula down to cell D8. The screen looks like this.

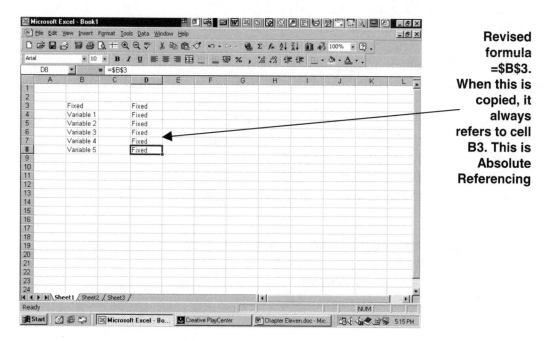

Revised formula =$B$3. When this is copied, it always refers to cell B3. This is Absolute Referencing

Copy the cells D3 to D8 to E3 to E8. The word "Fixed" still appears.

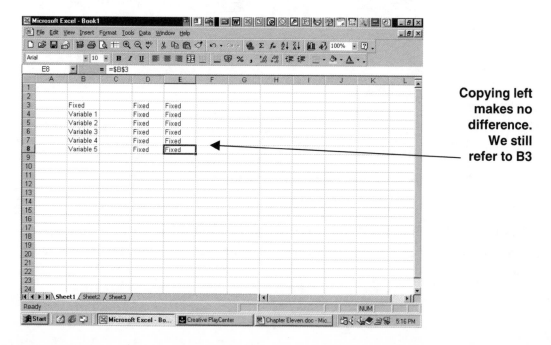

Copying left makes no difference. We still refer to B3

We will now demonstrate mixed referencing — keeping one item (column or row) constant, and making the other relative.

Delete the entries, and in D3 enter =B3. Press **F4** once, and the reference changes to =$B$3. Press **F4** again. This changes to =B$3. Copy the formula to D8, then to column H. The screen is shown below.

Explaining each column in turn:

- Column D   Referenced to Fixed in cell B3.
- Column E   Referenced to cell C3. The row (3) is constant at all times — the column (C) is two columns to the left of the current cell.
- Column F   Refers to cell D3, NOT cell B3. Type "Test" in cell D3 and prove this — the word "Fixed" in column F is replaced by "Test" in ALL cells in columns F and H, but not D.
- Column G   Refers to cell E3 only, so it is blank.
- Column H   Refers to cell F3. It also changes to "Test".

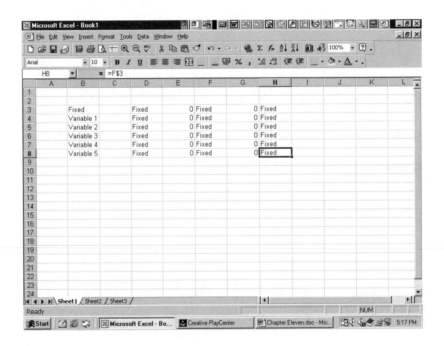

Delete the cells D3 to H8. Enter =B3 in cell D3, and press **F4** three times. The formula becomes =$B3. Copy to D8, then to column H as before. The screen looks like this.

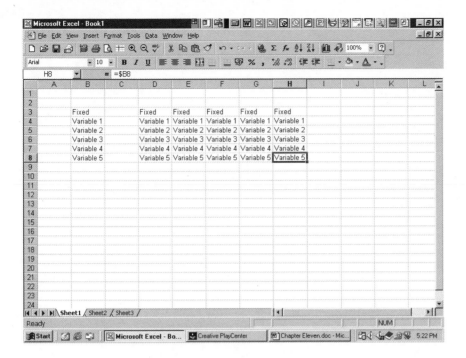

All cells refer to column B, but differ in the row they refer to.

Practice with cell addressing, and note the results — try entering the Fixed, Variable entries in cells B3 to H3, and work from cells B5 to H10.

As pointed out earlier, cell addressing is important when copying formulae. It is efficient, because it means a cell's formula does not need to be retyped. However, unless you are sure of the results of the mixture of constant and variable column and row headings, it can be dangerous, and produce incorrect results.

NEXT

In the next chapter, we look at how to maximize control of the spreadsheet by working with the screen.

Chapter Twelve

MAXIMIZING EFFICIENCY WITH SCREEN REAL ESTATE

In the land of DOS, one screen view was King . . .

We know how to input, we know how to control how the cell displays, we know how to print, how to save files . . .

We now want to practice working with the screen display, and taking advantage of the capabilities of Windows. This chapter is short but using Windows effectively, above all else, will provide you with the means to structure and work with your spreadsheet, and allow you to build a robust, error-free model.

Start Excel, and enter the following into the sheet:

Cell A1	100	**Cell G1**	200	**Cell Q1**	300	**Cell AA1**	400
Cell A15	25	**Cell G15**	35	**Cell Q15**	45	**Cell AA15**	55
Cell A28	71	**Cell G28**	72	**Cell Q28**	73	**Cell AA28**	74

Press **Ctrl + Home**. The spreadsheet looks like this:

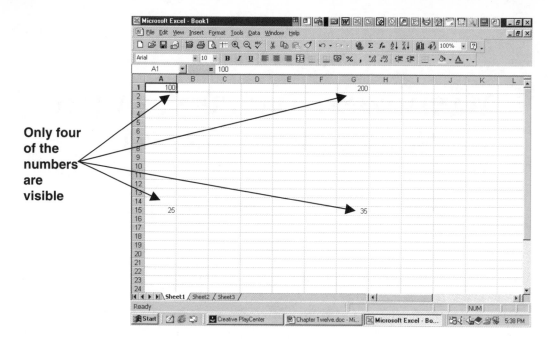

**Only four
of the
numbers
are
visible**

What we want is to have easy access to all of the numbers. First, we will take another window view.

In the current window, move to AA1 by pressing **Ctrl + →** repeatedly. Once AA1 is highlighted, press **Ctrl + →** to move to IV1, then press **Ctrl + ←**. This lines up AA1 on the left-hand side. Now select **Window** in the menu, then **New Window**.

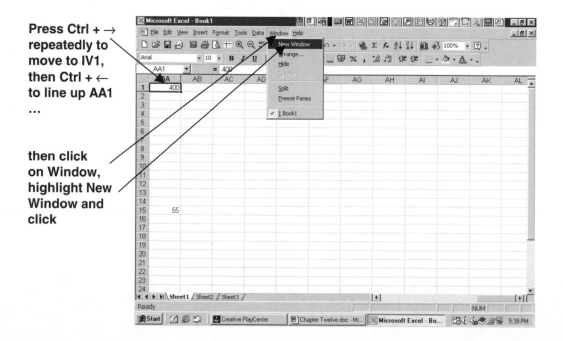

**Press Ctrl + →
repeatedly to
move to IV1,
then Ctrl + ←
to line up AA1
...**

**then click
on Window,
highlight New
Window and
click**

A new window appears. However, you will notice that the cell highlighter is on cell A1, not cell AA1. The screen is annotated to highlight important details.

The title has changed — the :2 indicates window 2

The two windows are displayed in the menu. The active Window is ticked

The two sheets are also included on the taskbar

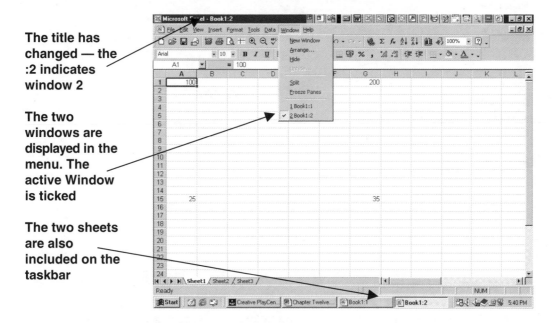

A new window always displays at cell A1.

We will now arrange the two windows side by side. Click on **Window** in the menu, highlight **Arrange** and click.

Click on Window...

highlight Arrange ...

and click

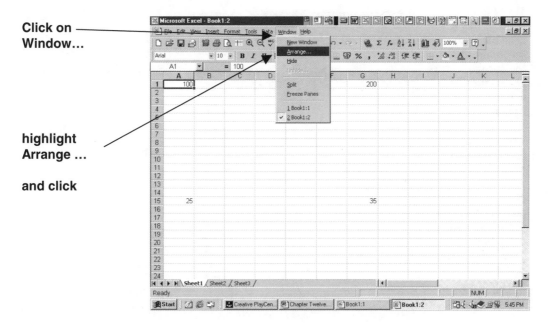

The following dialogue box appears:

**Practice
with the
choices ...**

**for most
purposes,
Tiled is
best ...**

**click OK
to accept**

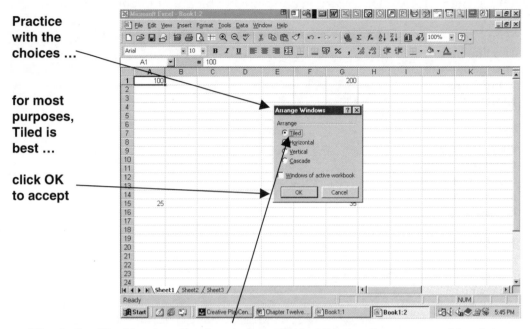

**The Active Workbook option has to be selected if more than one workbook is
open, and you only want to tile the active one**

We will accept the default — tiled. The screen changes to:

**The active
window has a
Blue bar with
the name of
the spread-
sheet, and the
window
number**

**The inactive
window has a
grey bar...**

**click
anywhere in
the window to
activate it.
This
deactivates
the other
windows**

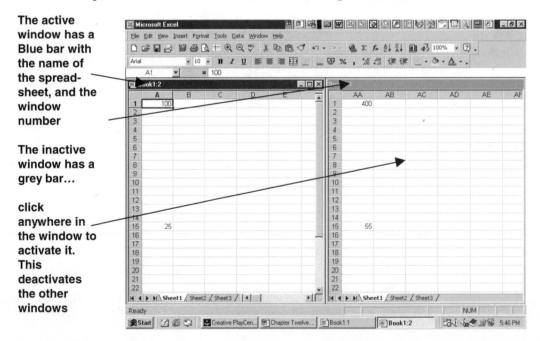

Not very useful on the face of it. What we gain by having two screen shots available, we lose by having a small working area that is not necessarily suitable for working in.

Change the magnification, first in the left pane, then in the right pane, until the numbers in the lowest cell are visible.

With the windows tiled, click the button to reduce magnification ...

click the button several times until all the numbers are visible

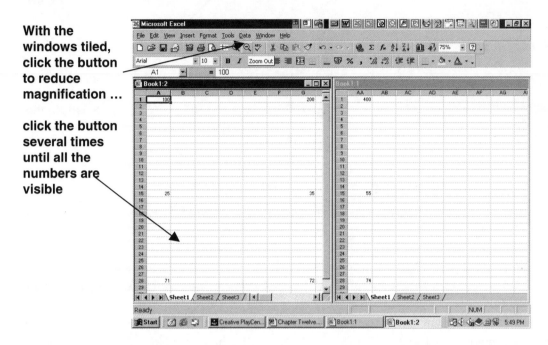

There is still one set of numbers that we cannot see because, even at this low magnification, the cells are too widely spaced. We will freeze the panes in order to get around this problem.

In the right pane, move to cell Q1 (**Ctrl + ←**) and, with the mouse in cell R2, click on the **Freeze Panes** button. A line appears in line with the left-hand side of cell R2 from top to bottom of the screen, and in line with the top of cell R2 from left to right.

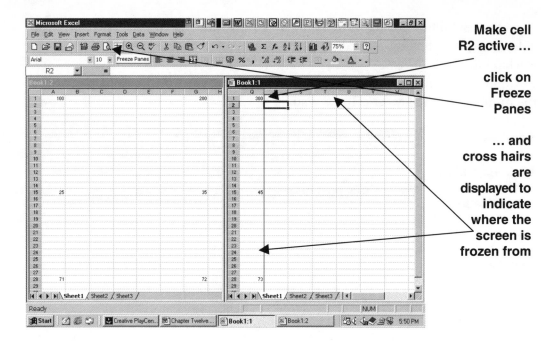

Now, make cell Q1 active and press **Ctrl + →**. Cell AA1 appears on screen. Press **Ctrl + →** again to get to cell IV1. Press **Ctrl + ←** and cell AA1 appears beside cell Q1.

The important point to note is that, despite the fact that the cell can only be maneuvered in the area to/from cell R2 with the arrow keys, you can use the mouse to make cells in the frozen area active. You can, therefore, easily move into this area to put in headings or change information without having to un-freeze and refreeze the panes.

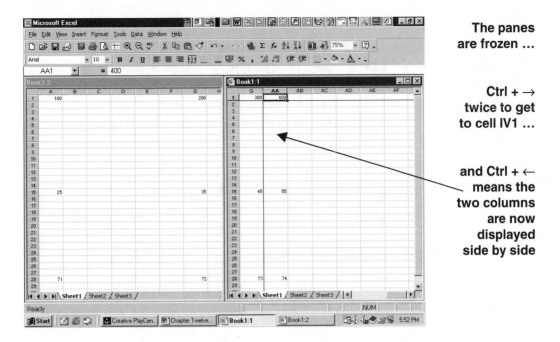

**The panes
are frozen ...**

**Ctrl + →
twice to get
to cell IV1 ...**

**and Ctrl + ←
means the
two columns
are now
displayed
side by side**

To display all of the cells again quickly, click in cell Q1 and, using the arrow keys, move one cell to the right. All of the column headings are now in sight.

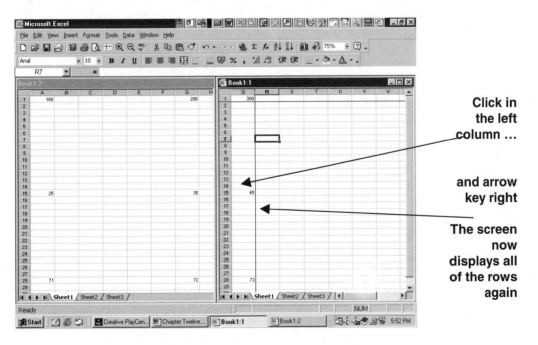

**Click in
the left
column ...**

**and arrow
key right**

**The screen
now
displays all
of the rows
again**

We can now view data in different parts of the spreadsheet at the same time, and we can change the amount of information shown on each screen shot. We will manipulate the screen a little more. We can quickly toggle a pane to minimized, full screen and default size by clicking in the **Window Resize** button. There are three buttons: a flat line, a box (or two boxes one on top of the other) and an X. Click on the center box on the left pane — it goes full screen. Click on the center box again (it now shows two boxes, one on top of the other) — it goes back to tiled.

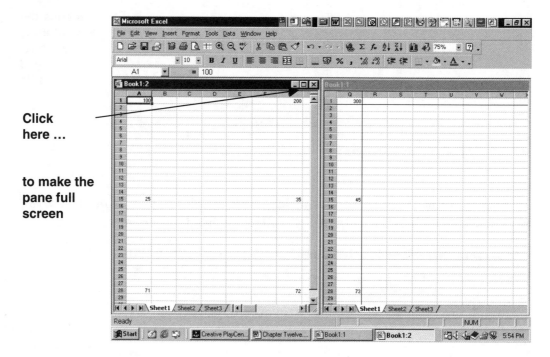

Click here …

to make the pane full screen

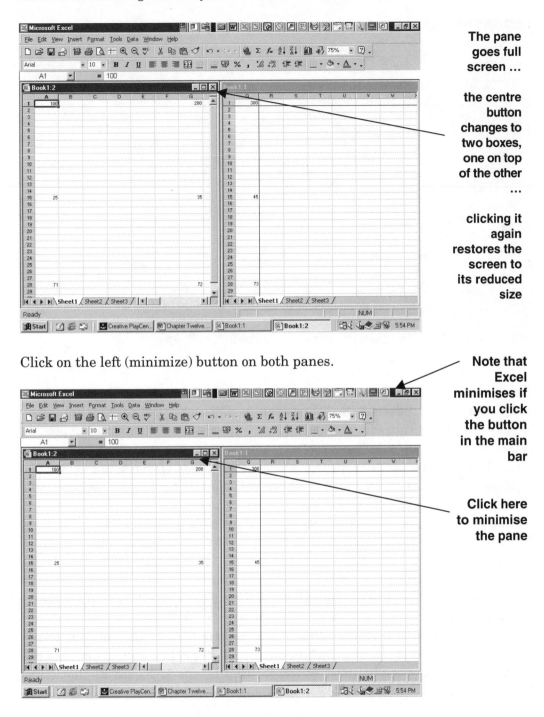

The pane goes full screen …

the centre button changes to two boxes, one on top of the other …

clicking it again restores the screen to its reduced size

Click on the left (minimize) button on both panes.

Note that Excel minimises if you click the button in the main bar

Click here to minimise the pane

When both panes are minimized, the screen looks like the one shown below. To restore the Window, or to switch between them without closing or minimizing, click on **Window** in the menu, and click on the pane you want.

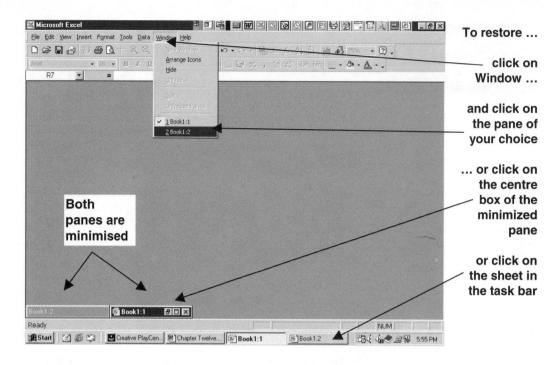

Being able to zoom down and display information in different sections of the same sheet, or in different sheets, or even in different workbooks, is extremely useful. Combining this with the ability to use the mouse on the panes to pick up cell references makes it indispensable.

In this example, we will copy the information in cells Q1, Q15 and Q28 to the equivalent reference in column C, and we will move the cell contents from cells AA1, AA15 and AA28 to the equivalent reference in column E.

Starting with the two panes, freeze the right-hand pane to show columns Q and AA as before. Reduce the magnification to fit everything in to the screen as before.

To copy the information from one cell to another, we enter a formula in the cell, in the form **=Cell Reference** (all Excel formulae start with an equals sign).

Therefore, click in the left pane and activate cell C1. Press = on the keyboard to enter it in the cell, then move the mouse pointer to the right-hand pane and click (this activates the pane). Click in cell Q1. A dotted line appears around cell Q1 to show it has been selected. Press **Return** on the keyboard so that Excel knows the operation is complete, and cell C1 now shows the contents of Q1.

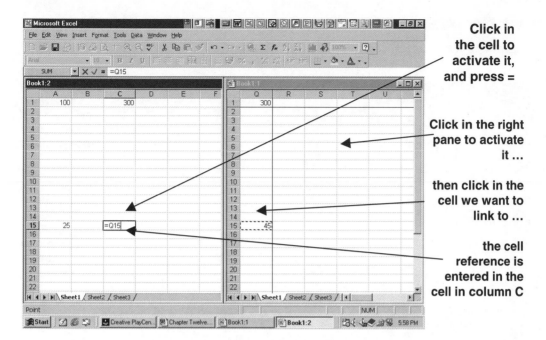

After the first cell has been completed, it may be quicker to use the keyboard for further entries. With the cell C1 highlighted, copy the formula to the Clipboard (**Ctrl + C**). Make cell C15 the active cell and paste in the contents of the Clipboard (**Ctrl + V**). The reference to the cell contents has been adjusted by Excel. The use of cell addresses is covered in **Section Four**, but the important point to note here is that there is still keyboard control available if you prefer.

We covered drag and drop in **Section One**. This is exactly the same, except that it is working across two panes.

Activate cell AA1. Place the mouse on one of the edges of the cell so that it becomes a pointer, left-click the mouse button and, holding it down, drag the mouse to the second pane. A shaded area, representing the cell, moves across. Move it to cell E1 and release the mouse button — the contents have moved.

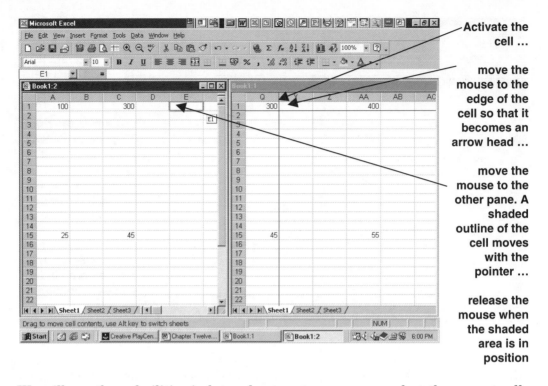

Activate the cell ...

move the mouse to the edge of the cell so that it becomes an arrow head ...

move the mouse to the other pane. A shaded outline of the cell moves with the pointer ...

release the mouse when the shaded area is in position

We will use these facilities in later chapters to ensure we select the correct cells in our spreadsheet.

HIDE

If there is more than one window in the spreadsheet and AutoSave is activated, then, when the file is being saved, the pane designated as window one is made active, irrespective of which pane you are working in.

This can mean that either you lose your place or the operation you are currently completing is cancelled. This is not a problem as such, although it is inconvenient. To avoid the difficulties, hide window one, and work by tiling windows two and three.

To hide window one, activate it (in preference to window two) and then select **Window** from the menu, then **Hide**.

The window can be made visible again by clicking on **Window** in the menu and then clicking on **Unhide** and selecting the window, although there is no advantage in this – if another screen-shot is required, it is quicker to open a new window.

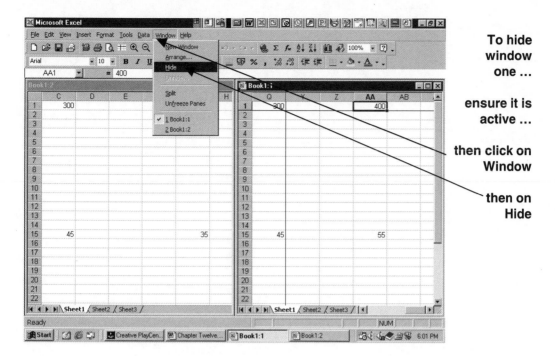

SPREADSHEET DESIGN

That almost concludes **Section Two**.

In **Sections One** and **Two**, we have seen how the mechanics of spreadsheets work. In **Section Three**, we look at some of the methods adopted to ensure spreadsheets are properly designed and tested. It is not a long section, but once again it is good background knowledge to possess, and we will put it into context when we build the spreadsheets in **Section Four**.

But first, in **Chapter Thirteen**, a quick look at some other features of Excel.

Chapter Thirteen

WITH EXCEL YOU CAN . . .

And there's more!

The purpose of this chapter is to act as a quick reference guide to the areas of Excel not covered elsewhere.

HELP

Excel comes with a substantial library of help files, providing information, advice and examples. Help is accessed in two ways:

- Start Office Assistant by selecting it from the Help menu.
- Click on Help in the menu, then select **Microsoft Excel Help.**

These are illustrated below.

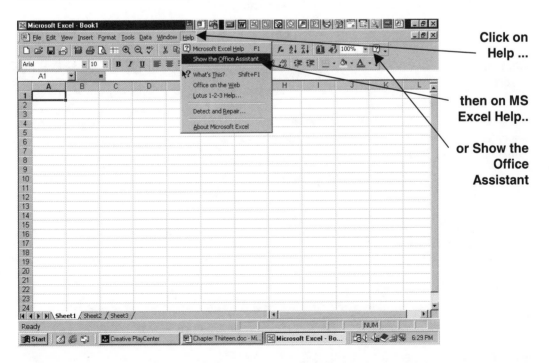

When Help is accessed the following screen appears:

**Help is organised
in three ways:**

**1.Contents (by
topic)**
2.Answer Wizard
3.Index

**In Index, type the
word
(for example, IF)**

**Or Select from the
list of keywords**

**Then select the
topic.**

**The Help file is
displayed.**

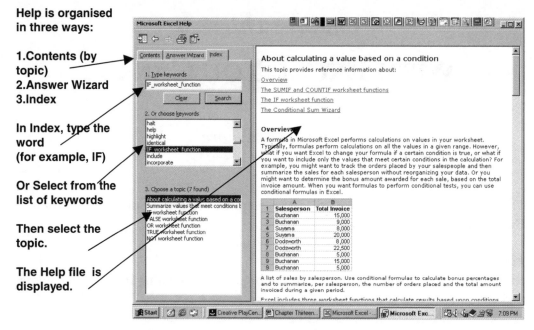

FUNCTIONS

There are many in built functions in Excel, and it is the flexibility of these items
that makes the spreadsheet such a useful analysis tool.

**Click on
Insert ...**

**then on
Function**

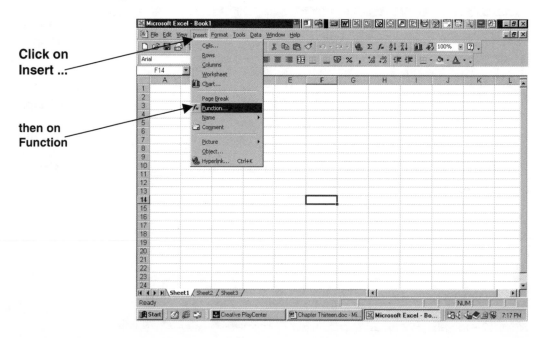

This displays the following dialog box:

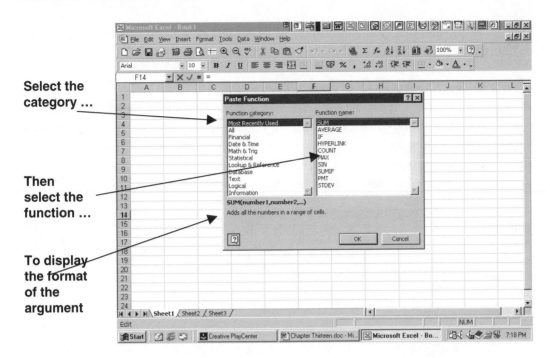

Select the
category ...

Then
select the
function ...

To display
the format
of the
argument

If you are not clear on how to use a particular function, access **Help**, and review the examples used there to illustrate it.

The more commonly used functions, from our perspective, are briefly explained below:

- IF   This tests IF a condition is met. If it is, the first part of the
                    expression calculates. If not, the second part calculates. The
                    format is =IF(condition, do this if it calculates, do this if it
                    doesn't).

- AND   This tests if part A AND part B are both correct. If so, it
                    returns TRUE (which has a logical value of 1) or FALSE
                    (which has a logical value of 0). Therefore, if you combine it
                    with multiplication of a cell's contents, it will give a value or
                    zero.

- OR   As for AND, except only one of the items need be true.

- ROUND   This rounds a number off to the required level of precision —
                    whole number, thousands, two decimal places etc. The format
                    is =ROUND (value or cell, level of precision). The precision is
                    a number, so 2 equals two decimal places, -3 equals the
                    nearest thousand etc.

These are used in the spreadsheet models, and are fully illustrated there.

There are also functions for calculating depreciation, internal rate of return, standard deviation, performing lookups on databases etc. See **Help** for your specific requirements. Some examples of using these built-in functions are given in **Chapter Seventeen** and the chapters following.

COPYING AND MOVING SHEETS

If you have set up a spreadsheet with certain formatting or formulae, you may wish to copy the sheet within the same spreadsheet, or copy or move it to another spreadsheet. You may also want to change the order of the sheets within a spreadsheet. The steps involved are explained below.

Place the mouse pointer on the sheet name tab and right-click.

With the mouse pointer on the name tab, right-click …

Select the Move or Copy option with the mouse and left-click

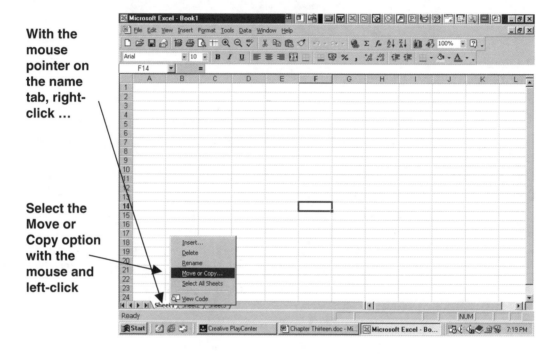

The same result is achieved by selecting Edit, Move or Copy Sheet from the main menu.

When the option is selected, the dialog box below appears.

The options within this are:

- Choosing copy. If not chosen the sheet is moved.
- Choosing the destination book. By default the current book is chosen. If it is to be moved, the second book must be open so that it is included in the list.

Select the sheet ...

click on the Create a copy option button ...

select the book (if it is copied or moved to another book) ...

click OK to complete the action

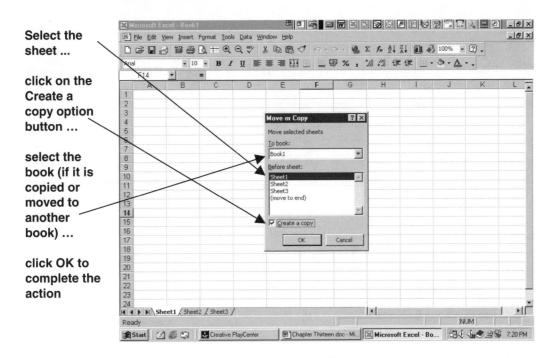

The new sheet is inserted, as shown below:

The copy of Sheet 1

Notice the name given

Double-click on the tab to highlight the name, then type in a new name

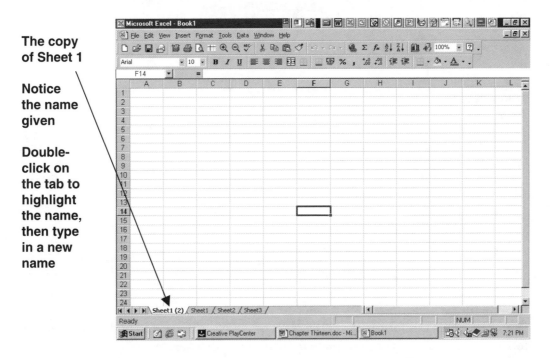

Naming of the new sheet is automatic. If the sheet is copied within the same book, it is named the same as the original, except that its name includes a bracketed number to distinguish it. If it is copied to another book, it is named the same as the original, provided the name is not used by another sheet in the new book. If it is, the bracketed number is inserted.

To move a sheet from one book to another, make sure the **Copy** box noted above is unchecked. To move a sheet within a book (to change the order of the sheets within a book), select the **Sheet** tab by clicking and holding down the left mouse button, and then drag it to the new position. Releasing the mouse "drops" the sheet in its new location.

DATA ENTRY FORMS

If a list is being entered in a spreadsheet, Excel can create a simple data entry form, instead of the user entering the details directly into the spreadsheet cells. It will also navigate through the list and display the corresponding entries.

To prepare a form, select the cells concerned, including the labels. From the menu, select **Data**, then **Form**.

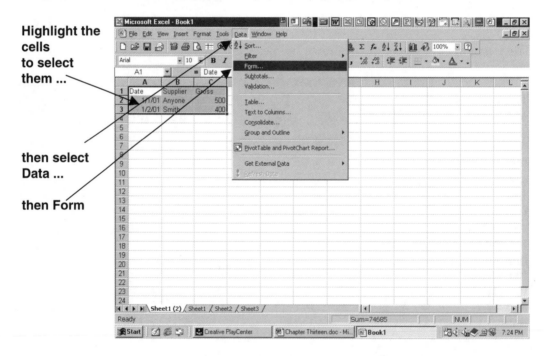

Excel generates the form automatically, and allows the user to add a new record, delete a record, scroll through the list, or undertake a search.

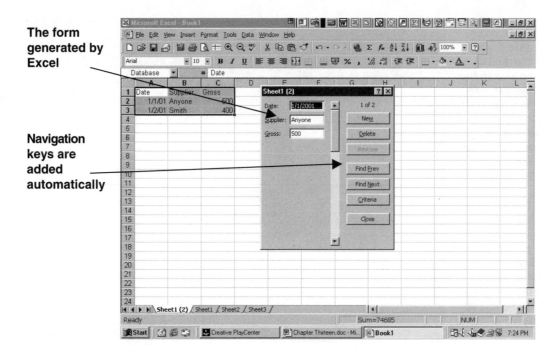

The form generated by Excel

Navigation keys are added automatically

Data entry forms provide a pleasant user interface, although there are drawbacks:

- Entry is slower than direct entry into the cells
- The form is only provided "as is" and it cannot be changed.

MACROS AND VISUAL BASIC CODE

The Office suite of programs has a common programming language running through it — Visual Basic. This can be coded directly, or Excel can generate it by recording the actions in a macro. There is no difference in the actual code, although there is better control when the code is written directly by the user.

To record a macro, activate the VB toolbar, by placing the mouse pointer in the toolbar section, right-clicking to display the toolbars available, and then selecting the VB toolbar.

The first two buttons that appear are Run Macro and Record Macro. The other buttons are VB-related items. Clicking on **Record Macro** and then entering the required keystrokes will create a macro, which is then converted to VB code. When Record Macro is selected the button changes to **Stop Recording** button.

Macros and VB code execute very quickly, and you must be absolutely certain that the code does exactly what you require — nothing more, and nothing less. An error generated by an incomplete or incorrect macro may not be immediately obvious.

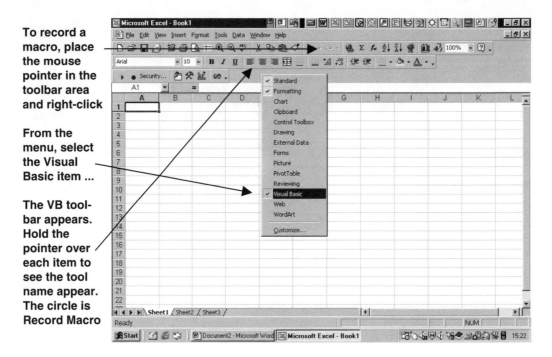

To record a macro, place the mouse pointer in the toolbar area and right-click

From the menu, select the Visual Basic item ...

The VB tool-bar appears. Hold the pointer over each item to see the tool name appear. The circle is Record Macro

GOAL SEEK

Goal Seek takes the guesswork out of working out numbers. Look at the spreadsheet below.

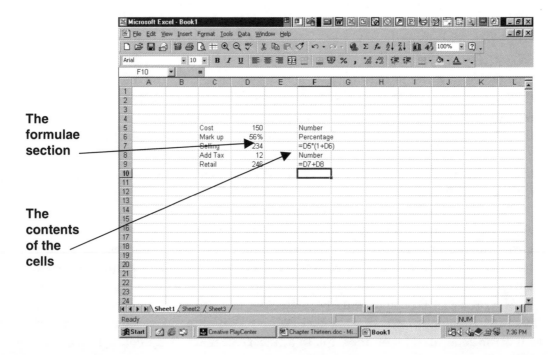

The formulae section

The contents of the cells

What is the Cost, if the Retail is £1,000?

To calculate using Goal Seek, click on **Tools**, **Goal Seek**. The following dialog box appears.

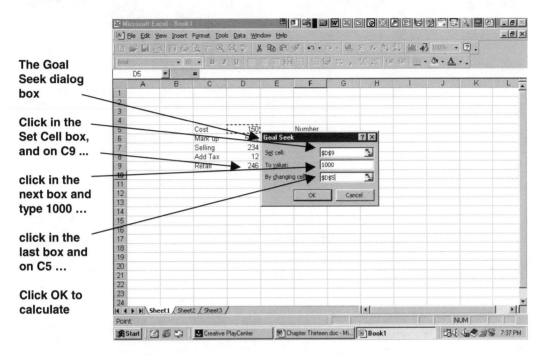

The Goal Seek dialog box

Click in the Set Cell box, and on C9 ...

click in the next box and type 1000 ...

click in the last box and on C5 ...

Click OK to calculate

When OK is clicked, cell C9 is changed to 633.333, and the result in C13 is 1000.

We use Goal Seek to calculate what the Gross Pay must be to produce required Net Pay in the spreadsheet we build in **Section Four**.

GRID LINES

By default, the spreadsheet shows gridlines on the screen, but does not print them on paper. Both of these defaults can be changed.

To turn off displayed gridlines, select **Tools** from the menu, then **Options**. A tab dialog box is displayed, one of which is headed **View**. This contains the display options, including gridlines on/off.

The screen shot is shown below.

To turn gridlines on/off when printing, go into **File**, **Page Setup**. Select the tab headed **Sheet**.

Click on Tools, then Options. The following dialog box is displayed

Select the View Tab ...

click on the check box to turn gridlines on/off

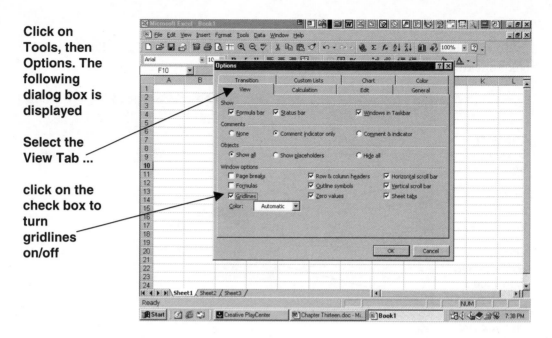

The Page Setup dialog box is shown below:

Select File, Page Setup

Select the Sheet tab

Select the Gridlines on/off check box

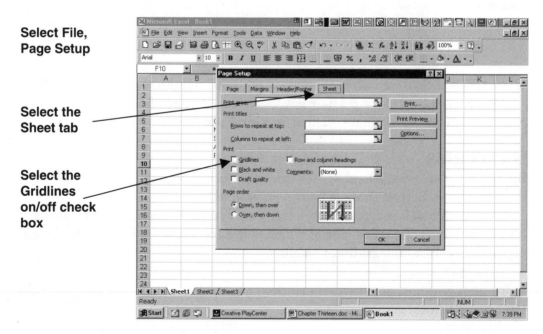

USING COLOR

Color can be useful for highlighting important areas of the spreadsheet — for distinguishing between input and output cells, or for making the spreadsheet look more attractive.

There are two types of color — the color of the text and numbers (the font), and the color of the background (the cell itself).

The default color for the font is black, and the cell background is white. To change these, select the cell or cells and select either the **Font Color** button or the **Fill Color** button from the toolbar.

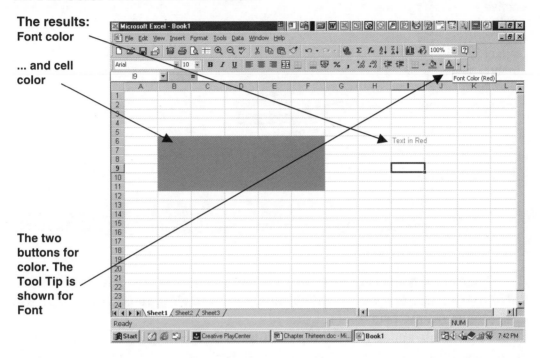

Click on the down arrow of the Color buttons for a full chart of the colors available, which will include **Automatic**, for the default font, and **No Fill**, for the default Cell Background Color. Clicking on these restores any highlighted cells to their original state.

DOCUMENTATION

Spreadsheet documentation comes in two types — the formal documentation written to explain how to use and maintain the spreadsheet, usually referred to as the Reference Manual and the User's Manual, and documentation written within the spreadsheet, consisting of notes and guidance.

The main difference between them is in scope and depth. We will look at how to attach comments to cells, but bear in mind that, whilst they can provide guidance to the user on what to input to that cell, or how to use that part of the spreadsheet, they cannot replace full and formal documentation procedures.

To insert a comment in a cell, activate the cell and place the mouse cursor inside the cell, then right-click the mouse. Highlight **Insert Comment**.

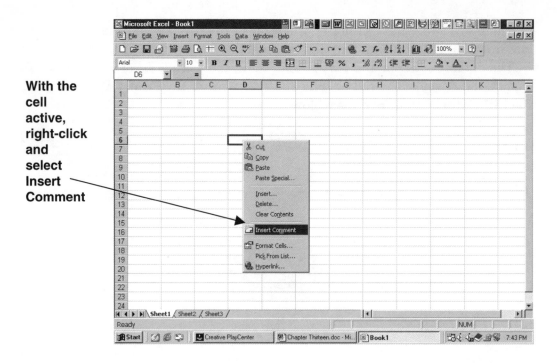

With the cell active, right-click and select Insert Comment

The Comment box appears and the note can be typed in. By default, the registered user's name appears. Highlight it and press **Delete** to remove it. You will also need to remove bold from the line

A red triangle appears in the top right-hand corner of the cell to indicate that a note is attached. Holding the mouse over the cell, whether it is the active cell or not, will cause the comment to be displayed.

If the cell with a comment attached is activated and, with the mouse pointer in the cell, the right mouse button is clicked, the menu list now displays **Edit Comment**, **Delete Comment** and **Show Comment**.

Edit and Delete are self-explanatory. Show Comment displays the comment permanently, whether the mouse is on the cell or not. If it is selected, right-clicking in the cell again brings up a menu choice of **Hide Comment**. This restores it to its default display (i.e. only visible when the mouse is on the cell).

**The
Comment is
attached to
the cell**

**Notice the
red triangle**

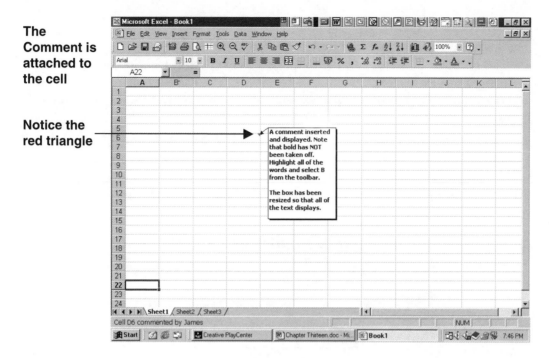

BORDERS

A border is one or more lines on one or more sides of one or several cells. Several
examples are shown below. The cell gridlines have been turned off to highlight
the various borders.

**Select the
down arrow
to display
the types of
border
available**

**Examples of
borders**

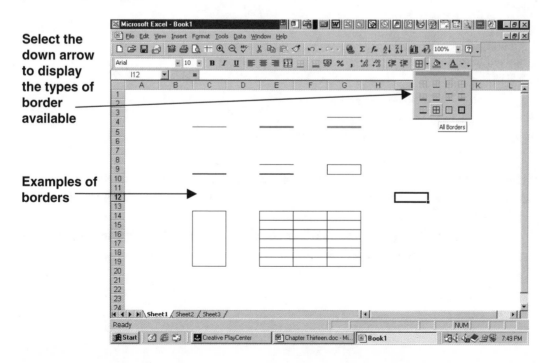

NAMING RANGES

There are several reasons for naming a range of cells:

- The named range can be used to quickly move to that location instead of using Page Down, etc.
- The named range can be selected, the print area set, and the range printed out.
- The named range can be used in formulae. However, this is not as useful as it appears.

To name a range, select the cells and click in the **Name Range** box. Type in a name and press **Return**.

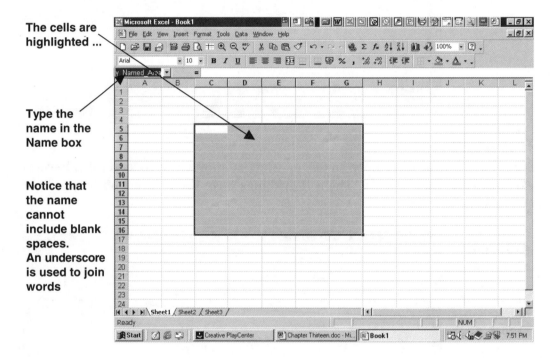

The cells are highlighted ...

Type the name in the Name box

Notice that the name cannot include blank spaces. An underscore is used to join words

The cells in the range do not have to be in one block. Holding down **Ctrl** as the cells are selected allows different sections of cells to be selected before the range is named.

To delete or change the named range, click on **Insert** in the menu, then on **Name**, then on **Define**. A dialog box allowing deletion etc. appears.

The screen below shows the menu.

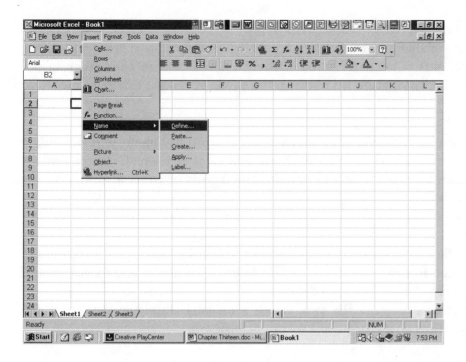

Once the **Define** option is clicked, the following screen appears. The named range can then be deleted or amended.

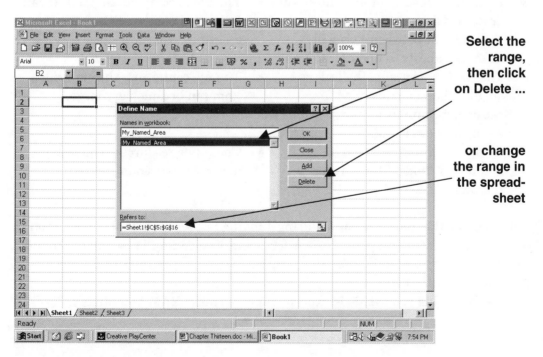

Select the range, then click on Delete ...

or change the range in the spread-sheet

OBJECT LINKING AND EMBEDDING

Linking and embedding are the terms used when information from one source (for example, part of an Excel spreadsheet) is placed into another program (for example, Word). The distinction between the two is explained briefly below.

Linking

The part of the spreadsheet that appears in the Word document is really only a reference to the original. When the Word document is opened, it accesses the spreadsheet on the hard disk and updates the figures or chart displayed in the Word document.

Embedding

The part of the spreadsheet that appears in the Word document is a copy of the original. It therefore exists within the Word document and it still exists, even if the original spreadsheet has been deleted.

The differences between the two, which are really the advantages and disadvantages of the two methods, are set out below:

Linked Files	Embedded Files
• The linked file updates when the original changes.	• Changed files must be recopied if changes are to be shown.
• Both the spreadsheet and the word-processed document must exist. Passing files between PCs will affect the ability to update the link.	• The file is complete in itself. It can be passed to other PCs without creating error messages.
• The file that contains the link is smaller than an embedded file, because it contains a reference, not a copy of the original.	• The file containing the embedded item can become very large.
• Computer resources must be greater for linked files to run at reasonable speed	• Computer resources required are lower, and speed is greater.

To conclude, the main reason for using Linking is to ensure that information is always up-to-date. The main reason for using Embedding is because computer resources are not adequate for the purpose — usually notified to the user as a "low memory" message.

The only thing you can do is experiment or increase RAM accordingly.

THE LINKING AND EMBEDDING PROCESS

The starting point for both is the same. The entire process is shown diagrammatically below.

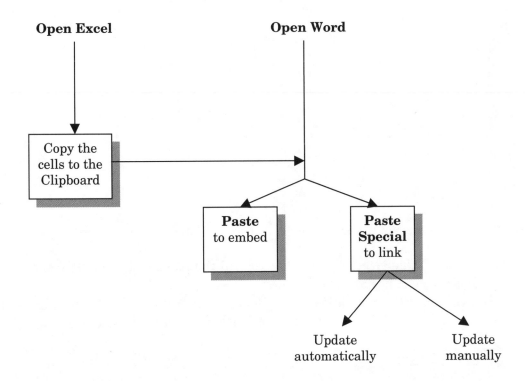

We will demonstrate embedding first.

Start Excel and Word, and type **Embed** in cell A1.

Copy cell A1 to the clipboard (**Ctrl+C**), then switch to Word.

Paste the clipboard into Word (**Ctrl+V**). Cell A1 is embedded in Word.

Enter 15 in A3, 4 in A4, and =A3 + A4 in A5.

Copy A3, A4 and A5 as one set of cells to Word.

For the purposes of the screen shot below, Word and Excel are tiled. In practice, using full screen is better, because more information is displayed.

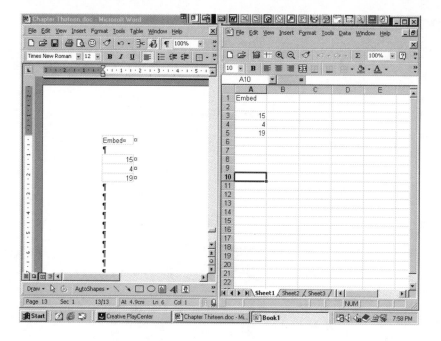

Now, in Excel, change cell A3 to 20 — cell A5 changes to 24. Look at Word, and you will see that it has not changed.

We will now link the cells to Word. Select A3 to A5 and copy to the clipboard (**Ctrl+C**). Activate Word and select the paragraph in which to place the cells.

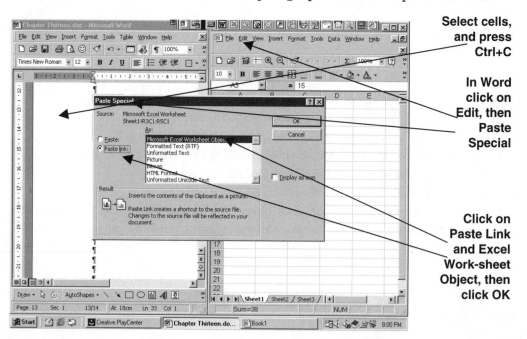

The link is set to update automatically. Now when you change the figure in cell A3 in Excel, Word updates the second (linked) block, but does not update the first (embedded) block.

To change automatic link updates to manual link updates, access **Edit, Links** in the Word menu. It is accessed in Word, not Excel, because this is where the link information is held.

SECTION THREE — SPREADSHEET DESIGN

That concludes the review of what Excel can do. We now need to look at how we can actually use the program in a controlled and well-managed way.

The next section lays down the foundation for designing spreadsheet models that will work, and that are suitable for the purpose — neither too unwieldy, nor too shallow. And after that, we will put it all into practice!

Section Three
SPREADSHEET DESIGN

SECTION INDEX

SECTION OVERVIEW

In this section, we will review the theory of spreadsheet design — in particular, how to ensure that the models built produce correct results, are manageable if changes are required and are prepared on a timely basis.

The term theory is used because, as with all things in life, the rules and stipulations are open to interpretation, amendment and the application of judgement.

It has been contended that, to be successful, anyone wishing to undertake spreadsheet modeling should follow the practices developed and adopted by computer programmers. **Chapter Fourteen**, therefore, reviews spreadsheet modeling from a programmer's perspective, and discusses the methods for undertaking a major development of a spreadsheet model. This chapter is from a complicated model perspective, looking down.

This would certainly change the approach of the majority of accountants, but in order to do this effectively an accountant should be in possession of substantially greater knowledge of programming procedures and skills than is likely to exist — or be reasonable to expect.

Thus **Chapter Fifteen** reviews spreadsheet modeling from uncluttered and uncomplicated models, looking up.

Chapter Sixteen gives us the background to why we need to build "real life" models. We will use the questions raised about spreadsheet modeling in **Chapters Fourteen** and **Fifteen** to build them.

Chapter Fourteen

SPREADSHEET DESIGN — PROGRAMMER-STYLE

E=MC², but are we programming in C, C++, Pascal, Visual Basic . . . ?

Programmers approach computer-associated tasks in a certain way, view the user in a certain light, and organize everything so that the program is available on time, at the right price and working properly . . . or so the theory goes.

However, over the years, the methods and techniques they apply in order to meet the challenge of producing the software can be, and have been, successfully applied to designing spreadsheet-based solutions to business problems.

There is no one answer to the question "What is the best way to approach . . .?". What we need to do, in order to be able to be satisfied that, later in the book, the methods and solutions we adopt are acceptable is to understand how this question is answered by a programmer (or purist, perhaps). In the next chapter, we will look at it from another perspective — that of hard-pressed accountants, with a tight time deadline and other pressing work to complete, preparing a simple model for use, mainly (and probably exclusively) by themselves.

THE DEVELOPMENT PROCESS — AN OVERVIEW

When programmers are going to write a program, they must do three things:

- They must find out what the business problem is, and decide whether it can be solved or properly represented in a program. This helps to provide them with a framework in terms of the complexity and size of the project, and they can consider whether the project is a computer-based one, or a managerial one.
- They will then define the calculation rules that they need to program the software, list the assumptions that will be inherent in the program, consider the format of computer generated output, etc. This gives them a solid brief around which their programming skills can be applied, and it starts to break

the process down into the logical, step-by-step approach needed to convert real life into a computer-based scenario.

- Finally, they consider the people who will input the data each day (or week, or month . . .), and design screens to ensure that the right data is input at the right time, in the right place and in the right format (date, text, numeric, alpha-numeric, etc.). The computer will process the raw data, via the new software, and developers must ensure that what is going in is tightly constrained, so that they can control, via the software, what is output by the system. Therefore, they design the screen layout, menus, sub-menus, toolbars etc. based on their assessment of the level of experience of the person who is inputting the raw data. Understanding the level, experience and knowledge of the person inputting is vital. This will dictate the level of flexibility that should be built into a program. Accountants will need fewer constraints from the program than clerical people, because they will understand what they are inputting, and how it will affect the output which will be generated.

Once these steps have been completed, programmers are ready to program the software. Test versions (sometimes called beta copies) will be produced, in order for the programmers to receive feedback from users about:

- Design issues, for example:
  - ➢ Does it fulfil the need it was intended for?
  - ➢ Are there any suggestions or changes required by the users?
  - ➢ Are changes needed in the way it operates?
- User interface, for example:
  - ➢ Is it user-friendly?
  - ➢ Is input easy to follow?
  - ➢ Are changes needed to menus, screens, or terminology? (e.g. Exit vs. Close)
- Test data, for example:
  - ➢ Is the program producing correct results from the test data?
  - ➢ Have users tried test data that is different from that expected?
  - ➢ Have users tried it enough to be sure that it is working the way they want prior to final sign-off?

When the test versions are accepted as "bug free", programmers are ready to prepare a plan to implement the new software and "go live."

This will involve:

- Writing technical manuals for the users
- Arranging training courses for users
- Providing a technical support help facility, agreeing responsibilities for answering queries, hours of operation, etc.

THE DEVELOPMENT PROCESS — DETAILED CONSIDERATIONS

The previous paragraph described in broad outline how programmers view the project from commencement to conclusion. Within this framework, the more detailed issues are:

- What is the budget for the project — both in financial cost and man-hours?
- Is the programming to be undertaken internally, or sub-contracted out?
- What risks attach to the business using the software? What would happen if it produced an incorrect result?
- Who are the users, and what are their requirements and expectations?
- Are there different user groups?
- Is the project feasible? Can a computer solution be found to the problem?
- What information (exactly) is to be input?
- What calculations (exactly) are required to be performed?
- To what level of accuracy is the output to be stated?
- How much "what if" flexibility is required in the output?
- What assumptions are inherent in the program?
- Are assumptions in the model fixed, or can they be changed by the user (for example, debt collection period)?
- What format of reports is required by the user base? Is this fixed, or is a report generator facility required?
- What test data will be used to confirm the software is operating correctly?
- How will the test results be documented and recorded for future reference?
- How often will the software be updated?

... and so the list goes on, almost *ad infinitum*.

These procedures imply that a substantial project is being undertaken, and there is a substantial investment in people (end-users) and in understanding what they wish to get out of the new software.

The other implication is that there is a substantial investment in time and effort to produce documentation covering:

- The technical specification of the software, so that programmers (either the same team or, if personnel leave and are replaced, programmers previously unconnected with the project) can amend, update or debug as necessary.
- The user manuals, so that users can find out how to complete tasks with the software, without the need to contact a technical help line.
- Training material, so that the current workforce can be trained initially, and that new employees can be trained when they join the organization.

After this, it is a question of mechanics:

- Which programming language should be used (including, but not restricted to, the Excel Visual Basic Applications language)?
- Will the software program call on a spreadsheet's functionality in the background, but be developed separately from the spreadsheet?
- Will a database, or other similar software, be used instead?

EXCEL PROGRAMMING

In **Section Two**, we discussed Microsoft's vision for users of the Office suite of software. In that discussion, we saw that the audience for the software falls into three broad categories, with accountants at one extreme and computer programmers at the other.

Let's assume that the programmer is using Visual Basic, which is a larger, broadened-out, programming language originally developed from the Visual Basic, Applications Edition, which is included with Excel.

From discussions between programmers and the users, the programmers will have established the broad approach that they need to adopt, they know what the program should achieve, they know the format of the input data, user groups (and therefore password protected areas, access, etc.)

The main screen shots, menus and program logic will all be controlled by Visual Basic, but for specific aspects programmers wish to pass information to Excel, have it make the appropriate calculations, then pass the result back to the Visual Basic program for further operations.

This is achieved by making a call on Excel from within Visual Basic.

Excel starts, but is instructed not to display on the screen.

The items are passed from a calculation or input box in Visual Basic to Excel, and the calculations are performed.

The value is returned to the Visual Basic program and is displayed on the screen by Visual Basic, or included in the next step in the program for background processing by the program.

Excel is closed.

The user is unaware that Excel has been closed, because they were unaware that it had been started.

Making the calls requires the following code to be included in the program:

```
...Sub Main()
Dim appExcel As Object
Set appExcel = CreateObject ("excel.application")
appExcel.Visible = False   'Excel starts invisibly - true or false confirms
...
...
appExcel.Quit              'To close Excel
```

End Sub

If you want to try this, you will have to learn a new language, with its own syntax and grammatical rules, as well a vocabulary that has a meaning different from the ordinary English word. The only way to learn how to use it properly and safely is to devote time and effort to it.

The other possibility is that the programmer is working on screen with Excel displayed. A lot can still be done to make it unrecognizable — the screen below is only the start...

Excel? Yes.

Recognizable? No.

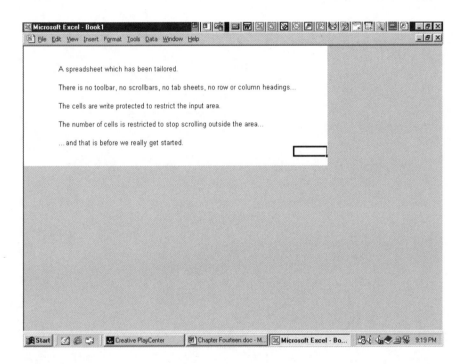

To Conclude

This chapter squeezes into only a few pages what is better covered in a substantial book.

As mentioned previously, the reason for including the above in this book is to explain what a programmer does, and to put it in context, side-by-side with accountants' perceptions of their needs — which is covered in depth in the next chapter.

The main point to remember is that, as regards methodologies, programmers have a lot to offer — covering the spectrum from concept, when they obtain the views of users, to final implementation, when they produce the manuals and documentation, and provide the training and support necessary to implement the solution. In this scenario, Excel becomes a (small) part of a greater whole, and it can be used in a variety of ways. However, in every case, operator control is limited, and user input is strongly controlled. You do what programmers want you to do, and you can only work within that environment. This kills initiative, but it forces accuracy . . . and there lies the catch-22.

AND NOW . . .

In the next chapter, we look at how we can bring common sense into our spreadsheets, and accommodate the two precious elements on which accountancy has been founded: Time, and accuracy.

Chapter Fifteen

SPREADSHEET DESIGN —
ACCOUNTANT-STYLE

The right figures, at the right time, at the right price.

Now that we have learnt the essential skills — how to use Windows and Excel — we are almost ready to learn how to apply those skills. But first, we need to understand how to use Excel's functionality in the real world, with all of its time pressures, quirks and difficulties.

That means designing spreadsheets that:
* **Minimize** the time necessary to develop them
* **Maximize** accuracy and faith in the model

Below is an example of the simplest spreadsheet possible.

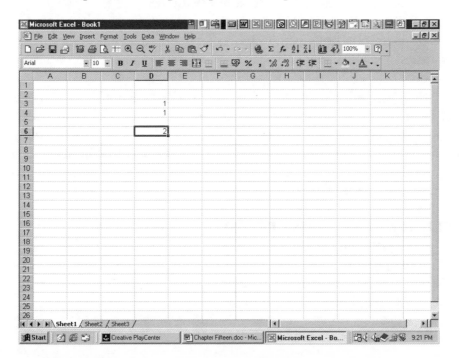

Does that count? There is:

* No heading
* No control check
* No formatting
* No thought as to where to position the figures — anywhere appears to do.

Is it really a designed spreadsheet?

Yes, it is! But this highlights a fundamental question.

WHAT IS THE DEFINITION OF A SPREADSHEET?

We have seen from **Section Two** exactly what a spreadsheet can do or, more accurately, what you can do with a spreadsheet.

But how you define a spreadsheet is the first constraint! Your definition limits how you will use the program — a programmer will define it by his ability to make calls on the "engine room" from other programs or procedures, an accountant will define it by what he produces, and so on.

I want to define the spreadsheet as:

"A scratch pad used to record text and numbers in a variety of formats."

Too simple? Look at the spreadsheet on the previous page. From an efficiency point of view, it cannot be beaten — **because the audience is the user, and the life of the spreadsheet is very short indeed.**

This definition also highlights that, from an accountant's point of view, a spreadsheet is an electronic pad of analysis paper! And that is fundamental for an accountant's view of spreadsheet programs, spreadsheet design and spreadsheet usage.

From this, you will also understand Microsoft's vision of how their software will be used in the real world: the computer is left on and available for use throughout the day; the spreadsheet is used as a calculator and scratch pad for work "on the fly"; the word-processor is used for memos; the database is used to interrogate the company database, etc. Not every project has to be a major exercise, or requires a great depth of formal procedures and documentation.

SIMPLICITY? YES! NAIVETÉ? NO!

Simplicity is a virtue in spreadsheet design. Naiveté is dangerous.

Whilst the majority of spreadsheets can be left in an unstructured and loosely documented manner, the dangers of adopting this approach *carte blanche* can be disastrous. Two true examples will suffice.

Embarrassing!

A partner in a large accountancy practice went to a client's bankers to discuss projections and cash flow requirements. The meeting progressed well, until the bank manager noticed that something seemed to be wrong with the figures. He pulled out his calculator and, sure enough, the spreadsheet did not add up!

Expensive!

At least in the first case, it did not cost money. In an another company, a spreadsheet was prepared to support a major investment decision. The firm lost $10m on the project and later, when they looked at everything again, they found the original spreadsheet model was defective. Several senior executives lost their jobs.

Something of a catch-22 here, I think. If you do not use spreadsheets and information technology, you cannot get the best jobs, and achieve your potential. Use them badly and it could cost you your reputation as well as your career.

So you have been warned! Now is the time for you to build a solid framework to control this monster and safeguard your health (and wealth)!

FUNDAMENTAL DESIGN ISSUES

The simple spreadsheet used earlier is an excellent starting point in deciding the issues that must be addressed. It is shown again below.

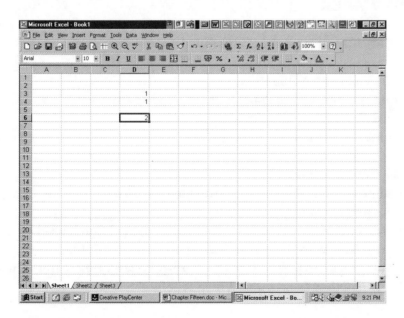

What is wrong with it? Perhaps the most important thing is the fact we do not have the correct starting point!

Before approaching the screen, we must first decide exactly what it is we are trying to achieve — therefore, we should design the spreadsheet off-screen first.

THE INITIAL DESIGN ISSUES

The issues to be addressed before approaching the screen (or the paper!) are:

- What file name will we use? It must be meaningful.
- Where will the spreadsheet be saved? On C: drive, floppy disk, network file server?
- Which file format will we save the file in? Excel 2000, Excel 95 etc.?
- Who will use the spreadsheet? You, more junior (inexperienced) staff, a qualified accountant, a Power User?
- How often will the spreadsheet be used? The spreadsheet example above is the "throw away" type. Will the model you want to build be used for months or years, again and again, a "template" type spreadsheet?
- What is the spreadsheet to be used for? How complicated is the issue we are reviewing?
- How important is it (professional indemnity, job security, etc)? The more important, the greater the need for a proper trail.

This provides the framework within which the spreadsheet parameters can be set (on paper). When we have decided these issues, the design stage can be approached with confidence!

DESIGN ON PAPER

Designing the spreadsheet on paper allows the project to be seen in broad detail, without the difficulty of becoming embroiled in the mechanics at too early a stage.

The aspects to address include:

- What period is covered in the spreadsheet? How many years? What are the break periods?
- Should annual projections be split one year per sheet, or all years on one sheet?
- What is the reporting period?
- The annual projections may be split into months. However, is the final report shown as an annual total?
- What will the final report look like? How many pages? Condensed or full size? How will it fit in to the rest of the report? Charts? Tables?
- Which headings will be pasted into the word-processed report from the spreadsheet? Are they to be bold? Which typeface?

DECIDE THE LAYOUT ON THE SCREEN

Still using paper, we are now in a position to prepare (again in broad terms) a rough map of the layout of the information on the spreadsheet. This map will identify:

- The main components of the spreadsheet
- The links between the sections, and the information within each section
- The grouping of information on sheets. Will reports be on a sheet of their own? How many sheets are needed? Is all detail on one sheet, or grouped (for example by date) and split across several sheets?

SET UP THE SPREADSHEET

Now the spreadsheet can be started.

The constraints of working on the screen are different from those laid down by the final report definition, because one is the working environment (the spreadsheet) and the other is the reporting environment (the paper product — perhaps developed through the constraints imposed by the word-processing environment).

Some of the issues to be addressed within the spreadsheet are:

- The width of columns — especially for headings
- The formats to be applied in cells for dates etc.
- The presentation of figures on the spreadsheet — Are negatives in brackets? Is a thousands separator used?

A further set of issues (sometimes referred to as "Real Estate", because they relate to the amount of available screen space compared with the amount of information to be presented) include:

- The tiling of window panes, and the number on screen at one time
- The lowest level of zoom possible. If zoom reduces below a cell display factor, the contents become hash (######). It then becomes difficult to control the flow of information from cell to cell.
- If zoom reduces, the figures in cells become rounded-off (subject to the formatting). The final report may report too much detail, and detract from the impact as a result.

LOGICALLY RELATE THE ABOVE TO THE SCREEN

With the knowledge gained above, the spreadsheet can be prepared — cells can be formatted, data input and formulae inserted. The full extent of the need for audit trails will at this stage be known, and therefore no "hidden" calculations will be happening — unless, of course, you are confident about the result!

Later in the book, this process is used from start to finish to build spreadsheet solutions. However, in the meantime, we will analyze what went wrong with the two spreadsheets, and how the problems could have been averted at the design stage.

THE BANK EXPERIENCE — INACCURATE FORMULAE

Without access to all of the facts, it is impossible to give a complete analysis. However, some things are certain:

- The audience is known. The projections were requested by the bank
- The projections were specific to the client, even if it was tailored from a template
- The reporting requirements were known, as was the period to be covered by the report.

All of the background was available to the designer. However, care was not taken at the design stage to identify the main components within the spreadsheet:

- What is the link between the accounts and the projected cash flow?
- How has the audit trail been constructed, or are totals completed within cells behind the scenes?

The second point is illustrated below:

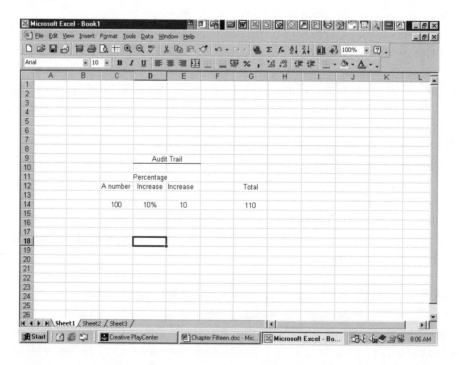

The summary information may not show the detail, but the printouts supporting the summary are easily reviewed to ensure they are accurate.

Compare this to the following:

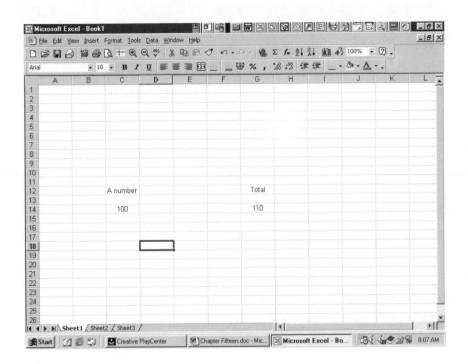

Obviously bad but this doesn't happen in the real world. Does it?

Providing a paper audit trail will be explored in the Accounts and Projections spreadsheet built in **Section Four**.

THE CORPORATE EXPERIENCE — BALANCED, AUDITED AND TOTALLY INACCURATE

The Corporate experience is slightly different. Everything appeared to be reasonable. However, the assumptions used in the projections did not correspond with the formulae and were therefore not properly implemented in the model.

Consider the following example:

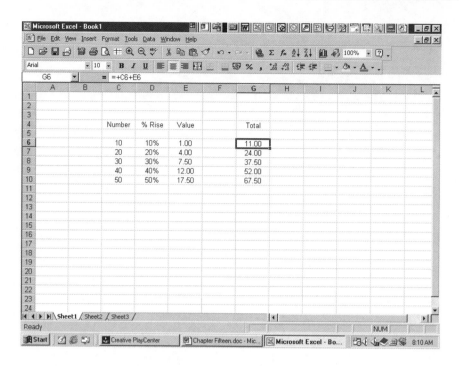

Dragging and dropping the total before copying the formula causes everything to miss by one line. Picking up the figures later in the spreadsheet produces erroneous results. This results in:

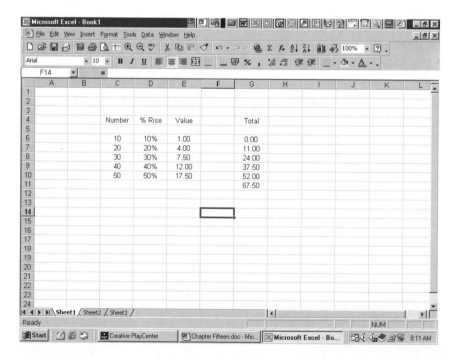

The person responsible for producing the spreadsheet must be aware of the dangers inherent in working with data — whether in input tables, detailed workings, summaries or anywhere else in the spreadsheet model.

The dangers inherent in some of the data manipulation tools were highlighted in **Section Two**, and they are also explored in the practical examples used in the following chapters.

NOW, PUT THEORY INTO PRACTICE

There are many traps for the unwary. The proper design of spreadsheet solutions is the cornerstone of robust, accurate models produced on a timely basis. There is also a need to be aware of efficient shortcuts available in the software, and any hidden dangers they present.

The following chapters show how to implement the theory. The solutions themselves are not a treatise on the single best method for achieving a result — rather, they are a blend of maximum accuracy and minimum development time. The cut-off point between the benefit of further time being spent in developing solutions compared with the increase in faith in the model is where your professional judgement comes into play. And the use of professional judgement is the hallmark of an accountant.

So, let's move on to **Chapter Sixteen** and put the theory into practice.

Chapter Sixteen

BUILDING SPREADSHEETS

To build, or not to build. That is the question.

We now have a knowledge of Windows, Excel menus, toolbars and screen real estate, how to manage software development, what to look for when we think about designing a spreadsheet . . .

Now is the time to draw this together in practical examples. The key to knowing any software is hands-on experience, so you are strongly recommended to follow these examples on your keyboard. The time you invest now is your investment in your computer skills for the next 30 years or more.

BACKGROUND TO THE EXAMPLES

For the purposes of all of the examples in this book, you are the accountant in Joe Bloggs Inc., based in a country called Lil.

Before each spreadsheet, an overview of the problem is given (tax legislation, time constraints etc.). We will design the spreadsheets from scratch. The disk enclosed with this book includes the pre-built solutions, complete to a stage. This means that you can check your results against the disk and, if necessary, use the disk version to move to the next stage.

LIL

Lil is like any other country in the world — a government trying to balance a budget, looking to every other country for ideas on how to squeeze money out of the people, and an annual budget to give it here, and take it away there. The tax regime is explained at each stage, but the taxes we are mainly interested in are:

- Sales Voucher scheme
- Wages tax
- Profits tax.

JOE BLOGGS INC.

It's like anything else really — nothing special. The work is easy enough most of the time, the deadlines are hectic at the month end, and the management team are, on the whole, okay. The pay is reasonable, but it could be better . . .

. . . AND YOU

As the accountant, you are expected to keep everything ticking over, there is an assistant to help, some clerical staff — the usual.

. . . BUT THEN . . .

It all happens at once:

- John Smith — the headman — wants the annual accounts and three years projections on his desk immediately. It has to be a full business plan, and he always says "Change this. What about that . . ."

- John Smith came back in and said he was hiring someone — "$10,000 in his hand. How much is that gross?" was his question. "In fact, give me a ready reckoner for working it out in future."

- John Smith's father owns a shop, and he decided to run a discount voucher scheme in order to boost sales. His computer system cannot calculate the amount of vouchers to issue to each customer, so one of his office staff calculated it manually, and sent out the vouchers to the customers. Several phone calls later and Mr. Smith knew he had a problem – some of them had not received enough vouchers, and you can be sure that if anyone received too many they won't be on the phone.

- To minimize bad will the voucher calculations need to be rechecked and compared to the clerk's original list – and with over 1200 transactions this is not a task to be undertaken lightly. Once completed, Mr. Smith wants the errors to be highlighted so that he can decide what action to take, if any.

His staff aren't up to the task. John Smith volunteered our services...

It was going to be one of those days . . .

Section Four

BUILDING SPREADSHEETS

SECTION INDEX

SECTION OVERVIEW

In this section, we see how to build spreadsheets from scratch, balancing speed with accuracy, sophistication with simplicity, and allowing a proper trail to be seen visually. Time wasted looking for errors on a spreadsheet is neither fun nor productive.

The aim is to teach the fundamentals of spreadsheet design and to show how to co-ordinate Excel with Word. Full automation using VB, whilst of great use to Power Users, is a full subject in itself and outside the scope of this book.

Once you have completed the section, you may wish to introduce greater sophistication into the models. Some pointers are included at the end of each example to help you in this.

Chapter Seventeen

THE SALES VOUCHER SPREADSHEET

If it looks right, it probably is right . . . probably.

Time is short for building this spreadsheet. No second chances, no messing —
just results. Therefore, the first thing we want to do is to organize one of the
clerical staff to complete the groundwork for the Sales Voucher calculation by
listing everything on a spreadsheet. If you need to check on how to use specific
aspects of Windows or Excel, refer to the appropriate chapter.

THE PROBLEMS

Chapter Sixteen gave us the background about how the sales discount vouchers
were miscalculated when the clerk manually worked them out. There are 2
problems that we have to deal with:

The first problem is that the computer program used by John Smith's father is
old, and it will not export the file so that we can pick up the invoices in Excel.
Therefore the invoices need to be re-input into our spreadsheet. If we could have
imported the file, the exercise would have been easy.

The second problem is that we do not have the time to input the information
ourselves, and we will have to delegate it to clerical staff. When we get the information back from the clerk, there are two possibilities:
- Perform a one-for-one check of what our clerk has entered
- Use the spreadsheet to highlight inputting errors, and only concentrate on
  the exceptions reported by the system.

We have to use the second option, because we do not have enough time to perform a one-for-one check and complete the other tasks we have been given. However, number crunching is what spreadsheets do best, and we should be able to
build a robust spreadsheet model that gives us the faith in the results that we
need.

We are going to start with this spreadsheet first so that the clerk can work on
it while we set up the Net Pay Calculator.

INITIAL DESIGN ISSUES

The first question we must ask is "Who is going to design the spreadsheet? A programmer, or us?"

The advantage of using a programmer is sophistication, documentation, full testing. The problem with using a programmer is that we don't have the time — it needs to be done now, or we will miss the deadline.

Having agreed that it is our problem, and that we cannot delegate it, we need to address the initial design issues we identified in **Chapter Fifteen**. These are set out below, together with the answers:

- What file name will we use? It must be meaningful.

  Sales Voucher Scheme July 2001.

- Where will the spreadsheet be saved? On C: drive, floppy disk, network file server?

  C: drive. It is a single-user spreadsheet, and it can be done on the local drive.

- Which file format will we save the file in? Excel 2000, Excel 95, etc.?

  Excel 2000. No computer is used at present, so compatibility issues do not arise.

- Who will use the spreadsheet? You, more junior (inexperienced) staff, a qualified accountant, a Power User ...?

  Clerical staff for volume work. Ourselves for pulling it together.

- How often will the spreadsheet be used? Will it be a "throw away" spreadsheet or will you want to use it for months or years, again and again, (a "template" spreadsheet)?

  Perhaps once, if John's father upgrades his system. Perhaps every year if not, or if his system upgrade means he cannot export the invoice details to Excel.

- What is the spreadsheet to be used for? How complicated is the issue we are reviewing?

  Volume processing. Speed of entry is important. The work is tedious rather than complicated.

- How important is it (professional indemnity, job security, etc.). The more important, the greater the need for a proper trail.

  If we do not reissue the vouchers quickly, customer goodwill will be adversely affected.

The risks (to us) are such that we cannot afford to take any chances. We do not have the time to check everything 100%, because we need to press on with the accounts. We need to build a spreadsheet that will allow us to quickly check the entries, and highlight anything dubious.

The next step is to design it on paper. The issues raised in **Chapter Fifteen**, and our answers, are shown in the table below:

• What period is covered in the spreadsheet? What are the break periods?	One month's invoices from July in this case. No breaks necessary — process everything *en bloc*.
• What is the reporting period?	Month of July
• What will the final report look like? How many pages? Condensed or full size? How will it fit in to the rest of the report?	A list of invoices, for the company's records. Condensed to fit all columns on one page.
• Is the report word-processed, or only done in Excel? Which typeface? Anything bold etc?	Excel only — it is working papers we need. There is no final report as such. Font, etc. we will decide below.

The final step is to decide how to lay the spreadsheet out on the screen. The questions from **Chapter Fifteen** are listed below, with answers:

• What are the main components?	Invoice details (number, customer, invoice amount) and discount as originally calculated. Separately, a section calculating the correct discounts. Error messages to highlight items for rechecking (both input errors by our clerk and calculation errors by staff).
• What links are there between sections etc.?	This is primarily a number-cruncher spreadsheet. High volume drudgery. There are no complicated links — it is being used to replace manual work, rather than providing highly complicated calculations.
• How is information to be grouped?	A list of invoices and the discount as originally calculated. A separate section for calculating the correct discount. This is done to minimize the visual screen for the clerk, in order to maximize their accuracy.

Next, we need to map out where the information will appear, and the headings we will use.

We said earlier that we need two sections – one as the input area for our clerk, and the second as a number-crunching section to calculate the correct discount, compare it with the clerk's input, and highlight any differences.

Let's sketch it out on paper below.

THE ORIGINAL PRINTOUT DETAILS

We need to enter the details from the list used by Mr. Smith's staff, and enter the amount of discount they calculated was due. We therefore need the list that was generated previously, and this will be the input source for our clerk.

The computer list of invoices is set out as follows:

Invoice number; Customer Name; Invoice Amount.

Another column, Voucher, was added and a hand-written entry was made against each invoice.

We are, in large part, transferring a substantial manual task onto a computer so that it will take out the tedium and increase accuracy and speed. The format used previously will therefore be mirrored in the spreadsheet, so that our clerk is picking up the information in the order it is presented – maximizing input speed.

BUILDING-IN CONTROLS

There are two levels of control that we want to build in – control messages for the clerk to recheck her input, and control messages for us that highlight errors in the original discount calculation.

CONTROL MESSAGES FOR OUR CLERK

If our clerk enters something incorrectly from the list, then all future calculations are going to be unsound – the "garbage in, garbage out" problem. We want to ensure that, as far as possible, the clerk has to recheck everything that is shown up as being dubious.

The potential errors, and their solutions, are noted below:

- An invoice line is missed.   AutoFill the numbers before starting. The clerk can periodically check that the details match the list.

- The wrong customer name is input.   Recheck names for all highlighted discount calculation errors. These are the only important entries.

- Invoice total and discount entries are switched.   Error message to be generated. Clerk to recheck all lines that generate the error message, and then input "Rechecked" as confirmation entry is correct.

• Incorrect amounts are entered.	The discount calculation within the program will calculate that an error exists, either in our input or in the original. An error message will request the clerk to recheck the amounts, and then input "Rechecked" as confirmation her entry is correct.

CONTROL MESSAGES FOR OURSELVES

Once the clerk has input all the invoices, and rechecked input for any errors, we will use the second part of the spreadsheet to review the errors arising, and to summarize the problem cases.

To assist the review, we will allocate the discount into four sales value columns – below $100; more than $100 but less than $200; more than $200 but less than $300; and $300 and above.

We also need to calculate the discount error (plus or minus the calculated amount). The list can then be used by Mr. Smith to decide what action he wants to take.

THE SPREADSHEET

We have identified the requirements of the spreadsheet, and we are now ready to approach the computer.

Start Excel, and save the file as **Sales Voucher Scheme July 2001** on C: drive in the folder **Practicing Spreadsheet Techniques**, which is in the folder **My Spreadsheet Folder** – we set these up in **Section One**. (If you have not set the folders up yet, do so now). See **Section One**, if you need to review folders.

Enter the headings in the spreadsheet as set out below, and adjust the column widths to display the entries fully. Format the columns as shown.

Cell	Entry
A1	Arthur Smith, T/A Smith's Store
A2	Sales Voucher Scheme July 2001
A4	Invoice
A5	Number
B5	Customer
C4	Sales
C5	Value
D5	Discount
E5	Query
F5	Agreed

We have started labels at A5 to allow two lines of text (rows four and five) and still give space between these and the heading — there is no point cramping the spreadsheet.

We now have a screen that looks attractive and that shows our clerk the information he/she is expected to input.

The spreadsheet is shown below, and is saved on the disk as **Sales Voucher Scheme July 2001a.xls.**

The formatting is also highlighted in the screen shot. If you do not know how to format, look at the appropriate parts of **Section Two**.

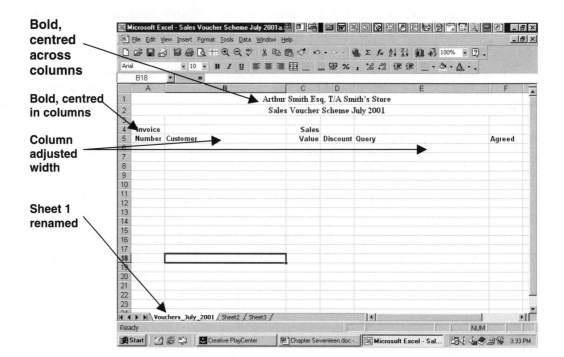

BUILDING THE FORMULAE
We will enter some test data, and then build the formulae for testing the clerk's input.

The test data we will use in the spreadsheet, and the reason, is given below.

Cell	Entry	Reason
• A6 to A 13	203470 to 203477	We can use AutoFill to insert the actual invoice numbers as per the list.
• B6 to B13	Various	Completeness.
• C6	$50	Below discount value. To test discount calculation below $100.
• C7 and C8	$100 and $195	1st band level.
• C9 and C10	$200 and $295	2nd band level.
• C11 to C13	$300 and $395	3rd band level.

Various amounts for discount, some right and some wrong have been entered in column D.

The spreadsheet is saved on the disk as **Sales Voucher Scheme July 2001b.xls.**

We want to build the formula for column E for checking the clerk's input.

COLUMN E - FORMULA
Earlier, we said that the potential errors we wanted to test for, and their solutions, were:

• An invoice line is missed.	AutoFill the numbers before starting. The clerk can periodically check that the details match the list.
• The wrong customer name is input.	Recheck names for all highlighted discount calculation errors. These are the only important entries.
• Invoice total and discount entries are switched.	Error message to be generated. Clerk to recheck all lines that generate the error message, and then input "Rechecked" as confirmation her entry is correct.
• Incorrect amounts are entered.	The discount calculation within the program will calculate that an error exists, either in our input or in the original. An error message will request the clerk to recheck the amounts, and then input "Rechecked" as confirmation her entry is correct.

The third and fourth items will be highlighted for the clerk by a tailored message in column E. There will be a different message, depending on the type of error.

In plain English, the messages will read:

1. Nothing appears to be wrong. Print dashes.
2. Nothing has been input in one of the columns (customer, invoice amount or discount). Display a suitable reminder.
3. The discount is greater than the invoice amount. Recheck the amounts from the list to ensure they are not switched around in error.
4. Discount does not compute at the amount entered. Recheck the amounts from the list.

Item 4 above will check the discount as entered against the discount as computed by us elsewhere in the spreadsheet. This part has not yet been built, so we will do this now.

DISCOUNT CHECKING

Our parameters for the complete spreadsheet design are:

- We want to minimize the display that the clerk sees, to minimize his/her visual distraction.
- We want to recalculate the discount as entered.
- We want a layout for the discount calculation that facilitates our physical review.
- We want a "reporting" section that will draw together the exceptions found.

We will therefore place the discount checking at AA1.

Enter the following headings in the spreadsheet as set out below.

Cell	Entry
AA1	=A1
AA2	=A2
AA4	=A4
AA5	=A5
AB4	=C4
AB5	=C5
AC3	Discount Calculation
AC5	<$100
AD4	>=$100;
AD5	<$200
AE4	>=$200;
AE5	<$300
AF5	>=$300

AG4   Calculated

AG5   =D5

AH4   Actual

AH5   =D5

AI5   Difference

We are using =A1 etc. as much as possible to ensure that, if we subsequently re-vise headings, they are consistently applied throughout the spreadsheet.

Also note that, for the purposes of our calculation, we are picking up invoice numbers in order to identify the item and relate it back to the original list. We do not, at this stage, need the customer name, and this redundant information is therefore NOT included in our calculation section.

The spreadsheet, suitably formatted, is shown below, and is saved on disk as **Sales Voucher Scheme July 2001c.xls.**

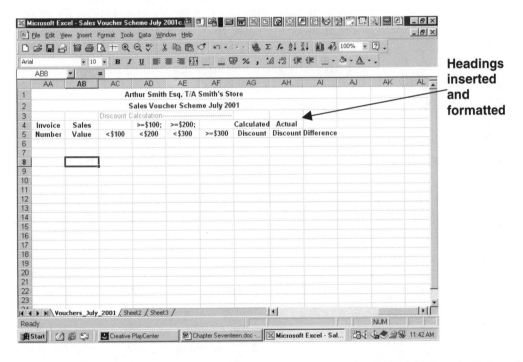

We now know which column we wish to use in our formula for the clerk but, in order to provide test data, we will finish building this part of the spreadsheet.

The formula in AA6 down will be =A6 etc. The formula in AB6 down will be =C6 etc. The formula in AH6 down will be =D6 etc.

We will now build the formula for column AC.

In English, the formula will read:

• If the sales value is less than $100 calculate the discount (as nil).

• If the sales value is more than $100 print a blank in the cell.

We could have decided to print a zero instead of a blank, and then formatted for Accounting, so that it displays as a dash. However, with this volume of transactions, a figure will stand out better amongst an empty screen, instead of a screen full of dashes in this column, the less than $200 column and the $300 and over columns.

Constructing the formula requires the use of IF statements, which have the format: =IF(Condition, True, False).

In the present context, this can be rewritten as: =IF(What is the sales value, if it is less than $100 discount is nil, if it is $100 or more print a blank in the cell)

We will now write the formula in a format that Excel understands, and give an explanation beside each part of the formula to help our own understanding.

A detailed explanation of the functions used is given in **Section Two**, together with details of how to access the functions from the menu and toolbar.

- =IF

  All formulas begin with =. The word IF tells Excel to produce one result IF a calculation works, and to produce a second result IF it does not.

- =IF(AB6<100

  If AB6 (the sales value) is less than $100.

- =IF(AB6<100, 0

  Enter a zero in the cell.

- =IF(AB6<100, 0, "")

  Otherwise enter a blank ("") in the cell.

Enter the formula in the spreadsheet, and drag it down to copy.

The spreadsheet is saved on the disk as **Sales Voucher Scheme July 2001d.xls.**

The formula for the next column has the same concept as the first formula, except it is expanded to test for a value from $100 to less than $200. The formula therefore becomes:

- =IF

  As before.

- =IF(AND(AB6>=100,AB6<200)

  If AB6 (the sales value) is $100 or more, and less than $200. AND is used because the figure must be both $100 or more and less than $200. If it was either the function OR would have been used. This is an example of a nested formula (a formula within another formula).

- =IF(AND(AB6>=100,AB6<200),5

  Enter $5 in the cell.

- =IF(AND(AB6>=100,AB6<200),5, "")

  Otherwise enter a blank ("") in the cell.

In the above table we said that Excel allows nested formulae to be put into a cell's formula. The same result could be achieved by using nested IF formula. The logic is explained in the diagram below, using English for clarity.

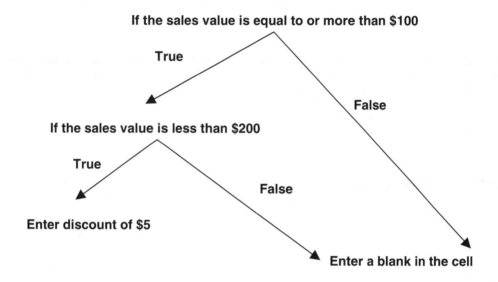

However, the formula is not as easy to read:

=IF(AB>=100,IF(AB<200,5,""),"")

The important point to note is that there is not necessarily only one answer to achieve the result you want.

The spreadsheet is saved on the disk as **Sales Voucher Scheme July 2001e.xls**. The next column in the spreadsheet has been completed. The formula is a variation on the one above.

The formula for the column AF has the same concept as the one above, except the amount of the discount is not fixed, but increases with the increase in sales value.

The amount of the voucher is in whole dollars, and Mr. Smith has said that unless the discount calculates to a whole dollar, the excess is not to be given. A sales transaction of $300 will receive a voucher for $18. A transaction of $313.26 will receive $18 + (£13.26 x 7.5%) = $18 + $0.99 rounded down to $18. A transaction of $313.27 will receive $19, because $13.27 x 7.5% rounds off at $1 to the nearest cent.

We will have to build this into our formula.

- =IF   As before.
- =IF(AB6>=300   If AB6 (the sales value) is $300 or more.
- =IF(AB6>=300, ROUND   Multiply the excess over $300 by 7.5%, and
  ((AB6-300)*.075),0)+18   round the figure to the nearest whole number.
                                                  Add $18 for the discount on the first $300.

- =IF(AB6>=300,ROUND   Otherwise enter a blank ("") in the cell.
  ((AB6-300)*.075),0)+18,"")

The spreadsheet is saved on the disk as **Sales Voucher Scheme July 2001f.xls**, and it is shown below. A total has been entered in column AG (the formula is =SUM(AC6:AF6), and the formula in column AI is =AH6-AG6. Column AI has then been formatted for Accounting, in order to show zeros as dashes, which then helps to highlight the difference.

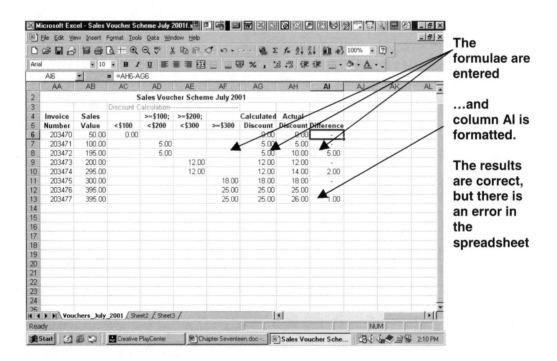

The formulae are entered

...and column AI is formatted.

The results are correct, but there is an error in the spreadsheet

However, this produces the wrong result.

Open the spreadsheet and extend the formula down to row 20.

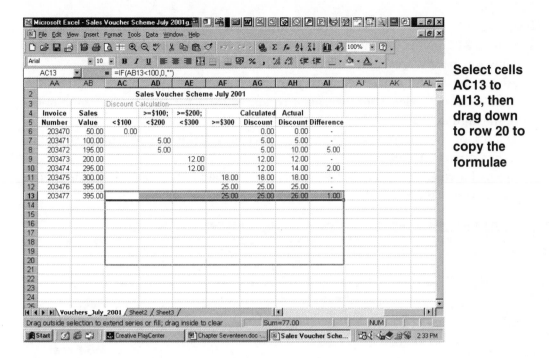

Select cells
AC13 to
AI13, then
drag down
to row 20 to
copy the
formulae

Insert the following test data in column AB, from AB14 to AB20:

AB14 313.25; AB15 313.26. AutoFill to AB20. The last cell should be 313.31.

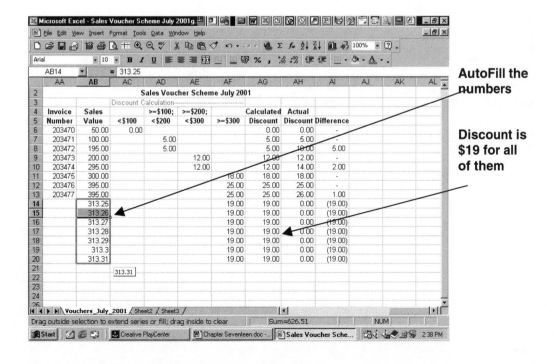

AutoFill the
numbers

Discount is
$19 for all
of them

However, Mr Smith had said that, if the sales value is $313.26, the discount should be $18 and, if the sales value is $313.27, the discount should be $19. Excel is using too great a level of accuracy to suit the reality of the situation.

Always be careful in the test data you pick.

To correct the calculation, we need to introduce a further level of sophistication. In English, it is:

If 7.5% of the excess over $300 gives part of a dollar, ignore the part dollar, and then process as before.

We will access Excel Help to find if a formula exists that will solve our problem.

Select Help, MS Excel Help.

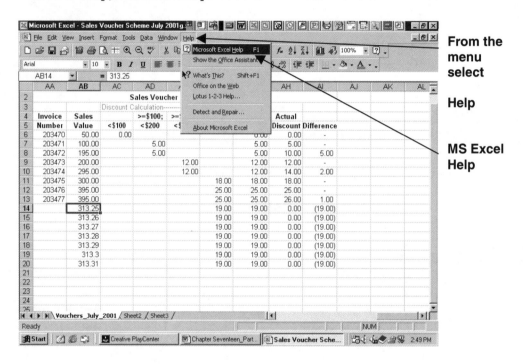

The help screen starts.

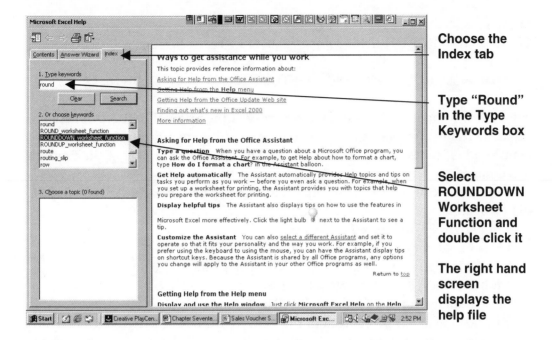

Choose the Index tab

Type "Round" in the Type Keywords box

Select ROUNDDOWN Worksheet Function and double click it

The right hand screen displays the help file

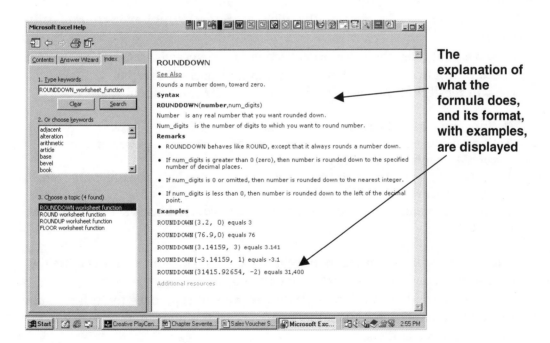

The explanation of what the formula does, and its format, with examples, are displayed

We therefore need to amend our original formula as follows:

Original
=IF(AB6>=300, ROUND((AB6-300)*.075),0)+18,"")
Revised
=IF(AB16>=300,ROUNDDOWN(ROUND((AB16-300)*0.075,2),0)+18,"")

There are two changes. The reported accuracy of the original ROUND function is increased from 0 (whole number rounding off) to 2 (two decimal places). This rounds up half cents to the nearest whole cent. The decimal part of the figure is then dropped.

In our spreadsheet, the two important figures are in cells AB15 ($313.26) AB16 ($313.27).

At full accuracy, $13.26 x 7.5% = 0.9945

This is rounded **down** to 0.99 in our ROUND formula.

The 0.99 is then dropped in the ROUNDDOWN function.

At full accuracy, $13.27 x 7.5% = 0.99525

This is rounded **up** to 1.00 in our ROUND formula.

The 1.00 is then left unchanged in the ROUNDDOWN function.

Our spreadsheet now properly calculates the value of the vouchers due to each customer.

The spreadsheet is saved on the disk as **Sales Voucher Scheme July 2001g.xls.**

We have completed the calculation section of the spreadsheet. Delete the test data, and return to cell A1 so that we can finalize the clerk's section.

You will recall that the messages we want to build into column E are:

1. Nothing appears to be wrong. Print dashes.
2. Nothing has been input in one of the columns (customer, invoice amount or discount). Display a suitable reminder.
3. The discount is greater than the invoice amount. Recheck the amounts from the list to ensure they are not switched around in error.
4. Discount does not compute at the amount entered. Recheck the amounts from the list.

Item 4 above will use the figure at column AI – the difference between the discount as entered and the discount as computed by us.

The actual formula is quite complicated, so we will reproduce the full formula below, and then analyze it in detail.

The formula in cell E6 is:

=IF(AND(ISBLANK(B6),ISBLANK(C6),ISBLANK(D6)),"",IF(OR(ISBLANK(B6),ISBLANK(C6),ISBLANK(D6)),"An entry is needed", IF(D6>=C6,"Discount is greater or equal to the sales value.", IF(AI6<>0,"The discount calculation is incorrect. Confirm figures","--------------------"))))

To analyze it properly we will separate the nested IF statements. They are split as follows:

First IF
=IF(AND(ISBLANK(B6),ISBLANK(C6),ISBLANK(D6)),"",

Second IF
IF(OR(ISBLANK(B6),ISBLANK(C6),ISBLANK(D6)),"An entry is needed",

Third IF
IF(D6>=C6,"Discount is greater or equal to the sales value.",

Fourth IF
IF(AI6<>0,"The discount calculation is incorrect. Confirm figures","------------------
-"))))

First IF

The first IF statement has the normal =IF(Condition, True, False) format. In English, it reads "If the cells for customer name, sales and discount are all blank then display nothing ["" in this case]. Otherwise run the next IF statement. The actual Excel function is analyzed below.

• =IF		As before.
• (Condition,	(AND(ISBLANK(B6),ISBLANK(C6) ,ISBLANK(D6)),	If B6, C6 and D6 are all blank then …
• True,	"",	Display the text (a blank cell).
• False)	Run Second IF statement	The statement is explained below.

Second IF

The second IF statement also has the normal =IF(Condition, True, False) format. In English, it reads "If any of the cells for customer name, sales value or discount is blank (but not all three at once – this condition was checked in the first IF statement), then print 'An entry is needed' in order to remind the clerk. Otherwise, run the third IF statement."

IF(OR(ISBLANK(B6),ISBLANK(C6),ISBLANK(D6)),"An entry is needed",
It comprises:

- =IF   As before.
- (Condition,   (OR(ISBLANK(B6),ISBLANK(C6)   If any of B6, C6 and D6
                 ,ISBLANK(D6)),"   are blank then …
- True,   "An entry is needed",   Display the text.
- False)   Run Third IF statement   The statement is ex-
                                                plained below.

THIRD IF

The third IF statement also has the normal =IF(Condition, True, False) format. In English, it reads "If the figure input for discount is greater than or equal to the figure for the sales value then print 'Discount is greater or equal to the sales value' in order to remind the clerk to recheck the input. Otherwise run the fourth IF statement."

IF(D6>=C6,"Discount is greater or equal to the sales value.",

It comprises:

- =IF   As before.
- (Condition,   (D6>=C6,   If D6 (discount) is greater or
                                                equal to C6 (sales value)
                                                then …
- True,   " Discount is greater or equal   Display the text.
                 to the sales value ",
- False)   Run Fourth IF statement   The statement is explained
                                                below.

FOURTH IF

As above, the fourth (and final) IF statement follows the normal =IF(Condition, True, False) format. In English, it reads "If AI6 (actual discount minus the calculated discount figure) is not nil (i.e. if they are not equal), then print 'The discount calculation is incorrect. Confirm figures.' in order to remind the clerk to recheck the input. Otherwise, print a line of dashes to indicate no errors arise."

IF(AI6<>0,"The discount calculation is incorrect. Confirm figures","---------------
-----"))))

It comprises:

- =IF   As before.
- (Condition,   (AI6<>0,   If AI6 (difference column in the
                                                discount checking section of the
                                                spreadsheet) is not nil then …
- True,   "The discount calculation is   Display the text.
                 incorrect. Confirm figures.",

- False)   "----------------------"   Display the text.
-)))   This closes off the previous three IF statements.

TEST DATA

The spreadsheet containing all of the above formulae is saved on the disk as **Sales Voucher Scheme July 2001h.xls**

Enter some test data from B14 to D22 to see how the spreadsheet will provide feedback to the clerk as each line is processed.

If errors arise, the error message will remain until the clerk enters "Rechecked" in column F. This is to provide a positive confirmation from the clerk that they have rechecked the details from the list. This will eliminate simple key press errors. However, we will ourselves recheck all entries highlighted as errors by the spreadsheet.

CELL FORMATTING OF COLUMN E

The only remaining aspect needed to make the clerk's input area complete is to ensure that all of the text in the error messages actually displays, and is not cut off by an entry in column F.

Select cells E6 to E65536 (F8 to anchor, and Ctrl ↓), right-click and select Format Cells from the menu. Choose the Alignment tab and click on the Shrink To Fit checkbox to select it. All of the text will now display at all times. In order to maximize the size of the text, adjust column widths accordingly.

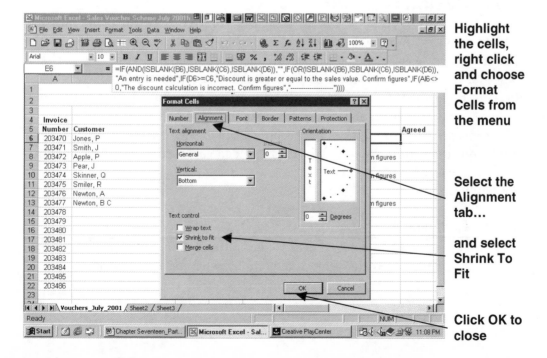

Highlight the cells, right click and choose Format Cells from the menu

Select the Alignment tab...

and select Shrink To Fit

Click OK to close

REPORTING THE ERRORS

After the clerk has input all of the invoices, we can review the spreadsheet and determine the extent of the problem. At that stage, we can use the spreadsheet to prepare a report for Mr. Smith. However, there is no point spending the time now in building a report structure into the spreadsheet when it may turn out that there are only a small number of errors that have arisen.

We will therefore clear the spreadsheet entries at B6 to D22 (including any test data you have entered), AutoFill the invoice numbers to equal the numbers covered by Mr. Smith's printout, and copy the formulae over the same range of cells. The spreadsheet is then ready for input by the clerk.

We are therefore now ready to work on the second spreadsheet – the Gross Pay Calculator. First, however, we will consider what improvements or changes we could have made in our spreadsheet design and our choice of approach.

IMPROVEMENTS AND CHANGES TO THE MODEL

The most important point to make is that there is no such thing as "the finished model" – improvements can always be made, evidenced by the continued and commendable improvements made in Excel with each version.

There is a balance between sophistication and knowledge and a diminishing return on increased sophistication and the extra time and effort involved. Where the cut-off point lies is for you to judge.

Some ideas are noted below.

EXCEL: OPTION 1

At present, if a text entry is put in each cell from B to D, an error message #VALUE displays. A variety of errors, including inappropriate display of the clerk's messages, arises, depending on whether the same two letters are in C and D, whether the letter in C is later in the alphabet than the letter in D, etc.

To trap the error requires testing of the input to determine whether it is text or numeric, and then to display an appropriate message.

However, provided the clerk is not receiving the dashes (all clear) message and will have to recheck their entry. Would the added complexity in the formula actually achieve any benefit?

Probably not.

EXCEL: OPTION 2

The clerk can use a Data Entry Form to enter the details. A Data Entry Form looks like this, and is activated from the menu by selecting Data, Form.

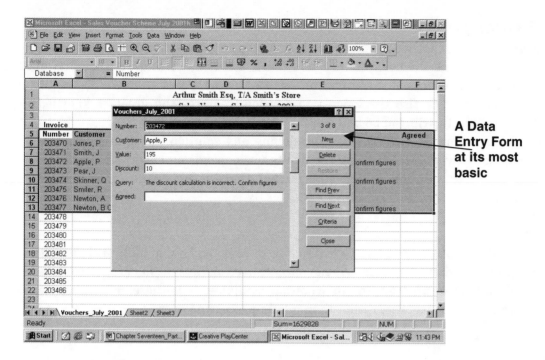

A Data
Entry Form
at its most
basic

However, it is slower for this type of work to use a form than to enter information directly onto the sheet.

EXCEL: OPTION 3

Use Excel Visual Basic Applications Edition to design on-screen commands. These are not visible if we scroll outside the immediate area and, therefore, are not useful for this type of work.

ACCESS

What we are processing in Excel in this particular case is a database. The software written specifically for databases is Access, and we would therefore expect to find it is much better suited to the task in hand.

However, our solution in Excel has been achieved relatively quickly, with strong control over the input and excellent testing of the accuracy of the data.

To achieve the same quality of solution in Access will take longer, because data tables must be constructed, forms designed for the input of the information, and VB code must be written to control the forms, automate the checking and process the data.

Whilst a lot of this is completed automatically by Access, there is still enough required from us to make this route unattractive.

There is also the question of the time required to learn Access, compared to the level of knowledge of Excel that we already have.

VISUAL BASIC

Completing the exercise from scratch in VB, using the same Jet engine used in Access, provides the most defined and "best" solution, writing the code and manipulating all events in the program.

However, it is also the longest to develop, requires the greatest knowledge and, ultimately, will you be better off?

Always remember that, when developing any solution, there are several different tools available. Choosing the one to use depends on experience, preference and the user, but the golden rule is that there is no virtue in unnecessary complexity.

NEXT

We will look at the Net Pay Calculator next, and see how to build it. It is different from the Sales Voucher Scheme spreadsheet, because it is being used to provide a single result from the information available. It is therefore a calculator-based computer exercise, rather than a bulk-processing exercise.

Chapter Eighteen

THE GROSS PAY CALCULATOR

I can go from A to B.
Going from B to A — now that's the problem!

The first spreadsheet is finished, and the clerk is processing the invoices. We will do the Gross Pay Calculator now, and then move on to the main spreadsheet — accounts and projections.

BACKGROUND

John Smith keeps hiring people on a "cash in your hand" basis, and then leaves the messy calculations to the payroll staff.

The problem is that the tax calculations are a mixture of fixed and semi-variable elements, so calculating backward from net pay to gross is difficult.

The tax allowances and rates applicable in Lil are:

Allowances

Personal relief	$3,500
Married person's allowance	$2,000

Tax Rates

Lower	10% on first $2,500
Basic	25% on next $22,500
Upper	40%

Employee and employer's National Health Tax (equivalent to Social Security) rates are:

National Health Tax / Social Security— Employee

Below $50 per week	Nil
$50 – $500 per week	2% of $50, plus 10% of excess above $50
Over $500 per week	No additional tax

National Health Tax/ Social Security — Employer

Below $50 per week	Nil
$50 – $99.99 per week	3% of the actual earnings
$100 – $199.99 per week	5% of the actual earnings
$200 – $499.99 per week	7% of the actual earnings
$500 – $749.99 per week	10% of the actual earnings
Above $750 per week	11% of the actual earnings

Although not actually requested, we will calculate the employer's contribution to National Health Tax. This will show John Smith the full implications of his decision when he is discussing pay.

INITIAL DESIGN ISSUES

As with the previous spreadsheet, the first question to ask is "Who is going to design the spreadsheet, A Programmer or us?"

This problem very much centers around the interface the person inputting is going to use and, to that extent, it is probably better for a programmer to design it. However, what we will do here is build a working model to show the programmer how we expect that it should run. We will also be able to use it to generate test data for the programmer's model.

The design issues identified in **Chapter Fifteen** are answered below:

• What file name will we use? It must be meaningful.	Gross / Net Pay Calculator Version 1.
• Where will the spreadsheet be saved? On C: drive, floppy disk, network file server?	Network, to be accessible to payroll staff, John Smith and ourselves.
• Which file format will we save the file in? Excel 2000, Excel '95, etc.?	Excel 95. John Smith runs Excel 2000, but the payroll department's computers have not yet been upgraded to run Excel 2000 at reasonable speed.
• Who will use the spreadsheet? You, more junior (inexperienced) staff, a qualified accountant, a Power User?	Computer-literate, but not spreadsheet-literate staff.
• How often will the spreadsheet be used? Will it be a "throw away" spreadsheet or will you want to use it for months or years, again and again, (a "template" spreadsheet)?	Reasonably often.

- What is the spreadsheet to be used for? How complicated is the issue we are reviewing?
- How important is it (professional indemnity, job security, etc)? The more important, the greater the need for a proper trail.

A single Goal Seek for each query. The grossing up of tax is a complicated calculation.
The actual payroll program will throw up any errors when it is first run. However, the embarrassment of getting the figures wrong should be avoided.

The risk (to us) is that the new employee will complain to John Smith if the payroll department calculate that our gross figure will not give the net pay agreed. However, a greater problem is that agreeing a net salary without really knowing what the true cost is can have quite an impact on the profitability of the company. Therefore, this is quite a critical spreadsheet for the business.

The next step is to design it on paper. The issues raised in **Chapter Fifteen**, and our answers, are shown in the table below:

- What period is covered in the spreadsheet? What are the break periods?
- What is the reporting period?
- What will the final report look like? How many pages? Condensed or full size? How will it fit in to the rest of the report?
- Is the report word-processed, or only done in Excel? Which typeface? Anything bold etc?

The spreadsheet runs per tax year. Break periods are 12-monthly.

Current week or month.
The final report will be a printout of the calculated sum, to be placed on the employee's personnel file.

Excel only — it is working papers we need. There is no final report as such. Font etc. we will decide below.

Finally, we must decide how to lay the spreadsheet out on the screen:

• What are the main components?	A section for tax rates, a section for the health tax rates, a trail for the calculation, an input section (name, etc.), an output section.
• What links are there between sections, etc.?	The gross is used to calculate tax deductions, to give the net pay. The computer will continually recalculate using Goal Seek, by changing the gross until we achieve the correct net. Therefore, link it together as a gross to net pay spreadsheet, NOT net to gross.
• How is information to be grouped?	Information is grouped onto one sheet. As we move from one tax year to another, a new sheet will be added, and we will change the tax rates as appropriate.

A schematic of what is going on is given below.

Initially we will use only straightforward spreadsheet techniques. As noted above, this particular task is more suited to programming, but it will be a useful exercise to draw out the areas that are the same in both, and the improvements that can be made through programming.

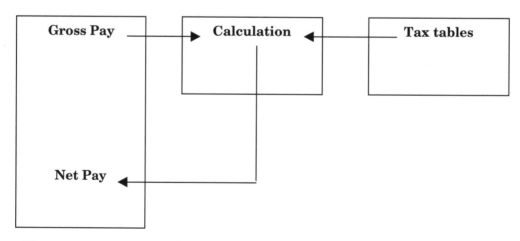

The report is printed, showing Gross and Net details

We will design the spreadsheet in this style, with each section as shown being in its respective part of the spreadsheet. Turning to the Input/Output section first, the spreadsheet looks like this:

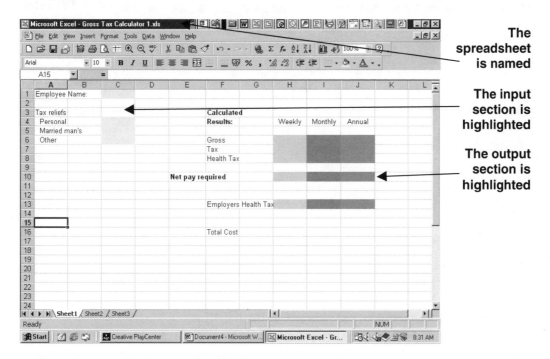

Highlighting above emphasizes where the input information must be placed, and where the output information is produced.

See **Section Two** to check how to apply background fill.

TAX TABLES

Keeping the same spreadsheet design as the rough diagram above, we will enter the calculation section at cell AA1, and we will place the tables at BA1.

The tables must show the rates and bands, and must be easily updated.

Using the information from earlier, place the table in BA1. The file is saved as **Gross Tax Calculator 2.xls**, and the screen is shown below.

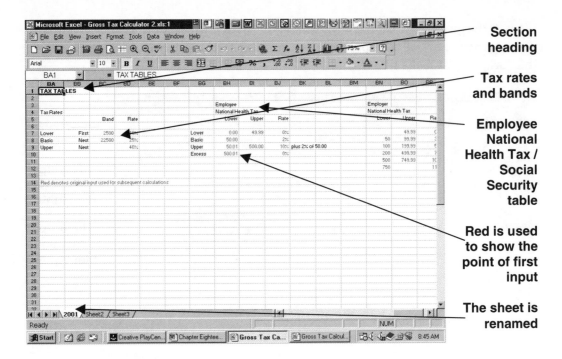

The exact positioning of the parts is not of itself critical.

Red has been used in order to show visually which entries are the original source from which other calculations and displays get their information. If these values appear elsewhere on the spreadsheet, they will be in black.

The Employer National Health part of the table is shown below.

This should be the only occasion we need to access this section of the spreadsheet, because it should only change as the tax rules change. There is no need for it to be accessed by John Smith, or anyone else using it, and we could hide it. However, in the meantime we will name range the section for our own easy access.

Highlight the area and click in the name range box. Type in **Tax_Tables** (note the underscore).

For detailed steps on naming ranges, see **Section Two**.

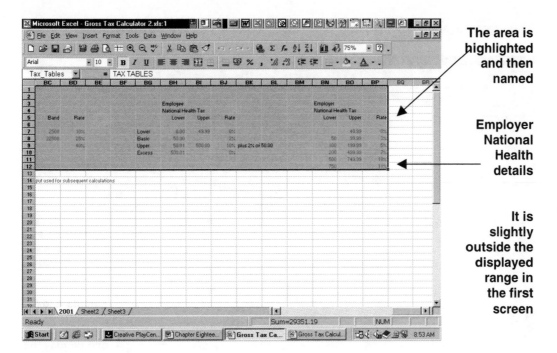

The table section is now complete.

CALCULATION SECTION

We will now build the calculation section. What we are trying to achieve is:

- A format that is easy to check visually
- A calculation style that is easy to follow (and therefore easy to correct).

We will start with the calculation of the tax.

Calculating Tax

We need to use the income after deduction of allowances, and then apply the tax rates to it. What we are trying to achieve, and the suggested layout, are:

• Calculate taxable pay	Display Gross and Allowances. Deduct one from the other and display the net.
• Calculate tax on the taxable pay	Split the gross across the bands, and apply the tax rates to each band.
• Display the total tax payable	Show how the total is arrived at, displaying tax falling within each band.

The screen is shown below, and is saved as **Gross Tax Calculator 3.xls**.

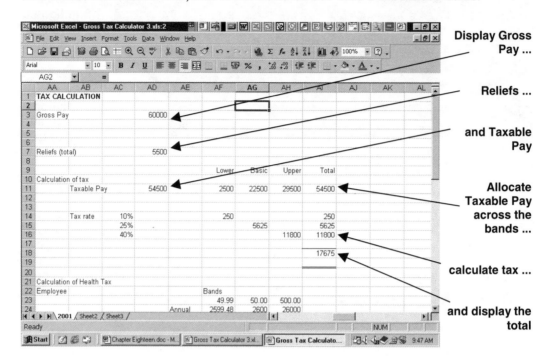

The space available on the sheet is substantial, and there is nothing to be gained by doing all of the calculations "behind the scenes." The layout above should help to identify visually whether any problems exist.

The formula in each cell is discussed below. Open the spreadsheet and review them:

- Gross Pay   =J6
  AD3   This is referenced to the input/output table. It is shown in order to give a full trail here, without having to scroll.
- Reliefs   =SUM(C4:C6)
  AD7   Totals the reliefs entered in the input/output section.
- Taxable   =IF(AD3-AD7<0,0,AD3-AD7)
  Pay   NOT =AD3-AD7 because this could be negative. The formula reads "If Gross minus Reliefs is less than zero, print zero, otherwise print Gross minus Reliefs."

This leads us to the allocation of Taxable Pay across the tax bands. The table headings of Lower, Basic, Upper and Total are inserted, and the following formulae are entered.

- Lower   =IF(AD11>BC7,BC7,AD11)
            BC7 is the value in the Tax Tables section. The formula is "If
            Taxable Pay is greater than the lower band, print the lower band,
            otherwise print the gross pay."
- Basic   =IF(AD11>(BC7+BC8),BC8,IF(AD11<=BC7,0,AD11-BC7))
            The formula is "If Taxable Pay is greater than the full bands in BC7
            and BC8 (lower and basic) then print the full basic band. If the
            Taxable Pay is less than or equal to the lower band print zero,
            otherwise print the Taxable Pay minus the lower band."
- Upper   =IF(AD11>(BC7+BC8),AD11-BC7-BC8,0)
            The formula is "If Taxable Pay is greater than the lower and basic
            bands print the Taxable Pay minus the lower and basic band limits,
            otherwise print zero."
- Total   =SUM(AF11:AH11)
            This is a cross-tot to visually show that all of the gross pay has been
            allocated.

The above are shown in cells across the page. Having allocated the Taxable Pay across the bands, we are now in a position to calculate the tax arising in each band.

Notice from the previous screen shot that the bands are shown in cells AC14 to AC16. They come down the page so that a simple table, easy to check visually, is produced. The formulae are:

- 10%   =AF11*AC14
            All of the formulae are simply band percentage multiplied by the
            value calculated by the formulae above.
- Total   =AF14
            Picks up the figure, and then totals the column.

To test the table, input a new gross in cell J6. As the gross moves between bands, the allocation of the gross between bands changes, and the tax arising changes accordingly.

Calculating Employee Health Tax

The screen layout is shown below.

The format is very similar to the Tax above, except that the lower band is nil, the middle band includes a split calculation, and the upper band has a finite maximum of $26,000. Above this amount, no additional employee health tax is payable.

The tax table at BA1 sets out the health tax as if there were a band at $50.00, on which tax at 2% is charged. This distinction is also used in the calculation table in order to maintain the ability to check the output visually.

Once again, the steps in the calculation — allocation across bands, calculation and display of tax within each band, total allocated and total tax — are all displayed to minimize the risk of oversight when it is reviewed.

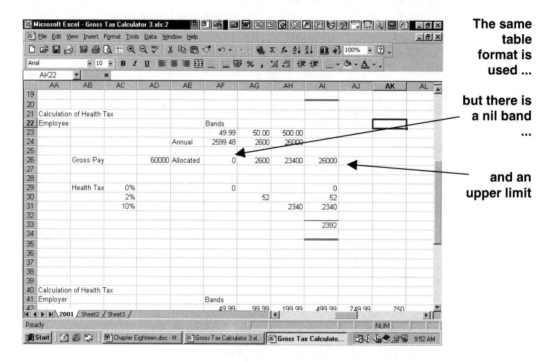

The same table format is used ...

but there is a nil band ...

and an upper limit

Check the formulae in the spreadsheet. They are reviewed below:

- **Annual**   =AF23*52
  Band   Increases the weekly band to an annual figure.
  AF24
- **Gross Pay**   =IF(AD26>AF24,0,AD26)
  Allocation   The formula is "If Gross Pay is greater than the annualized band
  AF26   print zero, otherwise print the gross pay.
- **Gross Pay**   =IF(AD26>=AG24,AG24,0)
  Allocation   The formula is "If Gross Pay is greater than or equal to the
  AG26   annualized band print the band value, otherwise print zero."

- Gross Pay
  Allocation
  AH26

  =IF(AD26>=AH24,AH24-AG24,IF(AD26<=AG24,0,AD26-AG24))
  This formula is more involved, because of the cap on the taxable
  amount. In English it reads "If the Gross Pay is greater than or
  equal to the maximum annual amount, print the maximum
  amount minus the 2600 band. If the Gross Pay is less than or
  equal to the 2600 band print zero, otherwise print the Gross Pay
  minus 2600."

  The cell reference is used instead of the value 2600 so that, if the
  band value changes, it only needs to be changed in one place —
  the Tax Tables.

Calculating Employer Health Tax

The final calculation we must perform is the amount of the Employer's contribution to the Health Tax.

The charge varies depending on which band the gross pay falls into. Once the
band has been identified, the tax is a straight percentage of the gross, so it will
only appear in one band at any one time. The spreadsheet is shown below.

The same table format is used ...

... but this time all figures should be zero except for one band

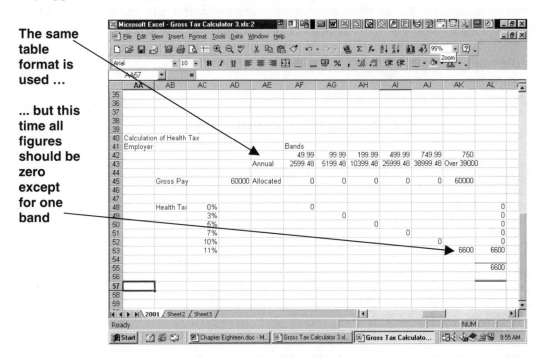

Look at the formulae in the spreadsheet. The main ones are reviewed below:

- Gross Pay   =IF(AD45<=AF43,AD45,0)
  Allocation   Very similar to earlier formulae, it reads "If Gross Pay is less
  AF45   than or equal to the band figure print the gross, otherwise print
                    zero."

- Gross Pay   =IF(AND($AD$45<=AG43,$AD$45>AF43),$AD$45,0)
  Allocation   In English, this reads, "If Gross Pay is less than or equal to the
  AG45   band, and it is greater than the previous band, print the Gross
                    Pay, otherwise print zero."
                    Note the use of the $ signs. $AD$45 is an absolute cell reference,
                    AG43 is a relative reference. This is done so that the cell can be
                    copied into the cells AH45 to AK45 without needing to edit them.

That completes the calculation section. The only things that remain to be done
are to highlight the area and to name the range. Call it **Calculation**.

DISPLAYING THE RESULTS

The calculations have now been done, and we are ready to pick up the results in
our table at A1. To do this, display two windows and tile them. See **Section
Two**, if necessary. Zoom down to display enough cells. The screen looks like this:

**Tile two
Windows
...**

**then, with
cell J7
highlighted,
press —
(minus
symbol) and
click in cell
AI 19 to
select it**

**Press Enter
to accept it**

**Repeat for
the health
tax (J8 and
J13)**

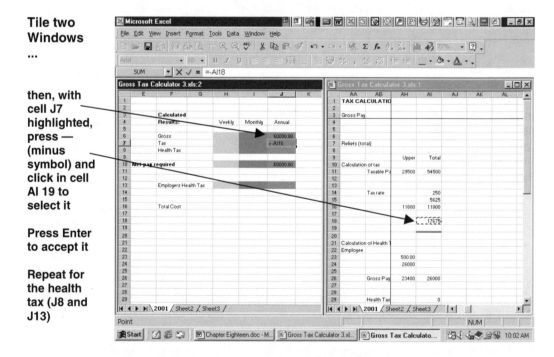

Enter the cell references as shown above, complete the Net Pay section [=SUM(J6:J9)] and the Total Cost section [=J6+J13].

The monthly and weekly sections are the annual figures divided by 12 and 52 respectively, rounded to two decimal places. The formula at I6 is therefore =ROUND(J6/12,2) etc.

Now that we have the final display, we can test data with the payroll department, to ensure it calculates correctly.

Once this is done, everything is ready for finalization. We will document the spreadsheet, date and author it, then show John Smith how to use it.

DOCUMENTING THE SPREADSHEET

We will document the spreadsheet directly, rather than making detailed notes and filing them.

The spreadsheet is shown below with notes attached. It is saved as **Gross Tax Calculator 4.xls**.

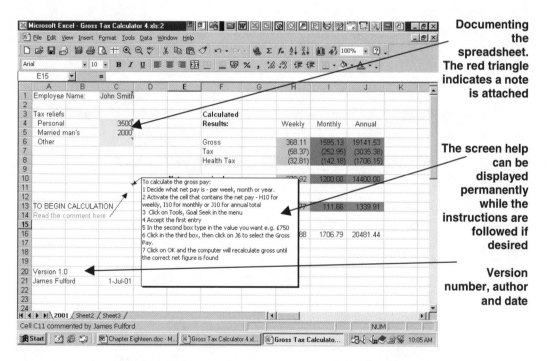

For an explanation of the detailed procedures, see **Section Two**.

PROTECTION

Finally, to finish, we will protect the cells so that they cannot be accidentally overwritten and the formulae destroyed.

Select the Annual Total cell and turn off protection (**Format, Cells, Protection Tab**, and remove the check mark from **Locked**). Likewise, unprotect the cells with the yellow background. All of the cells that are used for input are now unprotected.

Now switch on protection for the entire spreadsheet (**Tools, Protection, Protect Sheet**). Do not use a password. All of the cells other than the four above are now protected.

The spreadsheet is saved on the disk as **Gross Tax Calculator 5.xls**.

TRAINING

Five minutes training for John Smith on using Goal Seek and there we have it. (If you want to refresh on using Goal Seek before we see him, look at **Section Two**.)

SAVE AS...

We want to save the file onto the network drive, and we want to convert it from Excel 2000 format to Excel 95 format.

On the menu, choose **File, Save As...** The dialogue box is displayed. Click on the **Save As Type** box and select Excel 97-2000 & 5.0/95 Workbook(*.xls). **See Section One.**

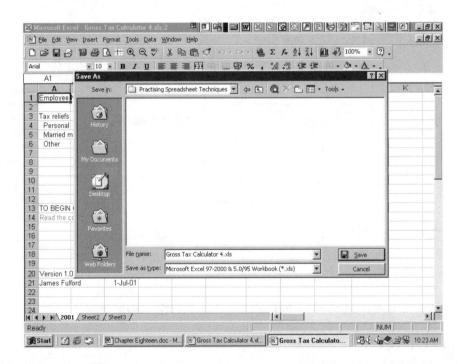

IMPROVEMENTS TO THE MODEL

We have designed a sturdy, documented spreadsheet that does everything we need. How can we improve it?

Improve the formulae

Name the various ranges in the tables and calculation section, then change the formula to meaningful English, for example:

=IF(Reliefs>Gross_Pay,0,Gross_Pay_Relief).

Improve the screen presentation

The problem with the spreadsheet is the "front end" — the part seen by John Smith, and used to provide the answers. The screen below has the gridlines and toolbars turned off and the rulers, status bar and scroll bars removed. It is saved on the disk as **Gross Tax Calculator 5.xls**.

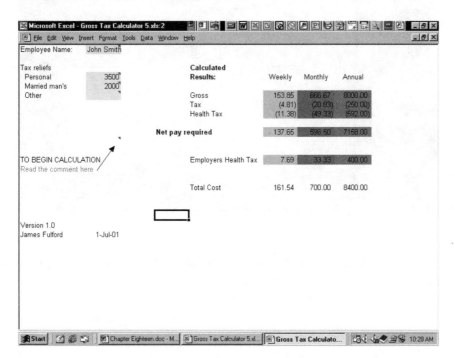

Even with the new formatting applied, it still looks clumsy and unattractive, and the main feature about quality Windows programs is that they should look pleasant and appealing to the user.

So what we are looking for is an improvement in the small area from A1 to J16. The choices are:

- Excel Visual Basic Application Edition
- Visual Basic.

The spreadsheet comprises tables for tax, etc. and, on the face of it, it would be well suited to a database solution. However, the Goal Seek facility option in the spreadsheet is the only reason for building the model, and this option is not available in Access. We would need to interact with Excel through programming in order to use the facility — not pretty.

The best option by far is to get a programmer to prepare a program using VB. One possible screen shot is illustrated below.

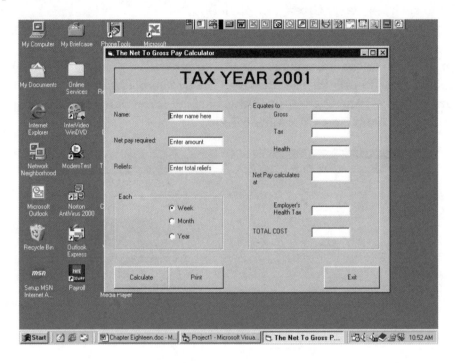

Even with Excel VBA, spreadsheets cannot be made to look as simple or as attractive as this.

Chapter Nineteen

ACCOUNTS AND PROJECTIONS

A balancing trick . . .

Two spreadsheets finished one more to go. This spreadsheet is to be used as the basis for the financials in a business plan to be printed in Word. We need to prepare the annual accounts and three years' projections and, knowing John Smith, everything will be changed and revised substantially before the business plan is finalized.

BACKGROUND

John Smith is an entrepreneur, an inspired businessman who can see opportunities where none appear to exist. He is also the most frustrating employer I have ever worked for — he doesn't understand the amount of effort needed to produce figures. He chops and changes figures part way through. He expects revisions to be completed there and then, and he expects it all to be updated in the report for the bank over lunch. Stress city.

The latest venture is a three-year expansion plan, moving into Whatsits, which he believes will be the biggest thing since Widgets were invented. There are a couple of other projects that he has mentioned in passing which may or may not need to be included, the usual vague brief we are always given.

When this sort of thing has arisen previously, the accounts have been generated by the computer and the projections have been prepared using one of the off-the-shelf packages. Everything has then been thrown into word-processing.

However, this has been very much a square peg in a round hole solution and we want to get a tailored solution once and for all.

The advantages of developing the spreadsheet are twofold:

- We can have a completely tailored solution
- We can use the Object Linking and Embedding (OLE) capabilities of the Office suite to bring everything together into a polished, professional document.

INITIAL DESIGN ISSUES

As with the previous spreadsheet, the first question to ask are, "Who is going to design the spreadsheet? A Programmer or us?"

This problem is interesting, because, on the face of it, it is very much in the domain of programming — the complexity of connecting years, built-in flexibility in each year, OLE to Word etc.

However, the crux of the problem is that the spreadsheet we are talking about is technical as regards the financial accounting aspects but, from a programming perspective, it is very simple. But trying to explain the accounting issues and the areas that need to be made flexible to the programmer and then expecting him to produce exactly the tailored solution that actually works is asking a lot. We should be able to produce a more accurate solution more easily and more quickly ourselves.

Let's look at the design issues identified in **Chapter Fifteen**:

• What file name will we use? It must be meaningful.	Accounts and Projections Template.
• Where will the spreadsheet be saved? On C: drive, floppy disk, network file server?	C: drive. The accounts and projections will be completed by us, and no-one else needs access. In addition, they are confidential.
• Which file format will we save the file in? Excel 2000, Excel 95, etc.?	Excel 2000.
• Who will use the spreadsheet? You, more junior (inexperienced) staff, a qualified accountant, a Power User?	Computer-literate and spreadsheet-literate.
• How often will the spreadsheet be used? Is it a "throw away" spreadsheet or will you want to use it for months or years, again and again (a "template" spreadsheet)?	Only John Smith knows — probably reasonably often.
• What is the spreadsheet to be used for? How complicated is the issue we are reviewing?	The spreadsheet is going to be central to convincing the bank to lend money. The accounting issues are straightforward — accruals, deferring income, tweaking.
• How important is it (professional indemnity, job security, etc.)? The more important, the greater the need for a proper trail.	Our professionalism with third parties is under minute scrutiny. Accurate projections, so that John Smith bases his intuition on solid figures, are critical to the company.

The risk (to us) is that if, for example, the balance sheet does not balance, our professionalism will be called into question.

The risk to the company is that John Smith asks, "What about this? What about that?" and our answers are inaccurate. He could then commit the company to a substantial investment that is badly founded.

The next step is to design it on paper. Let's turn that statement around. If we were preparing the accounts and projections manually, how would we do it?

ACCOUNTS

Think of the working papers on an accounts file. The accounts themselves are drawn together using an Extended Trial Balance (ETB), and the figures are then hand-written on last year's accounts so that the typist can produce this year's figures. The ETB shows the exact figures (to the penny), but the accounts are rounded off to the nearest whole number.

We therefore need:

- An Extended Trial Balance
- Journal Entries
- Accounts and notes.

In addition, we want the computer to do the work, but we want a visual trail so that, if necessary, we can trace any problems quickly and easily.

We will therefore have a Rounded Trial Balance table that rounds off the ETB, and then attach an allocation table to it to provide a trail for the figures into the Profit and Loss account (P&L) and the Balance Sheet (BS).

PROJECTIONS

From an accounts point of view, there is no difference between historical and projected data. They are summarized on the ETB in the same way, and they are processed into the P&L and BS in the same way.

We will therefore use the same spreadsheet design for the projected figures as for the historical figures. This means that we will have the same visual checking capabilities, and the same set of working papers for our file.

A schematic of what we are doing is:

Year 1

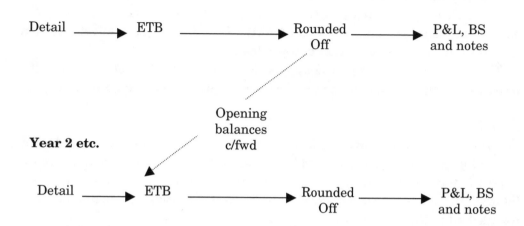

The issues raised in **Chapter Fifteen**, and our answers, are:

- What period is covered in the spreadsheet? What are the break periods?

  The spreadsheet covers four years — last year and the next three. Break periods are twelve-monthly for profit and loss and balance sheet, and monthly for cash flow.

- What is the reporting period?

  As above.

- What will the final report look like? How many pages? Condensed or full size? How will it fit in to the rest of the report?

  The final spreadsheet reports will be included in a word-processed business plan.

- Is the report word-processed, or only done in Excel? Which typeface? Anything bold etc?

  Times New Roman 12 pt. Bold etc. will be consistent with the word-processed report.

Finally, we must decide how to lay the spreadsheet out on the screen:

• What are the main components?	Headings, Extended Trial Balance (ETB), Journals, Rounded Trial Balance, Profit and Loss Account (P&L), Balance Sheet (BS), Notes, Cash Flow, Sales and Purchases details.
• What links are there between sections etc.	The figures link to the ETB, then to the Rounded Trial Balance, then to the P&L, BS and notes. The next year picks up the opening figures.
• How is information to be grouped?	One year per sheet. All years in the one workbook.

In the two previous spreadsheets, the actual report was a small area and the number of cells used was quite small. Exactly which sections we placed the various tables in was not critical, and there was plenty of room to spare. This is a much larger project, with its own particular quirks and problems, and although the size of each sheet is substantial we want to use this space logically in order to assist us later.

REPORTS AND WORKING PAPERS

There are two parts to the spreadsheet:
• Output for use in final reports
• Output for our file of working papers.

The difference between them is that we are constrained in our design for final reports, but not for working papers — we can condense print here, and are not excessively concerned with the appearance of this part of the spreadsheet.

THE SPREADSHEET LAYOUT

The placing of the sections, and the reasons, are given below:

• Account headings	A1. These are used in the ETB, Journals, P&L, BS etc. For easy access, they are placed at A1.
• Extended Trial Balance	A100. Working papers. No row or column formatting will be done. Leaves AA1 etc. clear.
• Journal Entries	A200. Working papers. No row or column formatting will be done. Leaves AA1 etc. clear.

- Journal Descriptions
  A500. Working papers. No row or column formatting will be done. Leaves AA1 etc. clear.
- Rounded Trial Balance
  A600. Working papers. No row or column formatting will be done. Leaves AA1 etc. clear.
- Profit and Loss Account
  AA1000. The report appears in the word-processed report, so column and row formatting will apply. Placing it so far down avoids clashes with other parts of the spreadsheet.
- Balance Sheet
  AA1100. The report appears in the word-processed report, so column and row formatting will apply. Placing it so far down avoids clashes with other parts of the spreadsheet. Leaves BA1 etc. clear. The same column formatting needed for the P&L will also be needed for the BS, so no conflict arises.
- Notes
  AA1150. The report appears in the word-processed report, so column and row formatting will apply. Placing it so far down avoids clashes with other parts of the spreadsheet. Leaves BA1 etc. clear. The same column formatting needed for the P&L will also be needed for the notes, so no conflict arises.
- Fixed Assets
  BA1500. The report appears in the word-processed report, so column and row formatting will apply. The formatting is different for a fixed asset note than for the P&L and BS, so BA is used.
- Cash Flow, etc.
  CA1, DA1 etc. These are used to provide easy and quick access to any tables built as part of the accounts and projections process. (**Ctrl+→** will allow us to move quickly from one section to another.)

By using the structure above, we can remember easily where the sections are, and use the speed keys to navigate around quickly.

BUILDING THE ACCOUNTS SPREADSHEET: ACCOUNT HEADINGS

Let's start building. The headings have been entered in the spreadsheet labeled **Accounts 1.xls**, and it is shown below. The range is named **Account Headings**.

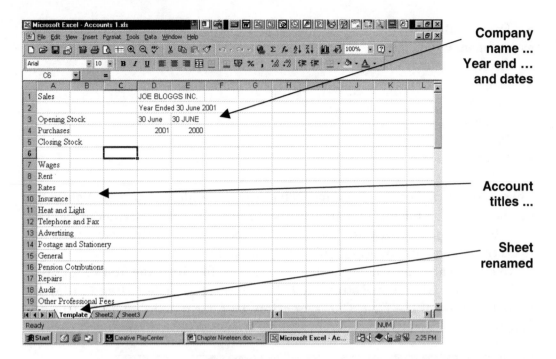

The table below analyses the highlighted areas:

- Account names   Typed. These will be referred to by formulae in the ETB,
                        Journals sections, etc.
- Company Name   Typed. These will be referenced from the ETB, Journals, etc.
- Year Ended   Formula. ="Year Ended "&D3&" "&D4.

                        The text is enclosed in quotation marks and is used to refer to
                        other cells to include in the text. The " " inserts a space
                        between the date and the year.
- 30 June   Text. Entered as '30 June. If the ' is left out, Excel converts it
                        to a date.
- 30 JUNE   To give an upper case version for use later.
- 1999 and 1998   This year, last year, for accounts headings.
- Sheet Name   Renamed to Template. It will be used for accounts and
                        projections.

EXTENDED TRIAL BALANCE (ETB)

To build the ETB, we need to set up the column headings, copy the account
names in from A1 and build the formula and format the numbers as necessary.

The column headings are:

- Opening Balances
- Payments
- Receipts
- Journals
- Accruals
- Prepayments
- Profit and Loss
- Balance Sheet.

There are several layouts in use for ETBs, so if you wish to change it slightly this can be done. The important aspect in the above is that each section of the ETB must balance and, by breaking the accounts process down in this way, the facility to check the computer information visually is available.

To pick up account headings, tile two windows, highlight the first cell, press = and select cell A1. Press **Return** and the cell displays Sales. Drag to copy the formula to rest of the ETB. Check **Section Two** for detailed steps to follow, if necessary.

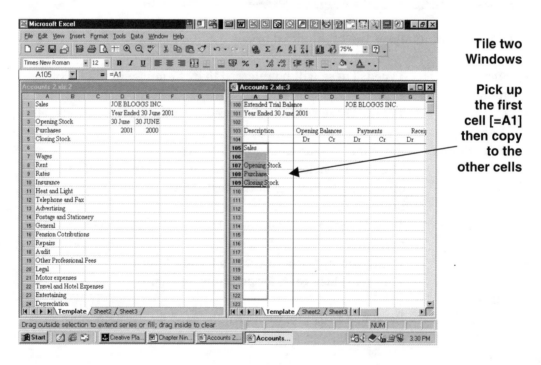

If the cell entry at A1 etc. is blank, the ETB shows zero. To display blanks, make a spacebar entry in A1.

By using =A1 etc. not only does it mean that, if the account name is changed, the other cell is updated, but it also ensures that the cells are in exactly the same relative position. This will be important in the Journals, for ensuring that the journal is picked up in the ETB in the correct place.

The next steps are to enter the formulae, and name the range. The ETB, completed except for the journals column, is shown below. We will pick up the journals once that table is built.

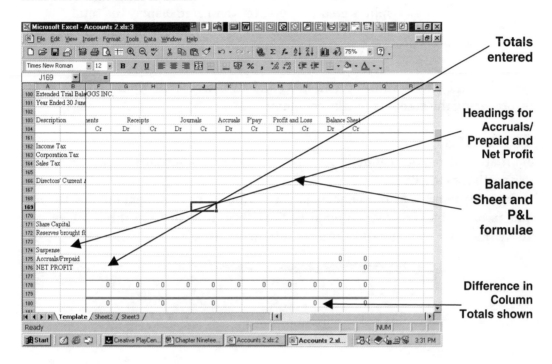

The formulae are explained in the table below:

- Totals
  C187 etc.   =SUM(C105:C177) etc. The cell borders are set above and below, to show it is a column total.
- Difference
  D180 etc.   =D178-C178. To confirm that the two columns are equal, or to identify the difference.
- Accruals/Prepay
  A175   Balance sheet heading, not in the Account Heading section because it is the transfer from P&L to BS
- Prepay
  O175   =L178. Picks up the total prepayments per the P/Pay column.
- Accruals
  P175   =K178. Picks up the total prepayments per the Accruals column.
- Net Profit
  A176   =IF(N180>=0,"NET PROFIT","NET LOSS")
                                 In English, If positive or zero print Net Profit, otherwise print Net Loss.

- Net Profit
  P176

  =N180. The transfer of the profit or loss to the balance sheet.

- P&L Cross-tot
  M105 etc.

  =IF(C105-D105+E105-F105+G105-H105+I105-J105+K105-L105>0,C105-D105+E105-F105+G105-H105+I105-J105+K105-L105,""). In English, if debits minus credits is greater than zero display the total, otherwise print a blank space. The credit side for the P&L and entries for the BS are similar.

We will build the Journals section now, and then test what we have done so far by preparing the accounts for the company.

JOURNALS

Journals will require columns for Account heading, Journal number and Total (for posting to the ETB).

In order to print at reasonable size, we can only have a maximum of 15 journals in one table. In order to build in flexibility, we will have three tables, one above the other, giving us 45 journals in total.

Named ranges ...

headings from A1 etc.

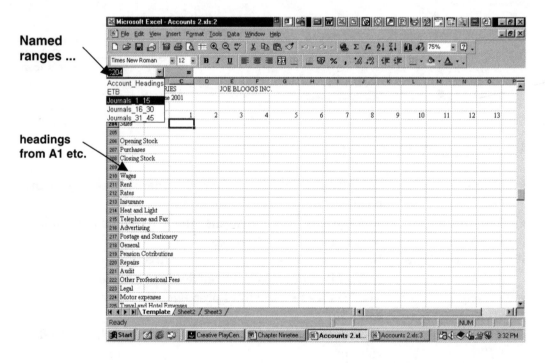

The Journal section and related formulae are shown below:

- Account Headings
  A204 etc.

  =A1 etc. This makes the names consistent, and always in the same place as they appear in the ETB.

- Totals
  R204 etc.

  =SUM (C204: Q204) etc. The journals will be posted to the ETB as one total, not individually.

- Total (should be nil)
  C421 etc.

  =SUM (C204: C420)-C275-C348. In English, Sum all cells in the three tables, then deduct 16 and 31 — the journal headings. 1 is at cell C203, and is outside the summed range, so it does not need to be deducted.

- C202

  =IF (C421=0,"", C421). In English, this checks whether the above total is zero — if it is, it prints a blank, otherwise it prints the figure. This provides a running total of the amount of the journal.

That completes the Journals. All we need to do now is pick up the journal figure in the ETB, and we are ready to check the accounts production. The formula is:

- I105

  =IF(R204+R277+R350>0,R204+R277+R350,0). In English, it reads, If the three journal totals is greater than zero, print the total, otherwise print zero.

To pick up the figures, two windows were tiled, and the cells were selected using the mouse. This saves time and increases accuracy. The cells are formatted for accounting, and show a dash if nil.

**Tile two
Windows**

**Building
the
formula
...**

**using
point and
click**

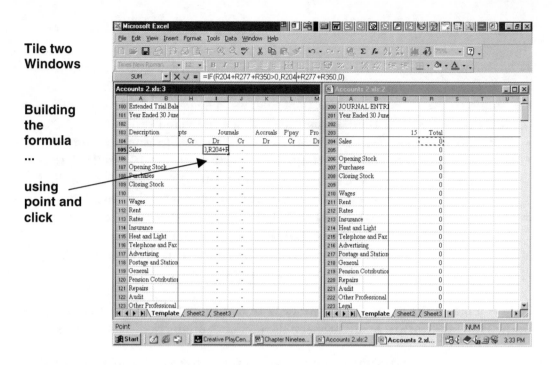

The spreadsheet is saved on the disk as **Accounts 2.xls**.

DRAFT ACCOUNTS

We will print a trial balance from the company computer and enter it in to the spreadsheet to test it. The trial balance is shown below.

Description	Dr	Cr
Sales		3691066.20
Purchases	2583746.34	
Wages	523532.90	
Rent	76000.00	
Rates	15200.00	
Insurance	17601.22	
Heat and Light	14122.30	
Telephone and Fax	9125.68	
Advertising	34197.56	
Postage and Stationery	44251.96	
General	6984.85	
Pension Cotributions	52353.29	
Repairs	4712.00	
Audit	1779.00	
Other Professional Fees	12500.00	
Legal	4758.00	
Motor expenses	27988.64	
Travel and Hotel Expenses	6899.60	
Entertaining	5477.63	
Depreciation	195000.00	
Bank Charges and Interest	17880.95	
Credit Card Charges	8772.45	
Hire purchase Interest	2500.00	
Loan Interest	3500.00	
Premises Cost	1900000.00	
Premises Depreciation		200000.00
Plant Cost	535477.00	
Plant Depreciation		133869.00
Fixtures Cost	312899.00	
Fixtures Depreciation		78225.00
Inventory	615178.00	
Trade Debtors Control	922766.55	
Petty Cash	574.69	
Trade Creditors		538280.00
Income Tax		14833.43
Corporation Tax		15766.94
Sales Tax		15447.63
Directors' Current Account		66000.00
Bank Current account		134766.54
Bank Loan		31643.00
Hire purchase Gross		23512.00
Hire purchase Interest Deferred	7837.00	
Share Capital		100000.00
Reserves brought forward		2920206.87
	7963616.61	7963616.61

The figures have been posted into **Accounts 3.xls**.

The year end adjustments are set out below.

Inventory is computerized, and is linked into the accounts package. The trial balance figure is therefore the actual inventory figure at the year-end. The opening inventory figure was £599,127.

Accruals are:

- Rent   £14,000
- Rates   £1,600
- Heat and Light   £2,250
- Telephone   £1,250
- Advertising   £4,250
- Carriage and Postage   £3,797
- Audit   £19,000
- Motor Expenses   £3,116
- Bank Interest and Charges   £970

Prepayments are:

- Insurance   £4,125

There are purchase invoices to be accrued of £17,117, and there are Sales cut-off adjustments of £35,119.

These are entered onto the ETB as follows:
- Inventory   Journal adjustment (JV1)
- Accruals   ETB column K
- Prepayments   ETB column L

Enter them in **Accounts 3.xls** to see how they update. This will be useful for the projections later. The ETB with the above entered is saved on the disk as **Accounts 4.xls**. You will notice that the ETB provides a full visual trail for checking that the balance sheet balances after all of these adjustments. The ETB screen is shown below.

Visual checking that Journals balance, BS balances etc.

Description changes to Net Loss

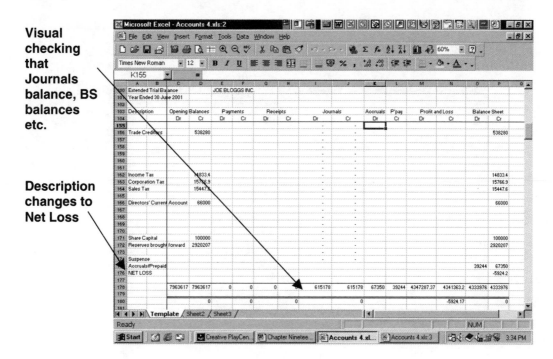

The net loss (before John Smith goes through the figures) is $5,924.17.

Play about with the model — delete accruals, insert prepayments, process Journals, to familiarize yourself. This will be useful for preparing the projections.

FINISHING THE DRAFT ACCOUNTS TRAIL

The last thing that we need to do in order to provide a full list of working papers is the Journal Descriptions section. This simply provides a written explanation of the reason each Journal is posted.

We will establish the Journal Description section below the Journals, starting at cell A500.

The requirements are simple enough — pick up the headings (=D1 for the company name, =D2 for the year end), type in the heading **Journal Descriptions** and enter Journal Numbers 1 and 2, then **AutoFill** to 45.

Once this is done, tile two windows to check — one for the Journals and the other for the descriptions — and fill in the details. The tiled screen, with the descriptions entered, is shown below.

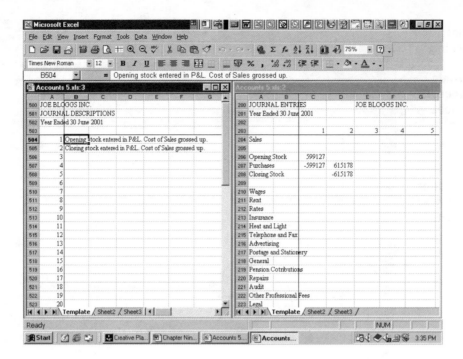

That finishes the accounts production aspects of the model – it allocates the amounts to Profit and Loss account or Balance Sheet as appropriate, Journal Adjustments can be entered as necessary, and Accruals and Prepayments are easily recorded. Visual checking is easy, and errors can be traced by using the ETB to identify whether the error is in the Trial Balance, the Journals, or some other part. A proper written detail of the reason for Journals being entered is available, and there is ample space on the spreadsheet for calculations and recording "on the fly". The spreadsheet is saved on the disk as **accounts5.xls**.

In the next chapter, we will put a front end on the draft accounts, as described earlier, prior to linking it into Word.

IMPROVEMENTS TO THE MODEL

We have designed the "back end" calculator for churning out the accounts, and can obtain the printouts and paper trail we need for our file. What improvements could be made?

Change the ETB headings

At present, the headings cover areas not applicable to accounts production. The opening balances, bank and cash transactions are included in the office accounts system. We have left the headings as they are because we will use the same format for projections. However, once the template is finished, the headings in the accounts sheet can be updated.

Protect the Worksheet

All of the formulae are unprotected at present, and they could be overwritten. To protect the cells, see **Section Two**. However, this step would be better completed once the full template is finished. Note that drag and drop on the ETB produces the #REF error whether the cells are protected or not.

ETB Cross-tot

At present, if a text entry is made on the spreadsheet, the error #VALUE is displayed. Error-trapping surrounding the P&L and BS cross-tot would identify it. The format would be =IF(ISERROR(cross tot), "Text Entry", [current statement]).

However, there is little advantage in displaying Text Entry compared with #VALUE, as long as you are aware of the problem and its cause.

Attach Explanatory Notes

It might be helpful to attach explanations of what we have done and why on the spreadsheet itself, by way of Insert Comment. See **Section Two** for information, if necessary.

Automate Moving Around

Provide a custom toolbar or menu for moving around, instead of using the range name section. However, the benefits are marginal as the number of defined areas increases and toolbar space is filled.

Chapter Twenty

ACCOUNTS AND PROJECTIONS: THE REPORTS

Presentation is professionalism personified.

We have the accounts in their raw, unformatted state. We will build the reports section, to make them appear as they do in the word-processed document. We saw in the previous section what we need to do, namely:
- Round off the figures to the nearest whole number
- Print the P&L, BS and notes
- Print a Fixed Asset note.

THE ROUNDING PROCESS
Rounding-off is not a particularly difficult process, and it could have been done in the ETB by adding =ROUND (Cross-tot formula , 0).

However, we want to achieve two things when we round-off:
- We want to show the rounded balances as they appear in the final accounts
- We want a show a visual trail to the figures that appear in the balance sheet. This is necessary because the balance sheet is a summary and amalgamation of the ETB figures. Greater detail is given in the notes, but some figures are still combined — and the notes neither give a full trail in one place nor do they provide an easy method for amending allocations.

We will build the rounded-off trial balance and attach an allocation table.

THE ROUNDED ETB
The rounded ETB is a straight copy of the P&L and BS headings of the ETB, rounded to whole numbers. A table is then attached to allocate the BS items across the balance sheet headings.

To build the table, move to A600, type in the heading **Rounded Trial Balance**, pick up the headings [**=D1** for company name and **=D2** for year end], then tile two windows and display the ETB in the second window by selecting **ETB** from the Name Range. Freeze panes, as appropriate, then copy the account headings from the ETB. We use the ETB, instead of A1 etc., because there are two headings (Accruals/Prepay and Net Profit/Loss) which only appear in the ETB.

The rounded figures will be picked up by typing **=ROUND(**, then selecting the cell with the mouse, entering comma and zero, then pressing **Return**. However, the formula must be encased in error trapping in order to function properly before it is copied to the rest of the cells.

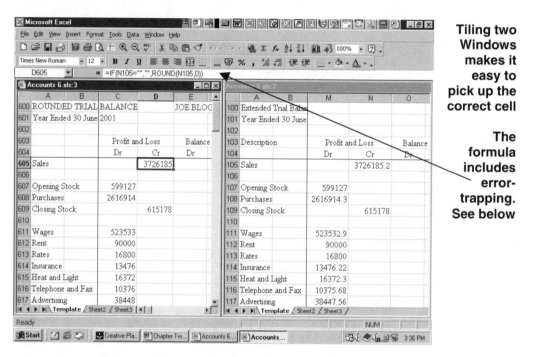

Tiling two Windows makes it easy to pick up the correct cell

The formula includes error-trapping. See below

The potential for error arises because, if there is no figure displayed in the ETB, a " " space is entered, and this is a text entry – you cannot round text, and #VALUE is displayed.

The formula tests first whether text is present and, if it is, it enters " " on the rounded TB. The formula is:

=IF(M105="","",ROUND(M105,0))   In English, if the cell in the ETB contains " ", print " ", otherwise round the number to zero decimal places.

If the ETB had been formatted to display zeros as dashes (accounting format), this would not have been necessary, but dashes would have appeared instead of blank cells. Alternatively, the window could be set not to display zeros.

ALLOCATING BALANCE SHEET ITEMS IN A TABLE

The table headings are the same categories as in the accounts. Individual entries are allocated by activating the cell and pressing **=**, then **Ctrl+←**. This moves the cursor over and, once the figure is selected, pressing **Return** places the cell reference in the correct place.

The screen below illustrates the table. The file is saved on the disk as **Accounts 6.xls**.

The headings are per the BS categories

The formula is straight-forward

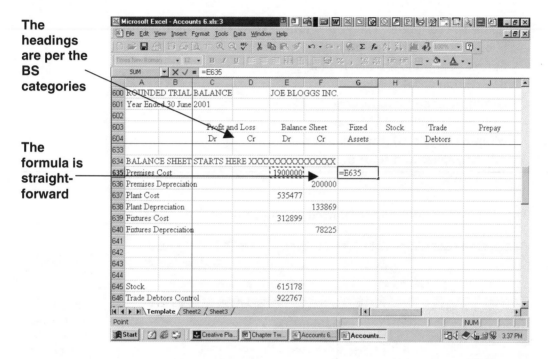

There are visual check digits below the totals – see **Accounts 6.xls**. They will be used when we build the P&L account, etc. Name the range **Rounded_ETB**.

THE PROFIT AND LOSS ACCOUNT REPORT

We will now build the first report. As background, the requirement for this report is that it must look and feel exactly like the original word-processed document. That means:

- It must be in the same typeface
- It must print at 100%, or near enough so that it is not noticeably smaller
- Underlines must be spaced with a gap, otherwise there will be a continuous unbroken line between columns.

As noted earlier, we start the report at AA1000. This allows us to change column width and row height without affecting other areas of the spreadsheet we might use.

The table below shows the steps taken to build the P&L report:

• Type in the title, and pick up the company name and year-end.	Type in "Profit and Loss Account". Enter the formulae =D1 and =D2
• Enter account headings and column headings.	The account headings come from the rounded ETB [=A605 etc.], column headings come from the years per D4 and E4.
• Space the columns to leave a small blank between each column of figures. Columns are needed for description (20.86), Note (standard), indented figures (standard), space (0.75), main column (standard), then space, column, space and column for the comparatives.	Drag the column width to the sizes noted.

The P&L report, suitably formatted, is shown below:

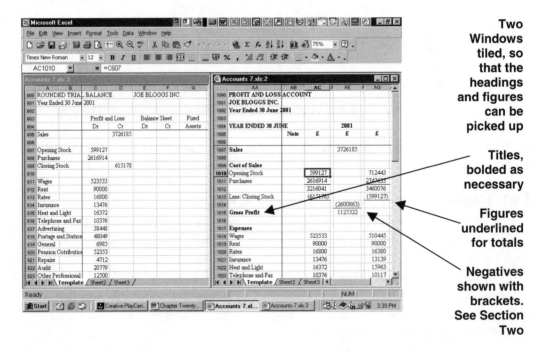

Two Windows tiled, so that the headings and figures can be picked up

Titles, bolded as necessary

Figures underlined for totals

Negatives shown with brackets. See Section Two

To display negative numbers in brackets, format the cell and choose the **Number** tab. Select **Custom** and, in the **Type** box, enter ###0_);(###0_);–____. There must be an even number of dashes, or an error message will be displayed.

Headings such as Cost of Sales and Gross Profit are placed directly on the report, because they are not used earlier. Note that the figures are not spaced on the ETB but are spaced and placed in columns in the report — the difference in approach relates to the difference between working papers and final report quality output.

Visual error-checking is built-in at the bottom of the P&L report. The total profit from the rounded ETB is displayed below the report figure, and the difference between it and the profit per the report is noted. We know that the ETB balances, therefore if there were a difference it could only arise because we have not picked up all of the figures from the ETB.

As emphasized previously, providing error-checking capabilities at each stage means that, should an error arise, it can be isolated quickly, and time is not wasted running through the entire spreadsheet.

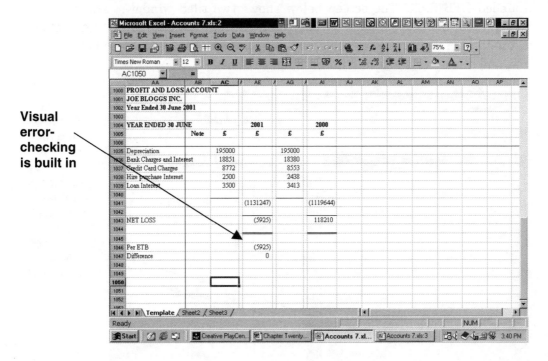

Visual error-checking is built in

To finish, the comparative figures must be typed in to 2000, and the name range **Report_PandL** must be inserted. This has been done for you, and the file is saved on the disk as **Accounts 7.xls**.

BALANCE SHEET

The Balance Sheet is placed below the P&L, so that it uses the same columns and column widths. It is prepared in the same way as the P&L, with headings being lifted from D1 etc. but, unlike the P&L, all BS account headings are typed in, the wording being taken from last year's word-processed accounts. This is because the BS is a summary page, with the detail being given in the notes to the accounts, whereas the P&L is a detailed document that does not have a supporting schedule.

If the P&L was a summary document and a schedule was provided behind it, a copy of the rounded ETB would have to be made and a further allocation table attached. The headings in this new table would equate to the headings in the full accounts.

A copy of the rounded ETB would be necessary, with a further table attached, because the size of a single table would be too unwieldy. To copy the table, use =A600 etc.

Once the headings have been inserted, the figures can be lifted from the rounded ETB table. The screen below shows two tiled windows, and the figure being lifted, using the mouse for point-and-click. In the case of the figure shown, a sub-total of accounts receivable and prepayments has been made below the table, and this total is inserted in the Balance Sheet.

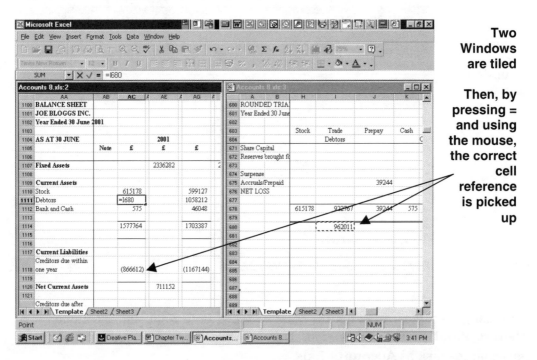

Two Windows are tiled

Then, by pressing = and using the mouse, the correct cell reference is picked up

Name the range **Reports_BS**. The completed balance sheet is saved on the disk as **Accounts 8.xls**.

NOTES TO THE ACCOUNTS

The report building is almost complete. The final step is to display the notes to the Balance Sheet, and then we will be ready to copy the template and use it as the core of the Projections template.

The notes are the detail to support the BS summary. The summary came from the rounded ETB, and, except for the fixed asset note, the detail for the notes will also come from the detail already in the rounded ETB.

Fixed assets are different, because they must show opening and closing positions and movement during the period.

The screen below shows how the accounts receivable note is constructed — the heading is typed in, the year-end is taken from D4 and E4, and the account descriptions are word-processed from last year's accounts.

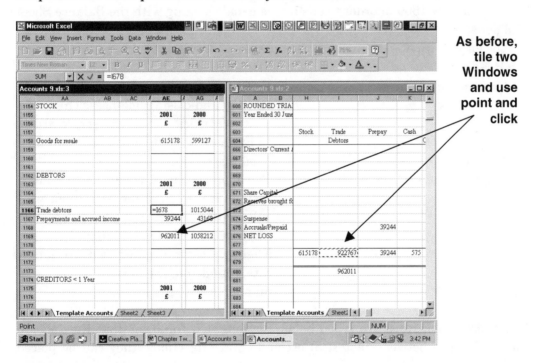

FIXED ASSETS

We need to build a fixed asset note. It needs some attention, because it shows opening balance, additions, disposals and closing balance. The choices within the spreadsheet as regards presentation are:

- Build one note that shows all lines, and display dashes if the figures are nil
- Build one note that shows all lines, but hide the rows that contain no figures when it comes to paste it into Word

- Build four notes, one for no additions or disposals, one for additions only, one for disposals only, and one for both additions and disposals. We would then use the note that applies in the circumstances.

We will use the second option — build one note and hide rows as necessary.

We can use the fixed asset note to calculate the depreciation charge, by entering a formula in the note. In addition, with the present layout of the ETB, we can pick up the opening and closing balances. However, we cannot pick up the additions/disposals split. To do this, we need an extra line in the BS for additions, which may or may not be used each year. The choices are, therefore, to pick the figure out ourselves and put it in the note, or to build in a buffer in the ETB to allow the figure to be picked up as part of the ETB process.

In this model, we will insert additions and disposals manually.

We will build the fixed assets note at BA1500 because the spacing for the fixed assets headings is different from the Profit and Loss Account and Balance Sheet. We start at row 1500 in order to ensure we avoid clashing with the Balance Sheet and notes.

The entries we need to make in the note are given below:

• Headings	=D1 etc.
• Account Headings etc.	Type in cost. Enter a formula for opening and closing balances. This is ="At "&$D$3&" "&$E$4&" and "&$D$4. In English "At [date and year from the headings section]
• Depreciation Charge for the Year	The depreciation is as per the accounts system. However, in the projections we will include the following formula: =ROUND(BD1511*BD1526,0). In English, Cost multiplied by depreciation rate, rounded to the nearest whole number.

The depreciation rates are typed below the note. On the basis that they should not be changed between historical accounts and projections, they can be placed here.

Name the range **Fixed_Assets_Note**. The fixed asset note is shown below.

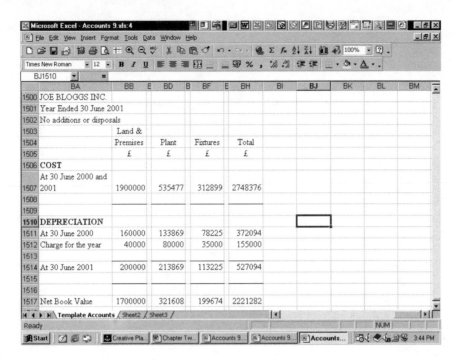

We are now ready to start work on the projections.

Chapter Twenty-one

THE PROJECTIONS

The same as accounts, only the future.

We set out our design for the Accounts/Projections template in **Chapter Nineteen**, and we have already built the elements necessary for the completion of the accounts. However, because we are using figures prepared up to TB stage in the accounts, it has not yet been necessary to use the capabilities of our visual system to its full potential. We will now complete the model, and then prepare the three years' projections, whilst maintaining the visual checking necessary to allow quick and easy identification of errors.

STARTING THE PROJECTIONS

The file **Accounts 9.xls** contains the template developed to the end of **Chapter Twenty**. We wish to change it from a template to actual accounts and projections, so we will amend it as follows:

- Rename the template **Accounts**
- Make a copy of the template and name it **Proj Yr 1**
- Delete the figures in Proj Yr 1 to leave it blank
- Enter closing balances from the accounts into Proj Yr 1 as opening balances
- Delete Sheets 2 and 3.

Diagrammatically, Proj Yr 1 will be expanded as follows:

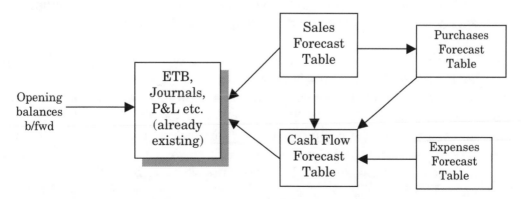

Open **Accounts 9.xls** and rename the sheet, delete sheets 2 and 3 etc. as set out above. See **Section Two** for detailed steps to complete these tasks, if necessary.

The amended file is shown below:

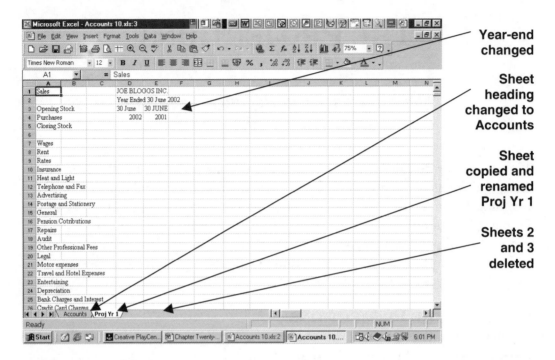

Figures have been deleted by highlighting them and pressing the **Delete** key. The amended file is saved on the disk as **Accounts 10.xls**.

We will now bring the opening balances into Proj Yr 1, and then build the Projected Sales table etc.

ENTERING OPENING BALANCES

Opening balances come from two places:

- Balance sheet items are taken from the Rounded ETB
- Detailed entries for Accruals and Prepayments are taken from the columns in the ETB, because only the grand total appears in the Rounded ETB.

The figures are picked up in the usual way — tiling two windows, pressing = and selecting the cell with the mouse. This is shown in the screen below.

As you can see from the diagram, the Accruals in the Accounts spreadsheet are in the debit column in the ETB in order to increase the P&L charge in that year, and the total of the column is carried forward as a credit in the balance sheet. We are splitting the balance sheet credit so we are showing the detailed entries as credits against the individual accounts when we bring them forward in the projected ETB.

Note that the rounding difference in the Accounts Rounded ETB was allocated to Accruals. We are carrying it forward in General Expenses in the projections, and it is therefore written off to reserves in that year. Also, remember that the reserves figure is the figure per the Rounded ETB plus the profit for the year.

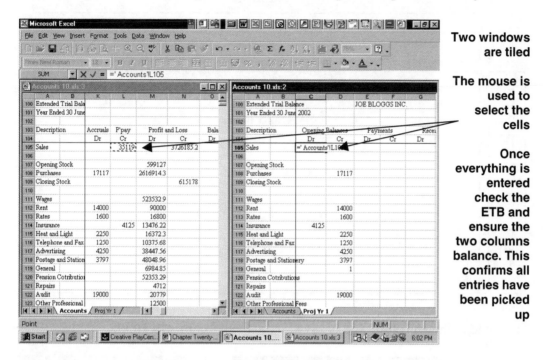

The file is saved on the disk as **Accounts 10.xls**.

PROJECTED CASH FLOW

The next two sections in the ETB are bank payments and cash received. We will look at Projected Sales and Projected Cash Received first. The principles from these will apply to purchases and creditors. Finally, we will look at Projected Overheads and Capital and Overhead/Capital Cash flow

PROJECTED SALES AND CASH RECEIVED

The schematic for the Sales cycle is:

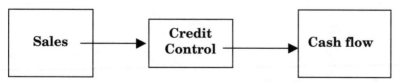

We want to reproduce this process in our spreadsheet, and to provide flexibility if assumptions are changed. The variables are Sales Forecast and Credit Control — cash flow is merely a consequence of the previous two. We will construct a table

structure that matches the above, and combines it with as much visual checking as possible. Diagrammatically, we will set up our table like this:

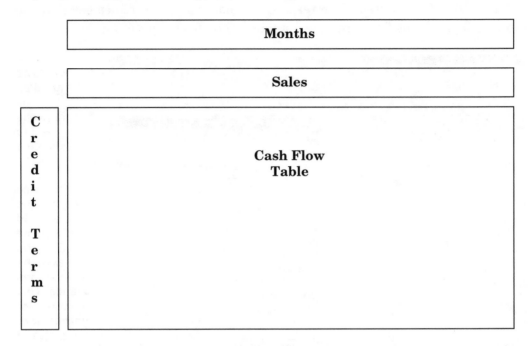

Months

Sales

C r e d i t T e r m s	**Cash Flow Table**

The table is shown below, and is saved on disk as **Accounts 10.xls**.

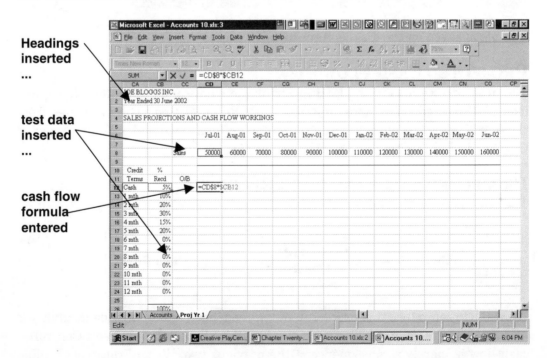

The formula used in the first cell is =CD\$8*\$CB12. In English, this reads, "Multiply CD8 by CB12. If copying, make the column CD variable but row 8 constant, and make column CB constant, but row 12 variable". See **Section Two** for absolute and relative cell addressing.

Filling out the entire area gives the cash flow over the next 12 months generated by each month's sales.

However, it is not an easy table to review visually. Cash flow in July 2001 is based on the value in cell CD12, Aug 2001 is based on CD13 plus CE12 etc. We will amend the table slightly. We will enter a column for the opening balance, drag each column to line up the receivable months, and enter the month ends.

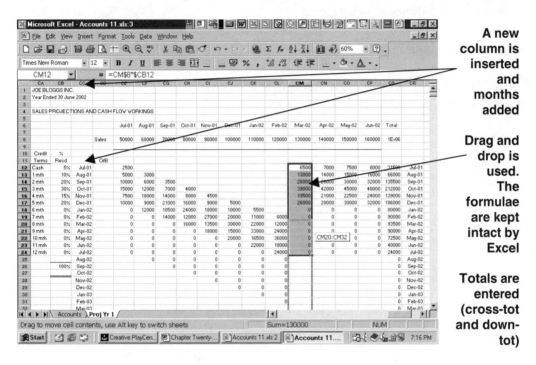

A new column is inserted and months added

Drag and drop is used. The formulae are kept intact by Excel

Totals are entered (cross-tot and down-tot)

The completed table is named **Cash_Sales_Table**, and it is saved on the disk as **Accounts 11.xls**.

The important aspects of the final table are:

- Sales are varied in cells CE8 to CP8, and the impact on cash flow is seen immediately.
- Credit collection success can be varied, and the impact on cash flow is seen immediately.
- The breakdown of any month's collections is easily ascertained
- The table will give an aged analysis of the debtor balance outstanding at the year-end, by deducting receipts from sales in each column at that time period
- All of the above is achieved without using long or complicated formulae.

The figures will be used as follows:

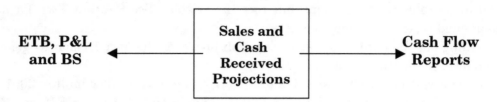

This layout means that the balanced accounts will agree with the figures generated in the cash flow, and that the cash balances per the Cash Flow reports will agree with the balance sheet figures.

However, we will build the other cash flow tables now, and then pass everything through the ETB and prepare the Cash Flow reports later.

PURCHASES, PAYMENTS AND STOCKING

The schematic for the Purchasing cycle is:

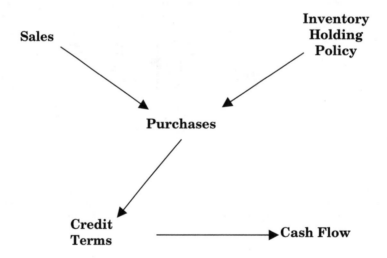

Therefore, when new products are introduced, cash flow is affected by stocking up. When products near the end of their life-cycle, there is de-stocking etc. Terms can be renegotiated with suppliers which lengthens (or shortens) the payment period, and the cost of the goods can alter if additional discounts are earned by early payment.

As previously, we will design a table that shows these aspects to feed into the cash flow, and that allows us to see the results visually.

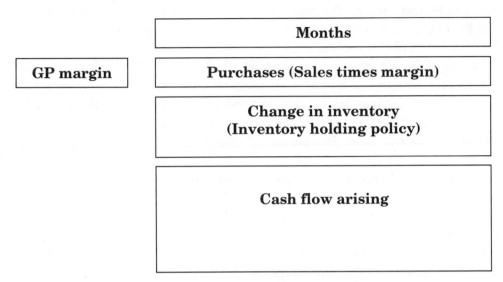

	Months
GP margin	**Purchases (Sales times margin)**
	Change in inventory (Inventory holding policy)
	Cash flow arising

The table is shown below, and is included on the disk as **Accounts 12.xls**.

A similar format to the previous table

Additional entries as required

... and space created by drag and drop

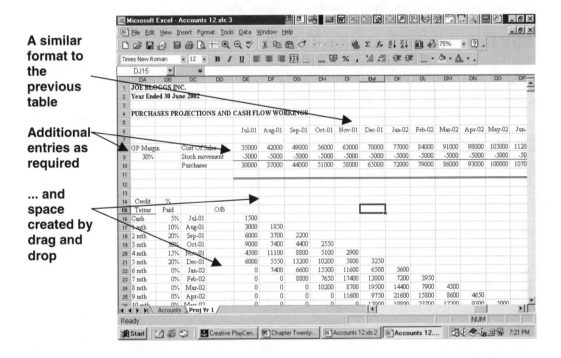

There are some fundamental differences between this and the previous table, and a straight copy will not do.

The headings all contain the formula =[cell]. This means that a change in the starting month in the Sales table will be reflected in the Purchases table.

The formulae in the cash flow section had to be deleted, re-input and dragged down to the correct month. The new line for inventory movement, and the new total of Purchases meant that cash flow would be based on the wrong cell, if a straight copy of the Sales table is used.

As before, the table gives us an aged creditor analysis. We can vary margin and payment terms to see how this impacts on cash flow. You will realize, of course, that the figures for margin, payment etc. are averages. If a more detailed analysis is required, further tables should be built and the results consolidated.

The range is named **Cash_Purchases_Table**.

The reason why we have included a stocking policy line is because, in the long term, the future for Widgets is not good. Sales are falling, and John Smith will be switching to selling Whatsits. The company will manage the decline in sales, and we will de-stock on the more exposed types of Widget so that we are not left with worthless inventory. If we ignored inventory levels, our cash flow would be fundamentally flawed. In addition, and the reason why we have to approach the bank, we will have to build up inventory of Whatsits, and sales will not finance the working capital requirement in the shorter term.

That leaves the Overhead/Capital Table to complete.

THE OVERHEAD/CAPITAL TABLE

The format for this table is different from the previous two — cash flow is dependent mainly on the overhead structure rather than on Sales, and cash flow is either monthly, quarterly or annual depending on the type of expense.

We need to build a table that allocates the annual projected overheads to the appropriate month as directed, and that then draws together the total cash flow. This will be achieved with IF statements.

The table is shown below:

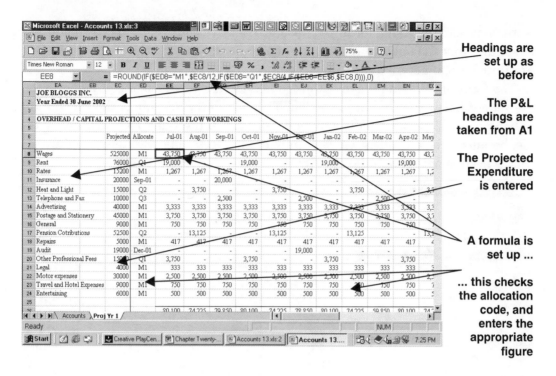

Headings are set up as before

The P&L headings are taken from A1

The Projected Expenditure is entered

A formula is set up ...

... this checks the allocation code, and enters the appropriate figure

The formula in each cell is discussed below:

- Wages etc.   =A7
  Cell EA8   The formula is dragged down, but excluding
                         Depreciation, HP Interest, etc.

- Projected   The figure is input here, for use in the ETB and the cash
  Expenditure   flow.
  Cell EC8 etc.

- Allocation Code   Typed in. The choices are monthly (M1), Quarterly (Q1,
  Cell ED8 etc.   Q2 or Q3, depending on the start month), Annual (enter
                         month paid).

- Month cash flow   =ROUND(IF($ED8="M1",$EC8/12,IF($ED8="Q1",$EC8/
  Cell EE8 etc.   4,IF($ED8=EE$6,$EC8,0))),0)
                         In English, the formula reads "Round the figure to the
                         nearest whole number. If the allocation code is M1, print
                         the total divided by 12; if it is Q1, print the figure
                         divided by 4; if the month heading equals the month in
                         the allocation code, enter the full amount. Otherwise
                         enter zero.
                         Cell EF8 uses Q2 instead of Q1, and EG8 uses Q3. All
                         cells are formatted for accounting, and display a dash if
                         the entry is nil.

Note the use of the $ sign for mixed absolute/relative addressing. The cell address is set like this to facilitate copying the formula across the rest of the table. See **Section Two**, if necessary.

The Capital elements (payment of loans and HP, purchase of equipment, etc.) are set out below the Overhead section. The only entry missing is the calculation of bank interest payable. This will be dealt with in the Cash Flow Summary table, because it is dependent on cash in and out. Cross-tots and down-tots are all that is needed now to complete the table.

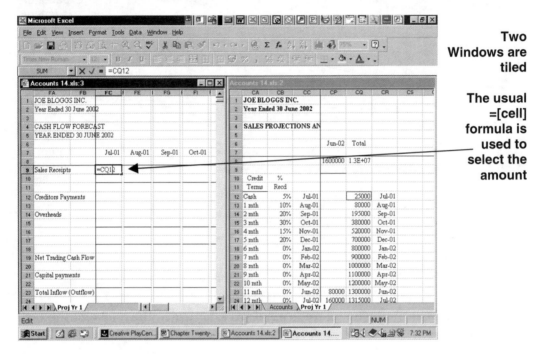

Two Windows are tiled

The usual =[cell] formula is used to select the amount

With the tables complete, a report can be produced, bringing together cash inflows and outflows. Once again, tiled windows will allow the proper selection of the correct cells. The cash flow report section is shown above, with the second window displaying the cash received section.

The completed spreadsheet is saved as **Accounts 14.xls**. Open the spreadsheet and study the tables. They are in the named ranges, so use this to locate them. There are several points to note:

- In the finished table, columns have been inserted and dragged to a width of 0.58 in order to give a gap between lines — otherwise, a single continuous line appears in the final printed report.
- I have decided to split the table in the final report, showing a summary first and the detailed analysis behind. Both are wider than A4 and we will set the

word-processor to print these tables as landscape (A4 on its side), and the rest as portrait (A4 vertical).

- Bank interest is calculated in the summary cash flow statement using a formula to work out the charge or interest receivable. This is explained below.
- The format for the cells has been amended so that zeros are displayed as dashes are displayed, but they are centered in the column. This is explained below.

BANK INTEREST

The formula calculates the interest based on the previous three months' balances per the cash flow. This avoids causing a circular reference. The full formula is: =ROUND((IF(FI25<0,FI25,0)+IF(FK25<0,FK25,0)+IF(FM25<0,FM25,0))/3*FC 32*3/12,0).

It is explained below:

• IF(FI25<0,FI25,0)	If month 1 is negative (overdrawn), include the figure; otherwise include zero. Likewise with months 2 and 3.
• IF(FI25<0,FI25,0)+IF(FK25<0,FK2 5,0)+IF(FM25<0,FM25,0)) /3*$FC$32*3/12	Divide the total of the above by three, to give a one month average. Multiply the balance by the interest rate for the year, then multiply it by 3/12ths to give the quarter's interest charge.
• =ROUND((IF(FI25<0,FI25,0)+IF(F K25<0,FK25,0)+IF(FM25<0,FM25, 0))/3*$FC$32*3/12,0)	Everything is encased in ROUND to ensure the result is expressed in whole numbers. The format of the ROUND statement is =ROUND(-----,0).

Note that an absolute cell reference has been used for the bank interest, and the others are relative. This is to facilitate copying.

DISPLAYING ZEROS AS DASHES

The custom format for displaying negative numbers in brackets is ####_);(####). We have amended this to ####_);(####); - _____ .

The ; followed by dashes spaces the placing of the zero dash. There must be an even number of dashes, or an error message will be displayed.

THE COMPLETED TEMPLATE

All of the structure is now complete. The same ETB and related sections are there for the preparation and printing of the reports. The cash flow tables are set up, and we are ready to meet John Smith to discuss finalizing the June 2001 accounts and to find out his views on the projected results to June 2004.

When we have this information, we will complete everything and blend it with the word-processed business plan.

The meeting with John Smith is dealt with in the next chapter. But first, some brief comments on how the model and our approach could be changed.

IMPROVEMENTS IN AND CHANGES TO THE MODEL

The problem with changing the model is that the edges of a square box start to appear, and flexibility is gradually lost. Whether the following are improvements is a personal matter.

Using Access

As mentioned in the previous models, anything that is built in a spreadsheet with a table structure can also be built in Access. Depending on how the model is constructed (using the Developers Kit to produce an EXE program, for example), it may be possible to enter figures directly into tables, although well-designed forms also will be necessary. The main differences between an Excel-based solution and a full, three-dimensional database solution are:

Excel	Access
Adjustments to relationships, formulae and layout can be made immediately, without fundamentally changing the template.	The complexity of the relationships between tables, and the problems of introducing new tables and, therefore, new relationships, means that changes cannot be easily implemented once the core structure has been set.
The converse of the above is that established relationships etc. can be overwritten in error.	The Access solution is difficult to tamper with and, therefore, if it is right, it will always be right.
There is no front end — entry is direct, simple and quick.	Entry is (usually) through forms. Entry is constrained and controlled.
The converse of the above is "More speed less haste".	The use of forms means that all input can be checked to ensure it is complete, before the user is allowed to progress.
Work "on the fly" in another part of the spreadsheet.	You can't.
Time to develop is relatively short. Testing is relatively easy.	Time to develop is relatively long. Testing is more difficult.

Using Visual Basic

Using VB, or Excel VB Applications Edition, provides programmable control, and more flexibility than is available in Access. However, development time and testing of data is more substantial, and undetected errors are more likely to arise.

The main advantage of using VB is that the shape of the box you are going to confine the user in is free-form — square, round, cathedral-shaped, whatever you choose. But, how much time do you have to develop your solution, who will use it, and does the finished product produce a proper return for the additional effort involved? Sometimes it does, sometimes it doesn't.

Section Five

THE BUSINESS PLAN

SECTION INDEX

SECTION OVERVIEW

In this section, we have our meeting with John, obtain all the information — projected sales, etc — and prepare the Business Plan. This changes the template into a fully working model, ready to produce reports for transfer into Word.

Chapter Twenty-two

THE MEETING

That's easy for you to say.

We have the templates built, we can prepare the accounts in Excel, we can produce projections, and we can link the projections to the accounts and to each other. We are ready to meet John Smith and to prepare the initial figures.

MEETING JOHN

John smiled warmly. "Oh, hello. And you've brought your colleague as well. Good." We all shook hands. "I've kicked a few figures around, so all you need to do is crunch them a little, then prepare the plan."

He picked up his papers. "You see, there are three main groups of Widgets, and the sales will fall like this." He showed us the table below.

	Year 1 $	Year 2 $	Year 3 $
Small Widgets	2,000,000	1,000,000	200,000
Medium Widgets	3,000,000	2,900,000	2,800,000
Big Widgets	2,000,000	1,800,000	500,000

"They will be replaced by the Whatsits."

	Year 1 $	Year 2 $	Year 3 $
Small Whatsits	500,000	1,000,000	3,000,000
Medium Whatsits	–	1,500,000	5,000,000
Big Whatsits	–	200,000	3,000,000

"The suppliers won't be geared up to start producing the medium sizes of Whatsits until the early part of the second year. The big ones should kick in at the end of year two. Small Widgets are as good as dead."

"We want to de-stock on the Widget lines, and stock up on the Whatsits. I have negotiated exclusive distribution rights but, as part of the deal, we have to up-grade our warehousing facilities and get new racking and storage in place. I expect the work on the building to cost $1,000,000 and the racking will cost $3,000,000 because it is highly specialized. The distribution agreement is cancel-able after five years, so write the whole thing off in that period. If we retain the distribution rights after that, we are laughing all the way to the bank.

"As well as that, we need to change the vehicles in the next 12 months, but I don't see any other major capital commitments. There shouldn't be any changes in debt collection, but I have negotiated new terms with the suppliers of the Whatsits. Here you are."

He handed us a sheet of paper setting out the contract terms. The important points are noted below, and the terms for Widgets are given for comparison:

- Whatsits (all from the one supplier)   Four months up to June 2000
                                           Three months up to June 2001
                                           Two months up to June 2002

- Widgets (five suppliers)   Historically this has averaged:
                                           Cash on Delivery 5%
                                           One month 20%
                                           Two months 15%
                                           Three months 10%
                                           Four months 20%
                                           Five months 15%
                                           Six months 15%

"We were able to gradually increase the time to pay suppliers of the Widgets, partly because there are a lot of suppliers and they want the business. If we do not pay for the Whatsits in the time-scale set out in the contract, the Distribution Agreement will be cancelled.

"Right," said John. "See you back here at, say, 3 o'clock to discuss the figures. Then we can get the business plan done before seeing the bank tomorrow."

That gives us four hours, including lunch.

Chapter Twenty-three

THE FULL PICTURE

WYSIWYG. What you see is what you get.

Let us look at the comments made by John at our meeting, and relate them to a spreadsheet. We will then know what fine-tuning we need to make in our model.

JOHN'S FIGURES

John's comments are shown in the table below, with comments as appropriate:

• Widget sales will fall, and Whatsits sales will increase	Debtor days should not change. Instead of using two Sales tables, we will put an extra line in the Sales table to distinguish Widgets from Whatsits
• Payments to suppliers	Credit terms are different between Widget suppliers and Whatsits. We need two Payment tables to reflect this.
• Hire Purchase and bank loan	Repayments will be included in the Overheads/Capital table. Depreciation and allocation of interest charges to the Profit and Loss Account will be made by journal entry.

We have already set up most of the spreadsheet, and we have tested to ensure that the formulae are working correctly. What we want to do now is:
• Insert a second Payments table.
• Drop the Sales table by four rows, enter the two sales lines and insert a total.
• To make life easier, we will include a new sheet and place all of the "point of entry" figures (sales, stock changes, overheads etc.) in the new sheet. Tweaking by John is then easily managed from the one place.
• Pick up the cash movement in the accounts.
• Copy the projections sheet twice, so that we can project years two and three.

We will adjust the existing sheet first. Open **Accounts 14.xls**.

INSERT A SECOND PAYMENTS TABLE

Highlight column EA, then press **F8** to anchor the point, and use the arrow keys to highlight the columns to EZ. Right-click the mouse and choose **Insert**.

Selecting the block from EA to EZ keeps everything from FA in logical starting positions, one set to the right.

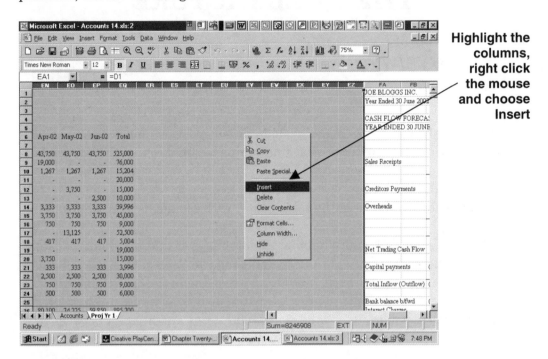

Highlight the columns, right click the mouse and choose Insert

Next, select the existing table and highlight the cells. Press **Ctrl+C** to copy them to the Clipboard. Move to cell EA1 and press **Return** to paste them in.

Correct the headings, which have changed because they were relative addressed instead of absolute addressed.

Delete the named range **Cash_Purchases_Table** and insert two new named ranges: **Cash_Purchases_1** and **Cash_Purchases_2**.

Leave the formulae for the purchases at present. We will amend this after the new lines have been inserted in the Sales Table.

INSERT NEW LINES IN THE SALES TABLE

Highlight from cell CA7 to CR10, right-click the mouse in the purple area and choose **Insert**. This time select **Shift Cells Down**.

When we move cells C8, etc. with the Insert command, Excel changes all of the formulae automatically, so the calculation part of the table does not need to be revised. The formula in CE15 has therefore been amended to =CE$11*$CB15 by Excel.

Finally, insert the titles Widgets and Whatsits in the sales section. Enter test data, and then change the entry in what is now CE11 etc. to total the column.

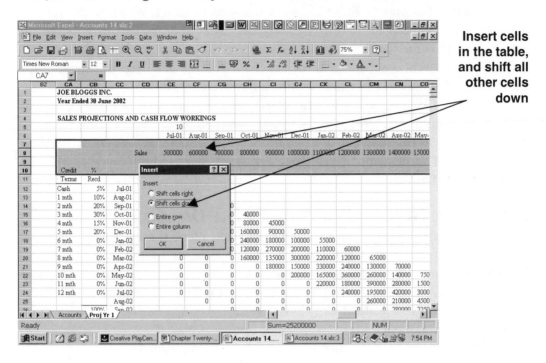

When the table amendments have been finished, it looks like this:

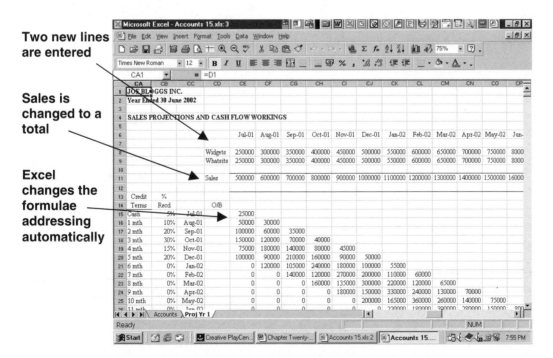

With the insertions made in the Sales table, two errors arise in the Purchases table. Excel revised the first table, built to reflect Widget purchases and cash flow, so that references to line CE8 were updated to CE11, which is the total of all sales. When we copied the Purchases table, Excel updated the formulae in the copy so that they now refer to the first Payments table, and not the Sales table.

Amend both tables so that the correct Sales figures are used to calculate the Purchases, and consequently the Creditors Payment schedule.

Take note of this error for future reference. This insertion of tables part-way through the building process and its (unforeseen) effect on the existing formulae is the single most common cause of errors in spreadsheets. However, irrespective of the potential error, we will use the ETB as an independent check on the correctness of the figures.

INSERT AND BUILD A POINT OF ENTRY DATA SHEET

To insert an extra sheet in an existing workbook, place the mouse on the sheet tab name and right-click. From the pop-up menu, select **Insert**, and then select **Worksheet**. Rename the sheet **Data**, and drag it to the extreme right if necessary, so that it appears after Proj Yr 1. See **Section Two**, if necessary.

Place headings in the sheet as follows:

- Cell A1   Joe Bloggs Inc.
- Cell A2   Data Entry Section — Accounts and Projections
- Cell A4   Widgets

What we want is a table that highlights the sales as per John's comments, then allocates them across the months. The table therefore has the following sections:

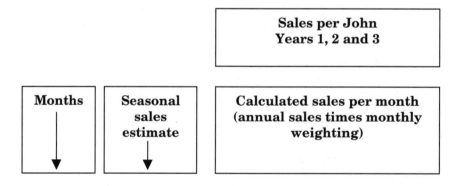

The table is shown below.

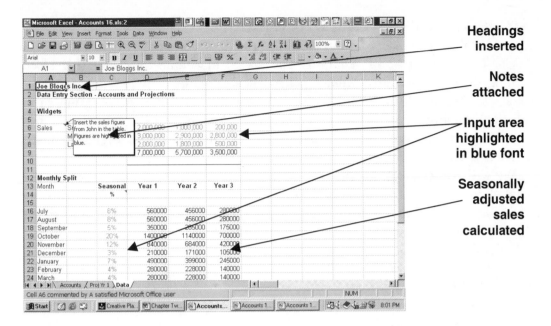

The areas of main interest are highlighted on the screenshot. The detailed steps to create the table are noted below:

- Month — Type in July, then drag and copy. A year is not inserted.
- Seasonal % — The percentage of sales each month is entered. The total must be 100%, so the last month (June) includes a formula (see below).
- % June formula =IF(C29-SUM(C16: C26)<0,"Negative" ,C29-SUM(C16:C26)) — The formula reads, "Take the sum of the 11 months and deduct from C29 (100%). If the answer is negative, print Negative. If it is zero or positive, print the number." If text prints, it creates an error message in the table and in the projections, and this highlights that there is a problem. It is an example of using text to generate an error message deliberately.
- Monthly sales =ROUND(D$9* $C25,0) — In English, total sales multiplied by the monthly %, rounded to the nearest whole number. For these figures, rounding is not necessary, but that may not always be the case. The mixed relative/absolute address is used to facilitate copying the formula. See **Section Two**.

A copy of the full table is made at AA1 (highlight all of the cells, **Ctrl+C** to copy, move to AA1 and press **Return** to paste). The heading Widgets is changed to Whatsits, and the figures for sales are amended. The amount for percentage of sales each month is revised to =C16 etc., so that if the seasonal sales spread is changed in the Widget section it is reflected in the Whatsits section.

STOCK MOVEMENT TABLE — WIDGETS

Finally, we want to insert a table to record the de-stocking of Widgets, and a table for the stocking up of Whatsits. The actual mechanics of calculating stock holding depends on the company policy on stock-outs, supplier delivery lead times etc. Technically, we could set up a table that uses statistical formulae to calculate the amount of increase/decrease in stock-holding dependent on the projected level of sales each month. However, for our purposes, this level of sophistication is of no major benefit.

We will reduce stock holding by a set percentage each month, based on the level of turnover each month. In order to show this in an orderly and visually clear way, we must highlight in the table that aspects are input here, and which aspects are taken from other areas of the spreadsheet. The format for the layout of the Widgets table is shown below.

Headings etc.

Sales (from the Sales table)	Reduce to cost	Calculate Stock reduction	Deduct from the month's opening stock figure

The spreadsheet looks like this:

Headings

Opening inventory position

Margin

Sales

% reduction in inventory holding

Calculated reduction in inventory

Table for year two

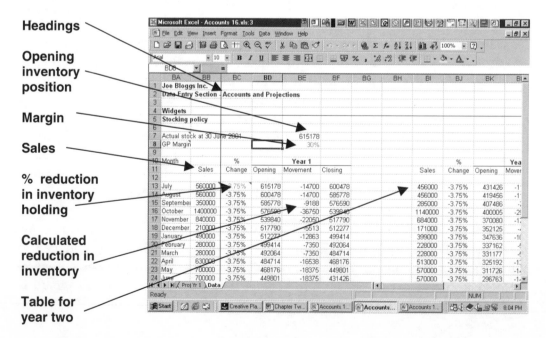

The structure of the table is set out below:

• Headings	=A1 etc. as usual.
• Opening stock	=ETB figure (Accounts sheet).
• GP Margin	Original entry, so shown in blue.
• Sales	=D16, then drag to copy.
• % Change	The first entry is in blue. The others are = the cell above, so they are black. Changing the first cell changes them all.
• Stock Movement =ROUND((BB13*(1-$BE$8)*BC13),0)	In English, Sales figure multiplied by the margin (one minus GP%), multiplied by the percentage. The figure is rounded to the nearest whole number.

Notice that the same result would be obtained by putting an absolute reference to the stock reduction percentage in BC13, and not showing a value in cells BC14, etc. However, by setting up the table in this way, we can change percentages in BC14, etc. by entering a number instead of =BC13, and we do not have to start revising the formula in BE14, etc.

A copy of the table is pasted into BI11 and BP11 (**Ctrl+C** to copy, **Ctrl+V** to paste). The references to the sales for years two and three have to be manually adjusted (Tile two windows, click to select. Once the first reference is selected, drag to copy).

Notes are added to cells to clarify what is being done, so that when we use the spreadsheet later we have a reminder of what we have done and why.

The range BA1 to BT26 is named **Data_Stock_Widgets** for easy access.

STOCK MOVEMENT TABLE — WHATSITS

The structure used for the Widgets table can be used for the Whatsits table. Select the Widgets tables (BA1 to BT26), **Ctrl + C** to copy, move the cursor to cell CA1 and press **Enter** to paste.

The table is inserted and, because the Whatsits Sales table was placed at AA1 (Widgets at A1), the relative references have adjusted to pick up the correct details (headings, Sales etc.)

However, the stocking policy for Whatsits differs from Widgets because we are in a start-up position. For our purposes, we will type stock values directly into the tables although, as noted above, formulae can be used if desired. We have taken closing stock as 1/6th of sales in the year and, except for the uplift in initial stock, have spread it evenly across the 12 months.

The table is completed by amending the blue color coding to show that all stock change cells are input points, and the comments are amended accordingly. The range is named **Data_Stock_Whatsits**.

The spreadsheet is saved as **Accounts 17.xls** (**Accounts 15.xls** and **Accounts 16.xls** can be checked for the transitions from **Accounts 14.xls to Accounts 17.xls**).

OVERHEADS TABLE

The allocation of overheads takes place in the Projections spreadsheet. All we are concerned about here is the treatment of increases in the period under review.

The input table will therefore list the names of the expense headings, and the annual amount for each of the three years, and provide an input area for annual increases if appropriate.

The table is shown below.

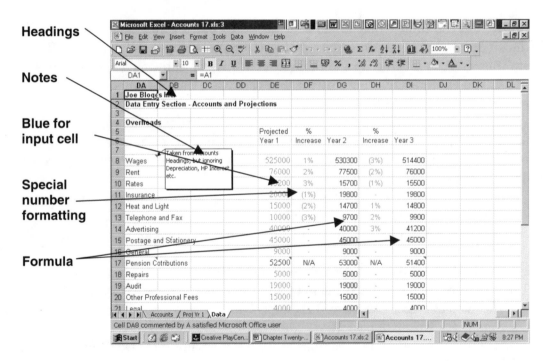

The main points of interest are:

- Account headings   Linked to the account headings section of the Accounts sheet. This ensures descriptions and the order of entries are consistent.

- % Increase

This is a custom format, so that the cell shows the figure and % sign in brackets for a negative figure, and a dash for zero. The format for the custom number is 0%;(0%);–. See **Section Two**, if necessary. The entire column has been center-justified.

- Year2 and Year3 amounts
  =ROUND(IF(DF8=
  "0",DE8,DE8*(1+DF8)),-2)

The formula in English is "If the amount is nil, enter the same value as previously; otherwise, multiply the previous value by one plus the % change. Round the answer to the nearest hundred."

Capital expenditure is, by its nature, infrequent. We will leave entry of capital items to the Projections sheet.

That completes the groundwork for the projections. We will now post the figures to the cash flow statements and the accounts for each year.

POSTING THE FIGURES

For the final stage, we need to tile two windows. Activate the Data sheet in one, and Proj Yr 1 in the other. Zoom down as necessary.

Post Sales to the Sales table:

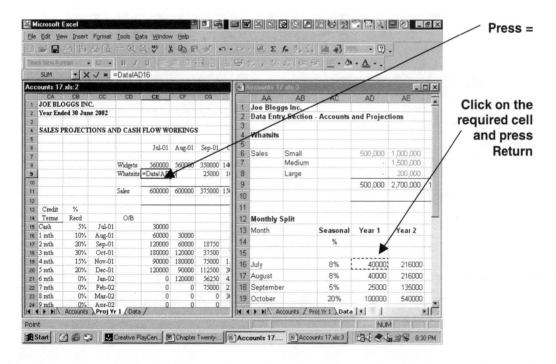

Post Stock Movements to the Purchases table:

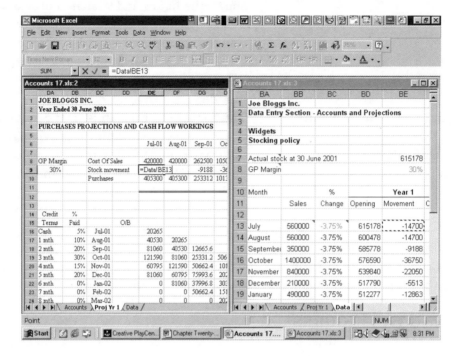

Post Overheads to the Overheads table:

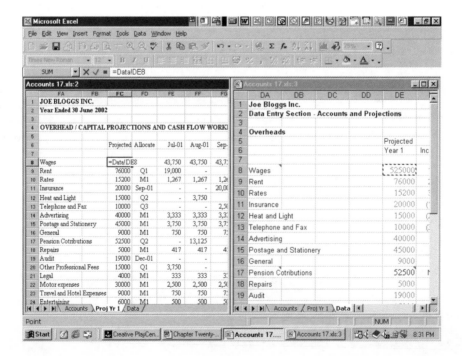

Enter the capital expenditure items in the Overhead table:

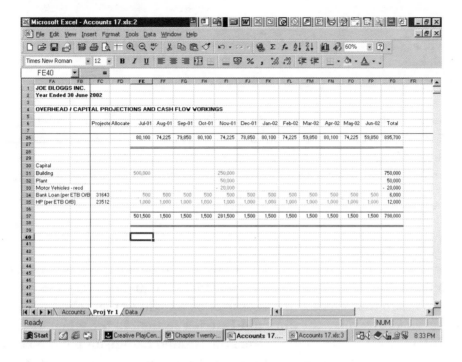

Link the Cash Flow table to the ETB:

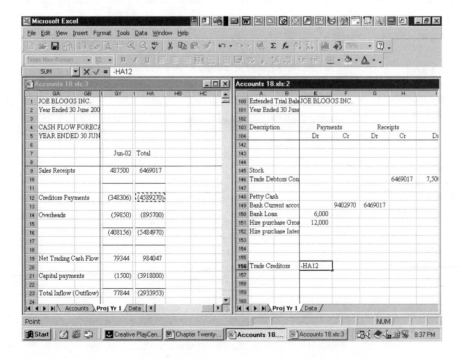

The figures are entered on the ETB as follows:

- Sales Cash Received   Receipts section of the ETB
- Purchases Payments   Bank Payments section
- Overheads   Bank Payments Section
- Interest and Charges   Journal Entry 1

The interest could be placed in the Bank Payments section, if you prefer.

The ETB produces the accounts, and we have two checks that we can make to ensure everything has been properly entered on the ETB:

- The balance per the bank should agree with the closing balance per the cash flow.
- The debit and credit columns of each section should balance. If they do, the profit and loss account and balance sheet will balance.

ENTER SALES AND PURCHASES

We have entered the cash flow in the accounts and the bank balance agrees with the cash flow items. Now we will enter the actual sales and purchases in the period in order to record the income and cost of sales on a credit, rather than cash, basis.

In one window, display the **Journal Entries** section. In the other, display the **Cash_Sales_Table** section. (Select from the **Named Range** drop-down box.)

Post the sales to turnover, and debit accounts receivable control. Post the purchases figure (which is after the stock adjustment) to purchases, and credit the accounts payable control. In the Sales table, total the cash received after the year-end. This equals the accounts receivable figure, and gives an automatic aging of the debt.

The Sales and Accounts Receivable Cash are posted in the ETB

The closing balance is found with an =SUM formula. It agrees with the ETB figure, so we know the two are correct. The ageing of the debt can be found from the table

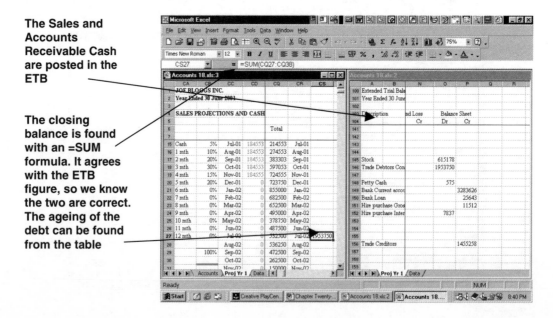

Similarly, the amount paid to suppliers after the year-end should equal the Accounts Payable figure in the ETB. The only difference is that there are two figures to add — the amount paid to Widgets suppliers, and the amount paid to the Whatsits supplier.

Finally, now that we are sure that the figures are being picked up correctly, we will change the credit period received from the Whatsits supplier so that it agrees with John Smith's earlier comments.

Go to the Whatsits Payments Table (click on **Cash_Purchases_2** in the **Named Ranges** drop-down box). Freeze the panes, then change the % payment schedule to Month 4, 100%, and delete the other figures.

You will notice that the payment schedule has not changed. The figures are linked to the percentages used in Table 1, and therefore they must be revised. The table looks like this when it has been amended. The spreadsheet is saved on the CD as **Accounts18.xls**.

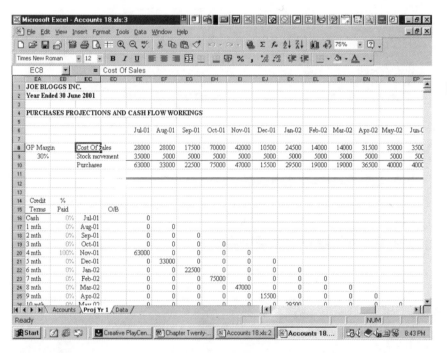

The two payment tables are now independent of each other

ENTER INVENTORY IN THE PROFIT AND LOSS ACCOUNT

The Profit and Loss Account must reflect opening and closing stock. This is entered through a journal entry, the figures being picked up from the opening balance in the ETB and the stock movement table.

Therefore, the figures will be:

- Opening Stock = ETB figure.(Debit)
- Closing Stock = Stock Table figure (Credit)
- Balance sheet entry = movement in stock (Opening minus Closing stock).

The entry is included as **Journal 5** in **Proj Yr 1**, and it is saved on disk as **Accounts 19.xls**. Check the GP margin to ensure it calculates at 30%.

Closing Inventory equals Whatsits and Widgets

Closing Inventory is picked up from the Stock table

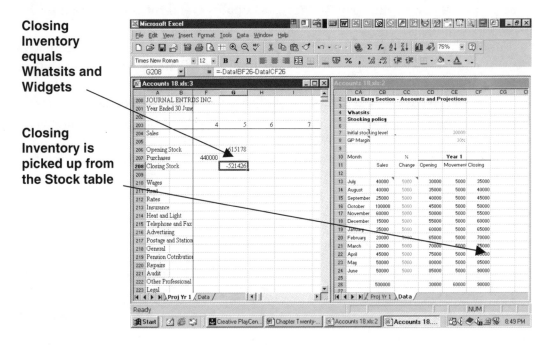

At this stage, it would be useful to enter the descriptions in the Journal Descriptions section. Tile two windows and enter the narrative.

Display the Journals ...

and the Journal Descriptions ...

then enter the narrative

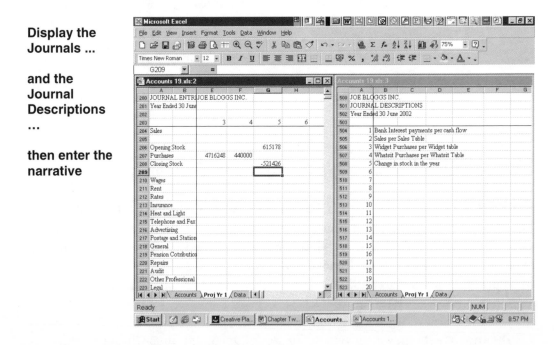

That finishes the cash flow statement and its co-ordination with the accounts. To complete the accounts requires dealing with the non-cash items — depreciation, sale of fixed assets, HP interest charge, accruals and prepayments, etc.

These items are dealt with in the next chapter.

Chapter Twenty-four

DEPRECIATION, ETC. TO FINISH

Money isn't everything!

The cash flow model is complete, it co-ordinates, and it agrees with the accounts. Now we must put the non-cash items (depreciation, HP Interest etc.) into the ETB to finish the financial figures and make them consistent with the accounting policies normally adopted by the company.

We will work on the Fixed Assets first.

FIXED ASSETS

The format for the Fixed Asset note is:

Cost

Opening Balance	From ETB
Closing Balance	From rounded ETB
Disposals	Entered in the fixed asset note manually
Additions	Closing balance minus opening balance, add disposals

Depreciation

Opening Balance	From ETB
Charge for year	Calculated, based on the closing balance of cost
On Disposals	Entered manually
Closing Balance	Tot of the above

The formula for calculating the depreciation is straightforward, and is:
=ROUND((BB1511-BB1528)*BB1526,0)

In English, Cost closing balance (less land in this case) multiplied by the depreciation rate. The result is rounded to the nearest whole number. Note that the accounting policy is a full years depreciation in the year of purchase, and none in the year of sale.

The depreciation charge calculated and the depreciation on disposals are put through the journals and thereby are added to the ETB figure of cumulative depreciation, so that the closing balance is the same as for the Fixed Asset note.

To complete the Fixed Asset note, enter the cost of the assets sold as $500,000 and the depreciation on those assets as $420,000 (both as negative figures).

Tile two windows. In the first, display the Fixed Asset note and, in the second, display the Journal Entries. Pick up the depreciation charge (=BB1516 etc.). In the next journal, pick up the disposal of assets (=BD1509 etc.).

The closing ETB figures now agree with the Fixed Asset note.

PRINT THE ETB FOR REVIEW

At this point, it would be useful to print out the ETB and review it for errors or anomalies.

Select **ETB** from the Named Range drop-down box. The ETB part of the spreadsheet is highlighted. Click on **Set Print Area** in the toolbar, then on **Print Preview**. Ensure the settings are **Fit To One Page** and **Portrait**, then print it out. Everything looks correct.

BANK LOAN AND HP INTEREST

These can be entered directly on the Journal Entry section, or "T" accounts can be created to provide a full set of working papers.

In our case, we will enter the interest charge directly on the Journal.

Select the window that displays the Journals section and post a Bank Loan interest charge of $3,164 and an HP interest charge of $3,919. Complete the Journal Description section.

OTHER ITEMS

We have ignored cash flow relating to Income Tax, Corporation Tax and Sales Tax. The same principles apply to these items as to other items discussed above as regards calculation and whether to include them in the existing tables, or build a new visual table. For our purposes, we have ignored them.

Accruals and prepayments are assumed to be the same as those in the (adjusted) historical accounts.

THE PROFIT AND LOSS ACCOUNT AND BALANCE SHEET

The accounts are now complete for the first year. Check the Profit and Loss Account to ensure it agrees with the rounded ETB. There is a $20,000 difference, which is the profit on sale of fixed assets — we did not have this heading in the historical accounts.

Fixing this is straightforward. Tile two windows, one with the Rounded ETB displayed, the other with the P&L displayed. Type = and select the cell, then press **Return**. The P&L now agrees with the ETB.

Check the Balance Sheet. It balances, and no amendment is necessary, because no new categories were created compared to the historical accounts.

TO CONCLUDE

The Projections template is now complete for year one. We have a set of cash flow tables for year one that agrees to the data table, we have a set of accounts for year one that balances, and the figures from the cash flow statement for bank balance, debtors and creditors agree with the accounts figures.

We can quickly and easily revise not only the cash flow elements, but also the accruals and prepayments to see the effects of amendments on both cash flow and profitability.

We are ready to copy **Proj Yr 1** to years 2 and 3.

Chapter Twenty-five

YEARS TWO AND THREE

More of the same.

We will now set up years two and three. This involves making a copy of year one, changing the references to opening balances and the cash flow data tables and reviewing the journals to ensure they are correct. Apart from that, everything should be accurate.

PROJ YR 2 AND PROJ YR 3

Activate **Proj Yr 1** and, with the mouse on the tab, right-click and select **Move** or **Copy**. Create two copies of the sheet, then rename them **Proj Yr 2** and **Proj Yr 3**. See **Section Two** for the detailed steps, if necessary.

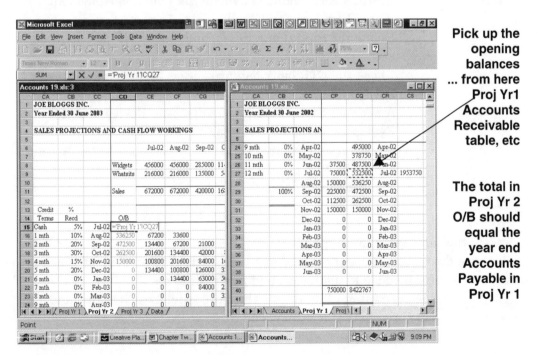

Pick up the opening balances ... from here Proj Yr1 Accounts Receivable table, etc

The total in Proj Yr 2 O/B should equal the year end Accounts Payable in Proj Yr 1

In Proj Yr 2, change the following:

- Headings   D4 becomes 2003, E4 becomes 2002.
- Opening   Tile two windows — one displays Proj Yr 1 ETB, the other
  Balances on   Proj Yr 2 ETB. Change references to Proj Yr 1 (select using
  the ETB   the mouse).
- Sales Table   Change the first date to July 2002, and drag to copy.
                       Pick up the opening debtor cash flow from the table in Proj
                       Yr 1.
- Sales Table   Select year two sales from the Data sheet. Tile two windows
                       and point and click.
                       The ETB debtors figure should agree with the Sales Table
                       year end debtors figure.
- Purchases   Purchases are based on Sales. However, we need to change
  Table Widgets   the Stock movement line. Tile two Windows and use the
                       mouse to select the correct cells from the Data sheet.
                       Pick up the opening creditor payments schedule from the
                       table in Proj Yr 1.
- Purchases   As for Widgets. In addition, change the payment terms to
  Table Whatsits   three months.
- Overheads   Change the references to pick up overheads in year two
  Table   (Data Sheet). Change payment date for single payment
                       items (Insurance and Audit).
                       Delete the capital purchases, and amend HP payments to
                       zero.
                       Check the ETB bank balance agrees to the summary cash
                       flow.
- Journals   Amend for Stock, Fixed Asset disposal. Review the others.
                       Revise the interest on loan as appropriate.
- ETB   Review it and ensure everything is correct. The GP margin
                       should be 30%
- Fixed Asset   Remove the disposal.
  Note

Complete the same steps for Proj Yr 3.

We have three years' projections and one year's actual figures, all of which are linked and easily amended for both cash and non-cash items.

The final thing remaining is to amend the Profit and Loss account and Balance Sheet in year three so that it displays all three years together.

THE THREE YEARS' ACCOUNTS SUMMARY

If we present the accounts in the same format as earlier, we will have six columns of figures (main column and indented expenses). This would be too wide for a Letter-size sheet in Word, and it is too long to change the paper orientation from portrait to landscape, and still fit it on one page.

We will therefore present each year in one column and use boxes to highlight sub-sections.

Open one window and display the Profit and Loss Account. Drag and drop the inset figures so that they appear in the same column as the turnover.

Once the figures are lined up, select the **Borders** drop-down tool button and place borders around the figures as necessary.

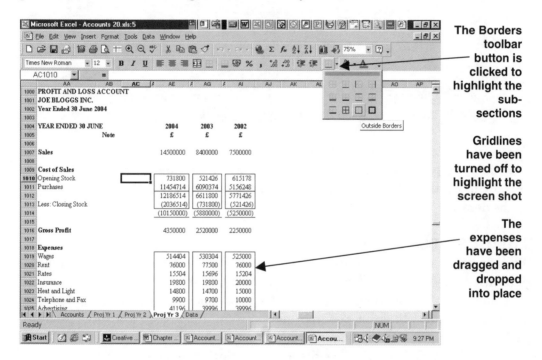

The Borders toolbar button is clicked to highlight the sub-sections

Gridlines have been turned off to highlight the screen shot

The expenses have been dragged and dropped into place

Tile two windows and pick up the figures for years one and two, using =[Cell].

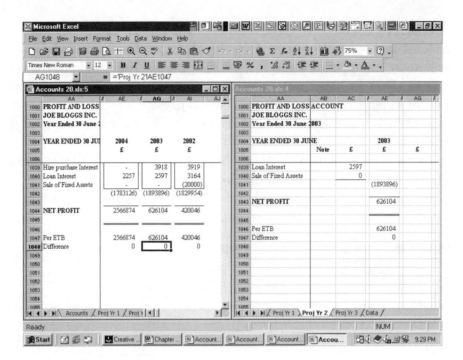

The same applies to the Balance Sheet.

Finally, prepare notes to the BS to break down the three years' summary figures, by using the ETB Rounded allocation table from each year in order to pick up the detail.

THE BUSINESS PLAN

We now want to draw the results into a report written in Word, ready for discussion with John Smith, prior to presentation to the bank.

It has taken us one hour to bring the spreadsheet to its present state, after meeting John and obtaining the information from him. There are three hours to go. We will prepare the business plan now, and then come back to the spreadsheet in order to pick up the accounts and cash flow statements as necessary.

We now have all of the information and results in our spreadsheet. The only thing we need to complete in the spreadsheet is to agree the format for the presentation on the information — the tables, summary information and presentational matters that are the cornerstone of a well-received business plan. We cannot really finalise these until we have sketched out the plan.

In the next chapter, we will look at how to get the Excel information to appear in Word.

Chapter Twenty-six

THE BUSINESS PLAN: OBJECT LINKING AND EMBEDDING

Broader than just one program.

We are going to concentrate on the more interesting parts of the business plan here — interesting in this context being anything that co-ordinates or impacts on the spreadsheet we designed earlier. Background information will be relevant to our understanding, and this is given below.

OBJECT LINKING AND EMBEDDING (OLE)

In **Section One**, we looked at the Clipboard, and its usefulness in transferring information from one place to another. The pasting of information applies whether it is placing a copy of information in the same program, or pasting it into another program — in the present situation, pasting from Excel into Word.

OLE is the next stage in the development of the process of sharing or integrating information from different sources. Although the format of Excel spreadsheets is different from Word documents, OLE provides a means to record the different formats seamlessly in the one document.

Looking at the term OLE, there are three components within the name:

- Object   This is the source information — the specific cell in the spreadsheet, etc.
- Link   A reference to the original spreadsheet is recorded in the Word document. The spreadsheet does not exist in the Word document as such, and any changes in the spreadsheet are reflected in Word when the link is updated. Automatic updating of links is the default setting.

- Embed   The cell range exists in the Word document. It is a clone of the original but exists separately from it. If either the clone or the original is updated, the clone will contain different information from the original. It is therefore a static view of the data as it existed at the time the embed was made.

Of the two methods, Linking is best, because the information in the Word document is always up-to-date.

However, the reason why the two methods of transferring the information are offered is because Linking is very processor-intensive and consequently slow. Embedded objects do not need to update when the Word document is opened and so are faster.

Which method you use is a personal decision. If Embedding is used, care must be taken to ensure that the latest version of all of the information is used.

We will use both methods, so that the mechanics of each is demonstrated.

THE BUSINESS PLAN OUTLINE

Amongst other things, the Business Plan will identify the market opportunity, the history of the company and the financial impact on the company of implementing the plan, and the impact on the bankers. The other items — SWOT analysis, etc. — are ignored for our purposes.

Within the above, we want the following financial details:
- A summary (to the nearest thousand) of the results
- A summary of the cash flow over the period
- The full accounts for the financial year just ended
- The full accounts for the period covered by the projections
- The full supporting schedules for the cash flow statement.

When combining typed information from several sources into one (seamless) document, pay attention to the following:
- The same typeface must be used for each. The defaults selected in Word may be different from those set in Excel, so this should be checked.
- The reports must be small enough to fit in the page margins in Word. If the report is not going to fit, it can be pasted in as a picture, and then scaled to fit.
- Headings (years etc.) should be typed in Excel and pasted in along with the other detail. If it is entered from Word, it will be difficult to line them up with the Excel parts.

We will start with Linking.

LINKING

When we want to link a spreadsheet to Word, we must complete the following steps:

- Select the cells (they will turn purple when selected)
- Copy the selection to the Clipboard (**Ctrl+C**)
- Activate Word (start it or click on the program in the Taskbar)
- From the menu choose **Edit**, then **Paste Special**.
- In the dialogue box, select **MS Excel Worksheet Object**, click on **Paste Link** and choose **OK**.

The link, once established, updates automatically. If, after all of the spreadsheet sections have been pasted into the Word document, the update process is too slow, the links can be changed to manual. The steps are shown after the screen shots below.

Select the Profit and Loss Account from **Proj Yr 3** and copy it to the Clipboard. In Word, select **Edit**, **Paste Special**.

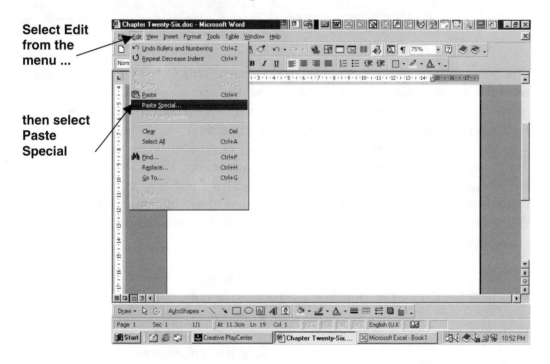

Click on **Paste Special**. The following dialogue box appears. Note that, if there is nothing to paste, Paste Special is dimmed.

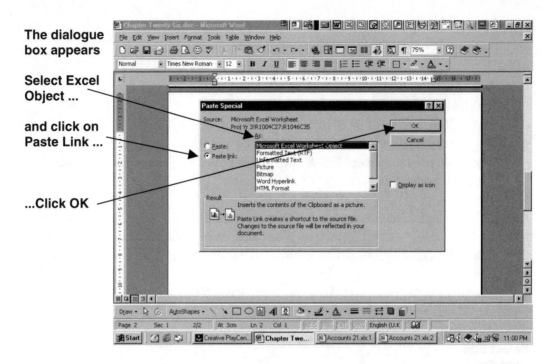

The Accounts are pasted into the Word document. This is saved on disk as **Business Plan 1.doc**. Note that, in screen view, the accounts show the spreadsheet gridlines. However, when it is printed out, it prints without the gridlines — only the borders (total underlines and boxes) are printed.

If the pasted object is too large, it can be resized in Word. Click on the accounts and you will notice that it becomes surrounded by a border and that, at the corners and the centers of the line, small white boxes appear. These are resize handles. If you place the mouse on one of these, it changes its shape to a doubled-ended arrowhead. Click and hold the left mouse button and drag. The accounts resize as follows:

- Corner white box   All sides in proportion.
- Top or bottom center white box   Stretches or reduces the length, but leaves the width unaffected (small and fat).
- Left or right center white box   Stretches or reduces the width, but leaves the length unaffected (tall and thin).

Do not change the original shape too much or it will look inconsistent compared to the rest of the document.

The resize handles allow minor adjustments to be made so that the Excel spreadsheet fits in

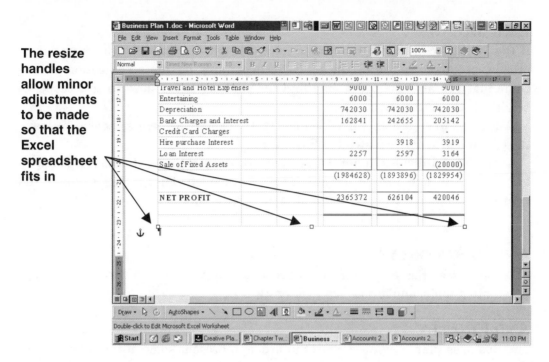

If you double-click on the spreadsheet section in Word, Excel is launched, and the original spreadsheet is loaded.

To change the link to manual update instead of automatic, click on **Edit**, **Links**. The following dialogue box appears. Click on **Manual**, then click **OK**.

Change the link to manual by clicking the option button

Then click OK to save the changes

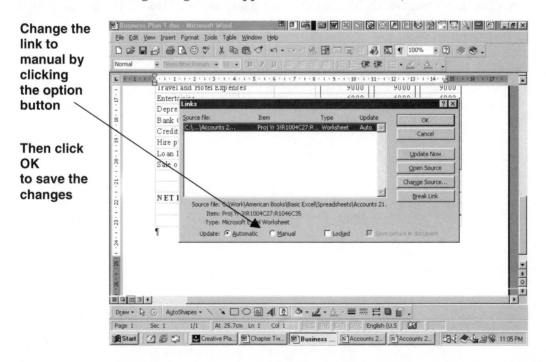

EMBEDDING

If the Word document is going to be moved between computers and the link is broken, problems can arise. In addition, depending on the specification of machine that you are using, you may find that linking is too slow. In this case embedding is the alternative.

The steps to create an embedded object are exactly as before, except we leave the option box at Paste instead of Paste Link.

If you have difficulties embedding the workbook, in the Paste Special dialogue box select **Picture** instead of MS Excel Worksheet Object. This changes the spreadsheet into a picture, and the file size is reduced accordingly.

AND PASTE ONLY?

The above uses Paste Special. If we use Paste only, Word converts the spreadsheet into a table, and it does not look pretty.

AND FINALLY ...

The Business Plan may need charts in order to present some of the information. Therefore, Charting is explained in the next chapter.

Rather than produce complicated tables, charts and other presentational inserts based on the data in the accounts and projections, we will illustrate the technique by itself, so that the methods do not become complicated unnecessarily. Once you have mastered the next chapter, you may wish to return to the projections to practice.

Chapter Twenty-seven
CHARTING

Good presentations are in the eye of the beholder.

We have reviewed how to build spreadsheets logically that are capable of being easily used and checked, and we have looked at how to prepare reports from the accounts and projections and paste or link that information into Word.

However, final presentation to the end user is a combination of imagination and interpretation — showing the information in a way that the reader will most readily assimilate. It is very much an art and not a science, because some users will want text, others will want figures and others will want pictures.

It is the presentation of information to the last group, those who prefer diagrams and charts, that this chapter is aimed at.

CHARTING AND DRAWING

There are two artist capabilities in Excel — charting (the presentation of data in the form of charts) and drawing (lines, boxes etc. drawn on the spreadsheet and used to highlight aspects of the spreadsheet).

Charting is activated from the toolbar either by selecting the Chart Wizard, or by displaying the relevant toolbar (select Yiew, Toolbar, Chart).

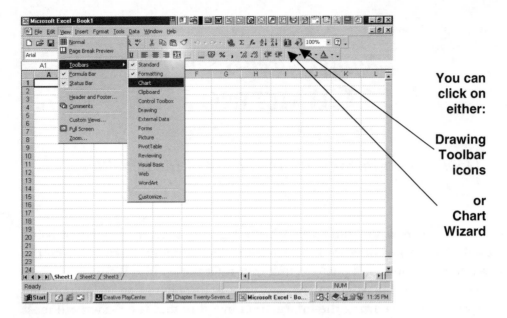

There is no drawing wizard, so if you want to illustrate and highlight, activate the toolbar and play.

CHART WIZARD

We will use the Chart Wizard to illustrate the possibilities. In a blank spreadsheet, type the following table:

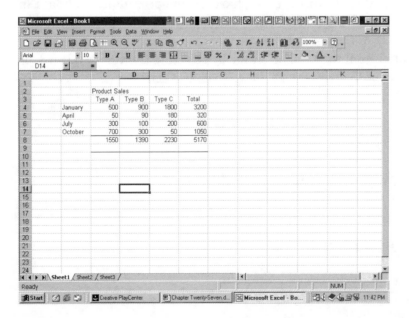

Start the Chart Wizard to guide us through the steps involved. Choose the Line type, and select the first example.

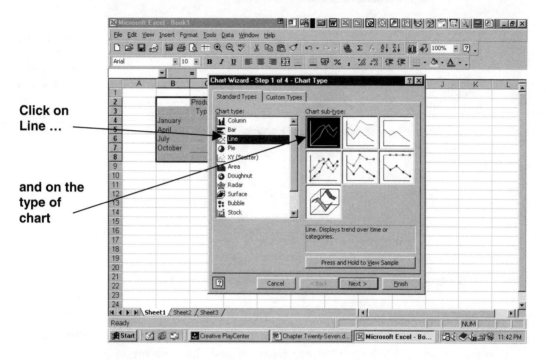

Click on Line ...

and on the type of chart

Click on Next. The anticipated chart shot does not look well. We will change the default selection of cells.

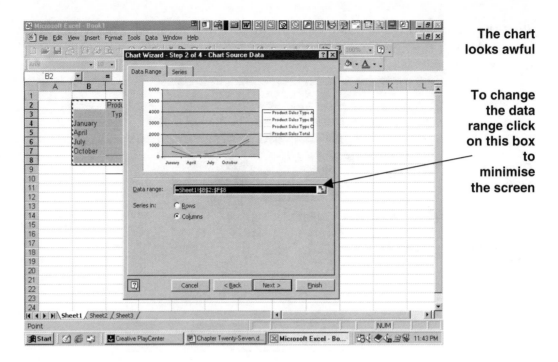

The chart looks awful

To change the data range click on this box to minimise the screen

The Chart Wizard is minimized. Click in cell C4 and drag to E7. A moving line of dashes surrounds the selection. Press **Return** and the new range is selected, and the Chart Wizard activates again.

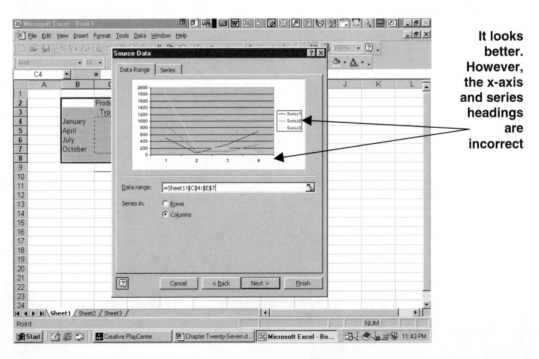

It looks better. However, the x-axis and series headings are incorrect

The line graph looks more sensible. However, because we have not chosen the full table, the headings for Series and the x-axis are no longer correct. To change these, click on the **Series** tab and either enter the cell reference for each item, or minimise the Wizard and select with the mouse.

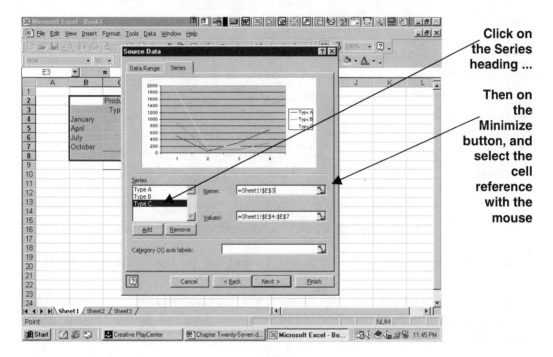

Click on the Series heading ...

Then on the Minimize button, and select the cell reference with the mouse

To select the x-axis headings, click on the **Minimize** button, then click on the first item in the series (January) and, while holding down the mouse button, drag it down to October. Press **Return**. The x-axis headings appear in the chart example.

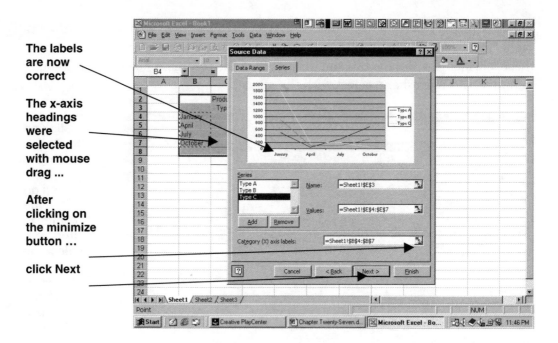

The labels are now correct

The x-axis headings were selected with mouse drag ...

After clicking on the minimize button ...

click Next

Click **Next**. The screen allows us to enter headings for the chart, and for the x and y axis.

Click in the relevant box and type in the entries required. The other tabs within the dialogue box allow options to be set as required. Leave them at their standard settings.

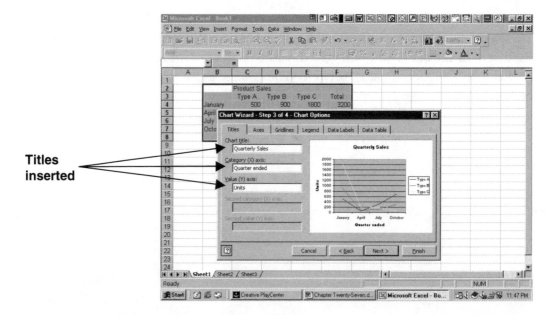

Titles inserted

Click **Next**.

There are two options presented:

- Place chart as new sheet
- Place chart as object in (named sheet).

If the chart is placed in the current sheet, it is located near the table to which it relates. However, it floats above the spreadsheet cells, and it can become tiresome navigating in the spreadsheet with the chart in the way.

If the chart is inserted in a new sheet, the problem does not arise, and normally this is the preferred option. Select the appropriate button and click on **Finish**.

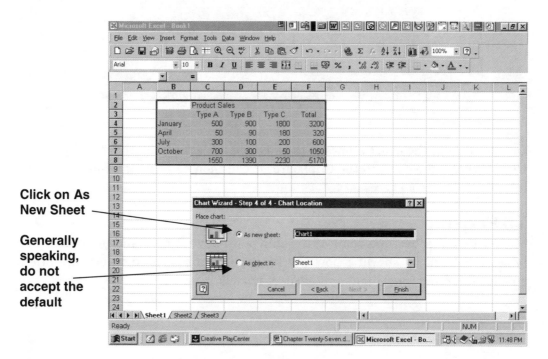

Click on As New Sheet

Generally speaking, do not accept the default

The final chart looks like this.

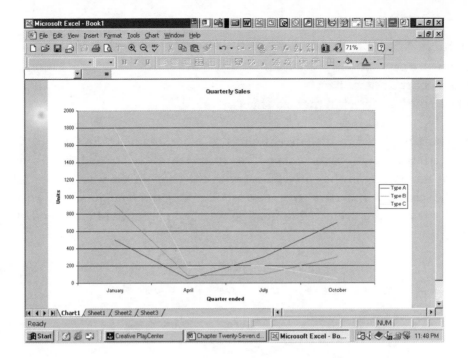

Double-clicking the chart allows it to be edited. Selecting the chart and pressing **Ctrl+C** copies the chart to the Clipboard. It can then be pasted, paste linked, etc. into Word. Resize as necessary.

TO FINISH

The next chapter reviews some of the things we have learnt, and puts them in a broader context, by showing how the knowledge can be used to prepare other, simple, quick and convenient spreadsheet models.

Chapter Twenty-eight
AND THERE'S MORE . . .

Complex tasks are simple tasks added together.

The three tasks that have gone before reflect three different perspectives on Excel — using it for volume processing by clerical staff, using it for manipulative calculations by an untrained end-user, and using it for detailed number crunching by the person that built the spreadsheet.

There are other uses to which it can be put, some tasks more technically complex than others. The purpose of this chapter is to explore some small self contained models, variations on what we have learnt already, in order to provide a different perspective. We will also look at some of the functions in Excel that we have not yet touched upon.

SELF-ANALYZING CHECK JOURNAL

We will build a self-analyzing check journal. We will use AutoFill to input checks numbers, the AutoComplete feature to enter the payee, and an IF statement to allocate the payment to the correct expenses column.

This is a variation of the overhead allocation table we built in the projections spreadsheet model.

Start Excel, and set up the headings as shown below.

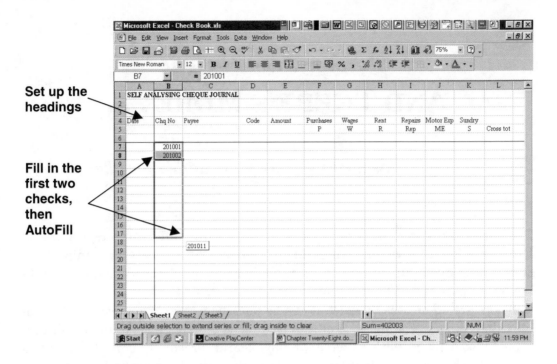

Use **AutoFill** to enter the check numbers, then enter the following details into the spreadsheet:

Date	Payee	Code	Amount
1 Jan 99	Smith, John	P	$1175.00
2 Jan 99	Smith, John	P	$500.00
2 Jan 99	Smith, S	R	$1000.00
2 Jan 99	Jones, Peter	Rep	$235.00
10 Jan 99	Jones Ins brokers	ME	$700.00
11 Jan 99	Powell	W	$417.33
11 Jan 99	Walker	W	$312.99
11 Jan 99	Stewart	W	$472.00
15 Jan 99	Jones, Peter	Rep	$117.50
31 Jan 99	Strains — petrol	ME	$120.00

Check numbers are not given in the table, because they are entered using Auto-Fill.

It is worth completing this exercise, to see how AutoComplete works. Entering the payee in line two, the full name appears after typing the first letter. Pressing **Return** accepts the suggested entry. You will notice that, with Jones, Peter for example, it blacks out only after entering enough letters to exclude the insurance brokers.

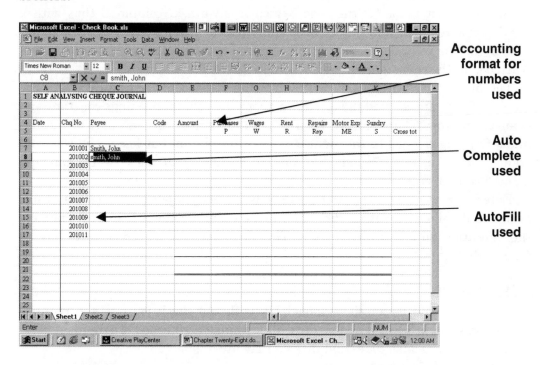

Accounting format for numbers used

Auto Complete used

AutoFill used

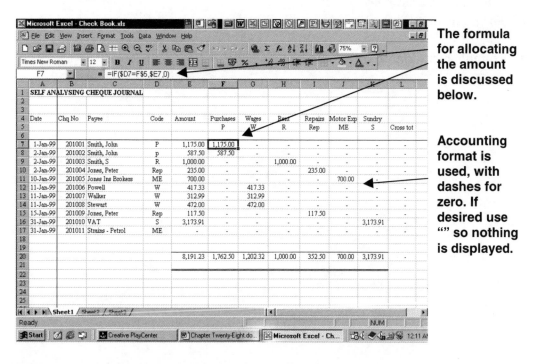

The formula for allocating the amount is discussed below.

Accounting format is used, with dashes for zero. If desired use "" so nothing is displayed.

The formula for allocating the net across the headings, using the code input in column D is: =IF($D7=F$5,$E7,0)

In English, it reads "If the code, which is always in column D (but with a varying row reference), is the same as the contents of cell F5 (always row 5, but with a varying column reference), put the contents in column E (always) row 7 (variable) in the cell, otherwise enter zero in the cell".

The absolute/relative/mixed cell addressing is used to facilitate copying the formula. To recap, copying the cell down keeps the column headings constant and changes the row. Therefore, we keep row 5 constant in the F$5 part of the formula. Copying the cell to the right changes the column, but keeps the row constant. Therefore, in $D7 and $E7, we are anchoring to the code column and amount column respectively.

Entering a cross tot ensures the code was correctly input and the amount has been validly allocated within the table. If the code in column D is now changed, the allocation automatically revises. The spreadsheet is saved on the disk as **Check Book.xls**.

TIMESHEET

We will now build a timesheet model. As with the check journal, the requirements are straightforward and no difficult formulae are needed. There must be:

- A list of chargeable codes and tasks (or clients)
- A formatted timesheet
- Formulae to total the timesheet.

An example of a formatted timesheet is given below:

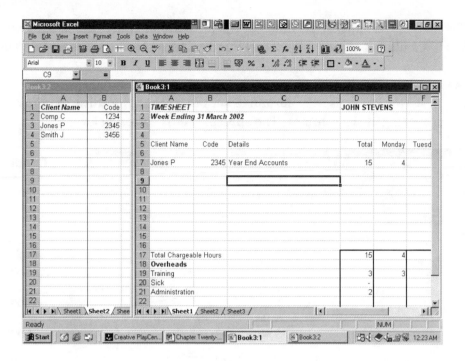

Note the formatting — no grid lines, rows or columns displayed in the second window, but they are displayed in the first.

The arrangement of client lists in another part of the spreadsheet, tiling two windows, but not evenly, and using this list to paste the name and code into the timesheet section is similar to the idea used in the Sales Tax spreadsheet.

Green borders have been added in the spreadsheet to highlight the lower part of the timesheet — the total chargeable time, sick leave etc.

The formulae are straight =SUM type.

THE EXPENSES CLAIM FORM

This model has been chosen, because it is a mixture of the two models above. The features of an expenses claim form will be:
- Recharge information — client lists and codes
- Analysis of the claim into constituent categories — travel, lunch etc.
- Highlighting of expenses in excess of agreed limits.

We are seeking to ensure the following controls over expenses claims:
- Any charges to a client in excess of $70.00 in total should be highlighted
- Individual expenses limits per client are Travel — $50.00, Meals — $20.00 and Sundry — $10.00

- The total travel expenses claimed in the month should not exceed $200.00, Meals should not exceed $80.00 and Sundry items should not exceed $30.00.

All amounts outside these limits must be signed for by a manager.

The first two items use the formulae set out above. The third requires conditional formatting of the columns. The spreadsheet is shown below:

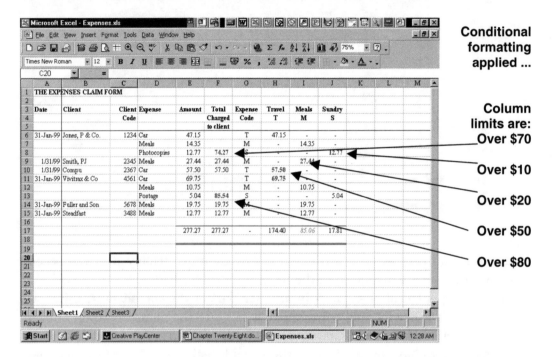

Conditional formatting is accessed from the menu. Select **Format, Conditional Formatting**.

The screen looks like this

Choose Cell Value Is

Greater than

Click in the box and enter 80

Then click on Format

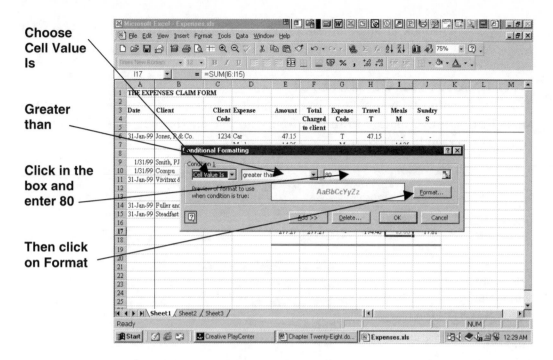

After clicking the **Format** button, the next screen appears.

Choose the style . . .

and the colour

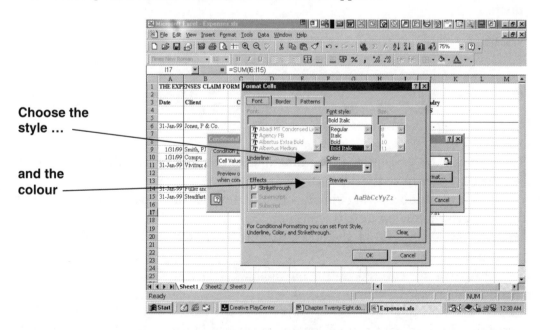

Conditional formatting is new in Excel 97. The above can be achieved in Excel 5.0 and 95, but programming must be used. Conditional formatting is a very good reason for upgrading to Excel 97 or Excel 2000.

Finally, we will look at some of the pre-defined functions in Excel. They are all accessed and activated in a similar manner, so only some are reviewed below.

INTERNAL RATE OF RETURN

The IRR function is available in Excel, and it is accessed from the menu by **In-sert**, **Function**. Choose **Financial** from the list on the left, and **IRR** on the right. The screen looks like this:

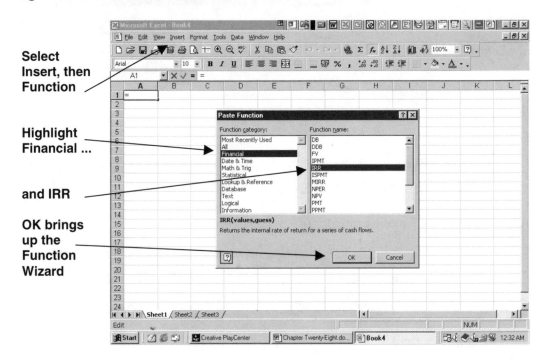

There are always two options with functions of this type — enter amounts, or select the cells that have the necessary values.

We will use the following simple example to illustrate how to select the cells that will provide the input to the formula.

Cash flow is –$1,000 at the start, $100 in years one and two, and $1,000 in year three.

The figures are entered in the spreadsheet below, in cells A1 to A4, and the IRR function wizard has been started.

Once the cells have been selected, pressing the **Enter** key on the keyboard restores the IRR box, with the cell reference entered in the Value box. Clicking **OK** accepts the formula.

The IRR formula would form part of a model, laid out with headings, coloured cells to highlight input areas etc.

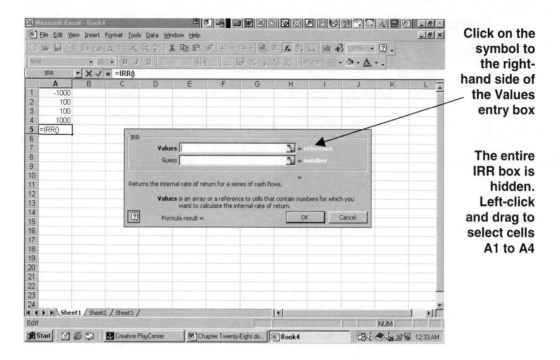

Click on the symbol to the right-hand side of the Values entry box

The entire IRR box is hidden. Left-click and drag to select cells A1 to A4

MORTGAGE INTEREST

A mortgage interest calculator will use the formula PMT or, if calculating it manually within Excel, Goal Seek.

For the purposes of the screen below:

- The font can be increased and colored as appropriate
- The Results box can be highlighted by shading the cell
- The PMT formula has been used, and the formula refers to the cells above, except for interest rates. A cell out of view is referenced to cell E6 (8%), and this is divided by 12 to give a monthly interest rate. In addition, by default the answer is negative and displays red, and is preceded by a negative sign. The Custom Number Format is used to make the negative number appear as if it is positive.

Additional cosmetics could be used to highlight the important detail:

- Gridlines could be turned off
- Row and Column headings could be turned off

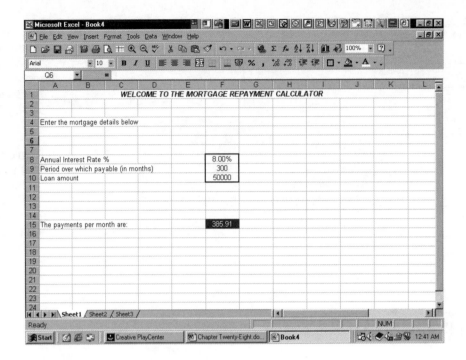

DEPRECIATION

There are several formulae to choose from, depending on the depreciation method adopted — straight line, reducing balance sum of the digits etc. Use the formulae headed DB, DDB, SLN, SYD and VDB.

A similar layout to the above will highlight input and output areas.

OTHER FORMULAE

Review the formulae available, and select those (if any) that are useful to your specific needs.

TO CONCLUDE

We have covered a lot of ground in the book, and the purpose of this short chapter is to show how the knowledge gained can be used to build small quick models, as well as large ones, and to identify some in-built functions that may be of use to you.

Always ensure a visual trail exists and the task of inspection and verification will be easier.

NEXT . . . THE END

In the final chapter, there is a review of how to proceed in the acquisition of further knowledge.

Chapter Twenty-nine

AND FROM HERE . . .

Where do you want to go today? The Microsoft slogan.

You have come through a long trail to see how the various pieces fit together to form a greater whole, and you have gained the confidence in using tools that are so vast they can never be completely mastered in all of their facets.

If you want to build on this knowledge, and lay solid foundations for the computer skills to take you forward through the next decades, I suggest that you may want to learn about:

- Advanced aspects of Excel, including its data analysis capabilities
- Visual Basic — and thereby gain a good insight into VB Applications edition
- Databases
- And, if you are not already familiar with it, word-processing.

All of the above are, to some extent, inter-linked. And, from an accountant's perspective, the more knowledge you have of how the programs can be made to dance to your own tune, the more you can get on with your real task — Accountancy. My suggestion is that, for your next step, you use **'The Accountant's Guide to Advanced Excel'** to put the next building block in place. [1]

But, whether you progress or whether you decide to finish here thank you for bearing with me. I hope that large oaks from this little acorn will grow.

Good luck!

---

[1] The Accountant's Guide to Advanced Excel by James Fulford. ISBN 1-86076-126-7. Available from Oak Tree Press, Merrion Building, Lower Merrion Street, Dublin 2, Ireland. Tel: +353 1 676 1600, Fax: +353 1 676 1644, e-mail:oaktreep@iol.ie, Internet: http://www.oaktreepress.com

Appendix A
THE EXTENDED TRIAL BALANCE

When preparing accounts manually, accountants use an Extended Trial Balance. This appendix is for those who have not used one before, perhaps because they have only prepared accounts from computer previously.

THE TRIAL BALANCE

When accounts entries are made in a set of books (whether manual books or computerized), a double entry is made in the nominal ledger — debit and credit. At a period end, the debits and credits are extracted from the nominal ledger and the trial balance is produced.

Preparing a set of accounts accumulates all of the Income and Expenditure accounts into one net figure (the profit or the loss) and this is carried forward in the balance sheet as Reserves. It must be carried forward because all we are doing in the Profit or Loss process is replacing a range of figures with one global total. The diagram below shows this.

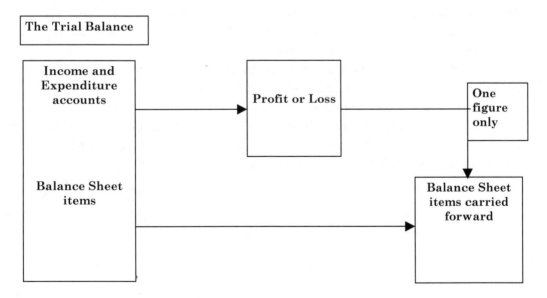

The last two columns in the Extended Trial Balance reproduce this process.

Nominal Ledger "T" Accounts

The individual entries in the nominal ledger are usually entered in a "T" account format as follows:

```
              ┌─────────────────┐
              │  Nominal Ledger │
              │     Account     │
              └─────────────────┘

┌────────────────────┐      ┌────────────────────┐
│ Opening            │      │ Opening            │
│ Balance            │      │ Balance            │
│                    │      │                    │
│ Payments           │      │ Receipts           │
│                    │      │                    │
│ Journals           │      │ Journals           │
│                    │      │                    │
│ Accruals           │      │ Prepayments        │
│                    │      │                    │
│ Closing Balance    │      │ Closing Balance    │
└────────────────────┘      └────────────────────┘
```

The headings in the ETB can vary, but in effect they are sectioning each of the lines in a "T" account and placing them across the page instead of down.

The Extended Trial Balance

The ETB is therefore, in effect, a summarized Nominal Ledger, with columns for Opening Balances, Total Payments, Total Receipts and Total Journals. The closing balances for the cross-tot is the Trial Balance, and this happens to be displayed in two sections instead of one.

When we enter the trial balance from the computer system, all we are doing is reorganizing the display of the trial balance into its two sections — Profit and Loss and Balance Sheet.

When we enter the cash flow items from the projections, we are posting the nominal ledger for that period, and using the nominal ledger to produce the trial balance, then splitting the trial balance into its two parts.

Appendix B
KEYBOARD SHORT-CUT KEYS

The main keyboard shortcut keys and function keys and mouse controls are noted below, to give a quick reference guide.

Movement	Up, Down, Left, Right	Arrow keys
	Screen up, Screen down	Page Up, Page Down
	Screen left, Screen right	Alt+Page Down, Alt+Page Up
	End of active cell group or first next cell used or end of spreadsheet if no cells used	Ctrl+arrow key
	Cell A1	Ctrl+Home key
	Left most column	Home key
	Next sheet	Ctrl+Page Down
	Previous sheet	Ctrl+Page Up
Mouse	Enter or Return	Left click
	Short pop-up menu	Right click
	Drag and drop, AutoFill	Hold left mouse button down and move mouse with button held. Watch the mouse cursor shape.
F Keys	Help	F1
	Lock the cell point	F8
	Change cell absolute/ relative addressing	With cell reference highlighted, press F4
	Edit the cell contents	F2
Clipboard	Copy	Ctrl+C
	Cut	Ctrl+X
	Paste	Ctrl+V

Menus	Activate menu	Alt+menu letter underlined
	Next menu heading	Left and right arrow key
	Items within a menu	Arrow down and up

There are other shortcut keys. However, for the rest, access the functionality using the keyboard or mouse. Accuracy is more important than speed.

Index